ATT

BORDERLANDS

D0723307

Diálogos Series

Kris Lane, Series Editor

Understanding Latin America demands dialogue, deep exploration, and frank discussion of key topics. Founded by Lyman L. Johnson in 1992 and edited since 2013 by Kris Lane, the Diálogos Series focuses on innovative scholarship in Latin American history and related fields. The series, the most successful of its type, includes specialist works accessible to a wide readership and a variety of thematic titles, all ideally suited for classroom adoption by university and college teachers.

Also available in the Diálogos Series:

For additional titles in the Diálogos Series, please visit unmpress.com.

AT THE HEART
OF THE
BORDERLANDS

*Africans and
Afro-Descendants
on the Edges of Colonial
Spanish America*

Edited by
Cameron D. Jones
and
Jay T. Harrison

University of New Mexico Press
Albuquerque

Library of Congress Cataloging-in-Publication Data
Names: Jones, Cameron D., editor. | Harrison, Jay T., editor.
Title: At the Heart of the Borderlands: Africans and Afro-descendants on
the edges of colonial Spanish America / edited by Cameron D. Jones and
Jay T. Harrison.
Other titles: Diálogos (Albuquerque, N.M.)
Description: Albuquerque: University of New Mexico Press, 2023. | Series:
Diálogos series | Includes bibliographical references and index.
Identifiers: LCCN 2022027174 (print) | LCCN 2022027175 (e-book) |
ISBN 9780826364760 (paperback) | ISBN 9780826364753 (cloth) |
ISBN 9780826364777 (e-book)
Subjects: LCSH: Africans–New Spain–History. | Africans–New Spain–
Social conditions.
Classification: LCC F1392.B55 A82 2023 (print) | LCC F1392.B55 (e-book)
| DDC 972.00496–dc23/eng/20220705
LC record available at https://lccn.loc.gov/2022027174
LC e-book record available at https://lccn.loc.gov/2022027175

Founded in 1889, the University of New Mexico sits on the traditional
homelands of the Pueblo of Sandia. The original peoples of New Mexico—
Pueblo, Navajo, and Apache—since time immemorial have deep connections to the land and have made significant contributions to the broader
community statewide. We honor the land itself and those who remain
stewards of this land throughout the generations and also acknowledge our
committed relationship to indigenous peoples. We gratefully recognize our
history.

Cover illustration adapted from Edward Walhouse Mark, "En el Río
Dagua," Watercolor on Paper, 1843. Credit: Art collection of el Banco de la
República de Colombia
Designed by Isaac Morris
Composed in Baskerville and Sybarite

CONTENTS

ILLUSTRATIONS

ACKNOWLEDGMENTS

This volume started in the most twenty-first-century way possible, as a late-night idea posted to social media. After the encouragement of several of our colleagues, especially that of Alex Borucki, we decided to go forward with it. It has not been an easy journey. With the outbreak of a global pandemic came isolation, difficult family and work situations, and closed archives and libraries. We as authors and editors, however, persisted especially in light of the death of George Floyd and the following summer of Black Lives Matter protests. We could see the need for more public and academic discourse on the history of Africans and their descendants in the Americas. It is for this reason that this volume exists.

As with any book, there are many people who are not named as authors who helped push the manuscript along. We are especially indebted to David Wheat and Ben Vinson III who helped us find many high-quality authors. We would like to thank Kris Lane for his support of the project not only as editor of the series but for his willingness to take on this project when it was in its early stages. We are also grateful to Spencer Tyce whose idea became the title of this volume. Finally, we would like to thank our families without whose time and patience none of this would have happened.

INTRODUCTION

AFRICANS AND Afro-descendants formed an integral part of the Spanish American Borderlands.[1] Compared to their actual presence, however, they were largely missing from histories of Latin America and the Borderlands for most of the twentieth century. While specialist scholars explored their presence, in most studies African contributions are still largely a footnote. Even when they enter historical narratives, they are but numbers, as the vast majority of records discussing Black bodies are those associated with economic production rather than their social and political lives. While absences of Black voices and lives in histories have been blamed on this lack of documentation, it is without a doubt also a function of continued systemic racism both in the academe of the United States as well as Latin America. Certainly, within the United States, educational disparities, combined with outright bias, have disproportionately barred people of color and African Americans in particular from the university professorate. Similar patterns can be seen in Latin America as Euro-descendants of mostly elite backgrounds had more opportunities to become scholars. Even when scholars, regardless of race or ethnicity, did produce scholarship on Africans and Afro-descendants, it was marginalized as specialized literature rather than as part of mainstream histories, making such subjects easy to ignore. Furthermore, Africans and Afro-descendants, especially in the context of Latin America and its borderlands, were difficult to place within prevailing historical narratives of both European triumphalism and indigenous resistance as a middle group who in many cases both defended and resisted empire. Ignoring such contributions for the sake of narrative clarity, however, only compounded cycles of neglect and erasure.

While there have been for decades groups of dedicated and excellent scholars calling for the increase in the awareness of Africans and Afro-descendants in the history of the Americas, the growth of popular movements both in the United States and Latin America has furthered the imperative for uncovering the prominent role people of African descent played in the history of the Americas. In the United States, while certainly much is owed to the civil rights movement in the 1950s and 1960s, the recent rise of Black Lives Matter in the last few years has brought to the forefront the erasure of Africans and their descendants from historical narratives. While cases of police brutality in the United States brought people to the streets, as the movement has progressed it has indeed moved to discussions of the perpetuations of certain historical narratives that have allowed systems of oppressions to persist. Evidence of this deliberative erasure for the sake of maintaining traditional narratives that erase

Black lives and other historically oppressed groups is abundantly clear in attempts by state legislatures and other groups to ban the teaching of the history of racism in the United States. In particular, Critical Race Theory (CRT) has emerged a particularly divisive issue. Although originally meant as a framework for legal reforms in the United States to dismantle structural racism, one of CRT's core tenets is that the social construction of race, in many cases through telling of histories, has been a means of oppressing non-European groups within legal structures. CRT, however, is widely accepted and utilized by historians of race and is essential to understanding the chapters in this volume. Indeed, attacks of CRT only serve to reinforce its basic framework.[2]

Incorporating Africans' and their descendants' contributions and voices in Spanish American historical narratives has followed a similarly difficult road. Like in the United States, most histories in the nineteenth century were centered on European triumphalism. When indigenous populations entered the narratives, it was a narrative of a defeated, savage people. Africans were almost completely ignored. This erasure was in line with ideas of some countries' official attempts to shirk or eliminate non-European cultures and even peoples. Argentina was probably the most notorious in these attempts with concepts such as "whitening the country" (*blanquear el país*), which sought to make their country more European through increased immigration from Europe. Some Argentine scholars from this period, for example, saw the inclusions of people of color in the nation as a remnant of the barbarism of colonialism that diluted European immigration with the inclusion of people of color.[3] While such machinations of erasing people of color from Spanish American nations was impossible given both demographics and resistance to such ideas, it had a profound effect on the writing of its history.

In the 1920s, '30s, and '40s studies began to emerge that sought to lessen the Eurocentricity of previous narratives. This was aided by movements such as *indigenismo*, which sought to emphasize the importance of Spanish American nations' indigenous history and culture over that of European traditions, though in many cases it did little to laud colonial or contemporary indigenous cultures. One of the problems, however, that arises from *indigenismo* is its tendency to ignore Africans in the construction of historical narratives. Only indigenous civilization mattered in the construction of the past.[4] Additionally, *mestizaje*, or racial mixing including offspring of persons of African descent, began to emerge as an important facet of historical narratives. One of the best examples of this new emphasis is José Vasconcelos's conceptualization of Mexicans as the *Raza Cósmica* (cosmic race), a race made up of the mix of the African, Asian, European, and Native American ancestries. While Vasconcelos tries to counter the conceptualizations of the European superiority coming out of an increasingly fascist Europe, his focus on racial mixing as national unifier tends to ignore differentiations in the ethnic and racial compositions of communities throughout Mexico, further exacerbating African cultural erasure.[5]

Probably the most important historical thinker of this transitionary era in terms of the inclusion of Africans in the Spanish American colonial past was the Cuban anthropologist Fernando Ortiz Fernández. Ortiz coined the term *transculturation*, a concept where instead of cultures of the colonized being erased by colonizers it mixes with them to form a new culture. Ortiz argued that Cuban culture is the result of mostly African and Spanish cultural mixing. Understanding the nation, therefore, requires understanding the role of Africans in its colonial past.

Reversing the erasure of Africans from Spanish American history in many places, however, did not start in earnest until the 1970s and '80s. A good example of these shifts toward reincorporating Blacks into historical narratives is the *La Tercera Raíz* (the third root) movement in Mexico. Led by anthropologist Luz María Martínez Montiel, La Tercera Raíz looked to incorporate the third root of Mexico's family tree, Africans, into its national identity and historical narrative (the first two roots were indigenous Mexican peoples and Europeans). Many Afro-descendants felt excluded from Mexico's cultural identity as it tended to emphasize its indigenous, and particularly Aztec, past.[6] Other such movements have begun in other Spanish American nations as well, such as Colombia's *Expedición Humana* (Human Expedition). Scholars within this movement went on to create the journal *América Negra* (Black America), which has served as a vehicle for incorporating Black voices into the historical narratives of Colombia and northern South America more broadly.[7] While these movements have begun to reverse the erasure of Africans and their descendants from historical narratives in Spanish America, just as in the United States, there is still work to be done.

This volume benefits from the perspectives of academics working mostly on colonial population centers. The majority of studies of Africans and Afro-descendants have focused on the settled centers of colonial power, or on the major economic engines of colonial hegemony: the haciendas, mines, and workshops where enslaved and free Blacks labored for colonial masters.

Exploring the history of the borderlands of Spanish America provides an excellent window into understanding the lives of Africans and Afro-descendants in the Americas. In borderlands it is easier to peel back the veneer of racial hierarchies of the colonial center. A lack of imperial control coupled with Spain's desperation for settlers and soldiers in frontier areas facilitated the social mobility of Afro-descendants. This need allowed African descendants to become not just members of borderland societies but leaders in those places as well. At the same time, this lack of control also facilitated Blacks resisting the colonization of the borderlands, thus becoming leaders in their own right outside of and against Spanish control. Africans and their descendants were essential actors in helping to shape the limits of the Spanish empire, both in collaborating with and resisting Spanish imperial power. Africans and Afro-descendants built, opposed, and shaped Spanish hegemony in the borderlands, taking on roles that would have been impossible or difficult in colonial centers due to the socioracial hierarchy of imperial policies and practices. Africans and Afro-descendants, these chapters will show, created a space, not just physically, but also economically, socially, and politically, that helped to define the contours of Spanish America. They were indeed at the heart of the borderlands.

While the exact definition of what constitutes the Spanish borderlands is still subject to debate, in practice the term has most frequently been applied to the region that became the southwestern states of the United States and the northerly states of Mexico. This definition was largely thanks to the Boltonians (students of Herbert Eugene Bolton) who saw it mainly as the space between the Anglo and Hispanic influence in the region. This book looks to be free of this Anglo-centric definition, refocusing instead on the borderlands of Spanish-controlled territories in America, rather than solely the history of what became the southwestern United States (in fairness, Professor Bolton envisioned and wrote of borderlands across a hemispheric view of the Americas).[8] This broader definition allows us to understand the borderlands in a Spanish American context, which better reflects the actual experiences of the subjects of this book rather than a reconstruction of historical facts framed by current national borders. Furthermore, we define the borderlands not just as a geographic space, but also as a cultural space where the weakness of Spanish institutions allowed for the development of hierarchies and interactions that were anathema to the colonial regime's core values of subjugation and acculturation of non-European populations.

In line with that way of imagining borderlands as spaces where Spanish control waned, we recognize in this volume that there were internal borderlands as well. By the term *internal borderlands*, we mean those spaces that otherwise existed within the well-established areas of colonial administration and power that the colonial state failed repeatedly to control. Examples addressed in the present book include maroon communities on the fringes of established colonial centers. Such sites of *marronage* existed on Caribbean Island colonies, in Andean centers of Spanish power, and in places where the wealth of the Spanish empire passed from the Pacific Ocean to the Caribbean, and thus to the Atlantic Ocean. So-called internal borderlands operated as sites of refuge but also as sites of purposeful resistance, planning, and execution of intentional acts against the Spanish authorities. And these sites were not isolated from frontier borderlands as persons in internal borderlands often found themselves in frontier zones as well, as historians have noted the mobility of Africans and Afro-descendants between these places and metropolitan centers. To be clear, such movement is what enabled such persons to exert authority in some places and negotiate their existence in others, and we should be vigilant in recognizing this phenomenon in the colonial context.

The volume offers additional ways of reading lives on the borderlands of Spanish America. While the order of the essays follows the landscape of the Americas north to south, the essays may also be read from a variety of other perspectives.

Comparative regional perspectives exist within and between the essays, some taking transregional approaches. Gender is an important lens in some chapters, while others examine or expose caste fluidity for Blacks in borderlands. Many of the essays feature marronage and sanctuary; the reader may find it useful to examine these themes in differing spaces within the greater Spanish American landscape as meanings of sanctuary varied and indigenous peoples played a role in ensuring the same more in some places than others. Likewise, the reader may wish to compare the use of rival geographies as a mechanism for understanding Afro-descendants' roles in border regions and how their experience proved similar. In sum, while the book is organized with a specific geographical framework, temporally and thematically the reader will find other manners of engaging these essays if so desired.

Chapters

The book is organized geographically, from the far north of Spanish America in California to the far south in Patagonia. This special emphasis is to demonstrate how widespread African and Afro-descendants presence was in the Spanish American Borderlands. While certain chronologies were factors in the construction of Black lives in the Borderlands, the spare nature of documentation in so many different regions makes it difficult to create an integrated timeline. While this volume is by no means geographically comprehensive, it is designed to give the reader a sense of the far-reaching presence of Africans and their descendants in Spanish American frontiers.

The first chapter, by editor Cameron Jones, examines the lives of Afro-descendants during the Spanish colonization of California. The true impact of Afro-descendants on early California has been little understood, because many Spanish Californians of African descent hid their origins in church records by referring to themselves as "gente de razón," or people of reason. Some came as settlers, but many were soldiers assigned to the missions to protect against indigenous uprisings. For Afro-descendants the anonymity that came with distance from the centers of political power provided an opportunity to raise their social position. They hoped that the Crown's desire for Hispanicized settlers could overcome their perceived inferior origin that elsewhere barred them from passing in the higher echelons of society. In some cases, it did, leading to Afro-descendant leadership in California on the cusp of Mexican Independence.

In the second chapter, Christina Villarreal explores how Black fugitives from slavery forged their own geographies and routes of emancipation in the Gulf Coast borderlands of the eighteenth century, from Texas to Florida. By paying close attention to colonial practices, and by observing other runaways, Black fugitives learned how and where to achieve asylum and/or liberation within Spanish-claimed spaces. In the process, they influenced how Spanish colonial officials exercised control over their territory, administered legal manumission, and enforced religious sanctuary. This essay explores how and where enslaved individuals fled captivity along the Gulf Coast throughout the eighteenth century. Using interdisciplinary methods from feminist and critical geography, the chapter reconstructs geographies of resistance to understand how challenges to colonial oppression shaped imperial territory and created alternative spaces for asylum. Specifically, it traces the movements of Black runaways to map the different routes and sites fugitives created to pursue emancipation. It makes use of archival material from Spain, Louisiana, and Texas to consider the question: how did landscapes of self-emancipation impact the borderlands of Spanish America?

The third essay by Joseph M. H. Clark investigates the linkages between New Spain's northern borderland and the Caribbean world in the late seventeenth and eighteenth centuries, focusing in particular on the way political and economic changes in both spheres affected Africans and their descendants. The end of the seventeenth century brought sweeping changes to the landscape of European colonization in the Americas. In some scholarly accounts, these developments portend the emergence of two discrete paths of colonial history: one in the Caribbean, typified by the dramatic expansion of plantation slavery, and one in the North American borderlands, typified by border disputes between European and indigenous empires and societies. Clark argues that understanding early North American borderlands as the extension of an existing maritime frontier in the Caribbean allows us to better contextualize African experiences. As demographics and slave regimes underwent stunning transformation in the Caribbean islands, precedents drawn from earlier Caribbean societies informed racial customs in the North American mainland. As in the earlier Caribbean, in new frontier settlements, free and enslaved African diasporas fulfilled a myriad of social and labor roles and used overlapping and contested jurisdictions to access social and physical mobility and to construct distinctive cultural identities. By emphasizing the continuities between Caribbean and mainland settlements, we not only better understand Black experiences in the borderlands, but we also begin to see coherent diasporic identities across times and spaces that often appear fragmented.

The fourth chapter examines the fluidity of racial categorizations in the hinterland of Jalisco, New Spain. In particular, Anne Reid looks at the life of María Faustina who in parish records was labeled as a *mulata* or a mestiza with her child ultimately being labeled as Spanish. This case of racial (mis)identification speaks to the larger practice of church officials who assigned, sometimes randomly, racial caste categories based on the phenotypes of their parishioners. These racial categorizations suggest that other factors may have also influenced how persons of African descent, like mulatas, could birth Spanish (español) children, despite the rigidity of socioracial hierarchy. Contrary to the dominant eighteenth-century narrative that persons of African ancestry and their descendants could not achieve whiteness, the phenomenon of transcending racial categories from Black, to indigenous, and to white, was much more common in practice than the rigid *casta* system hierarchies admitted, especially in the borderlands.

Continuing south, in the fifth chapter Mark Lentz examines the intrepid founders of San Benito, Petén, Guatemala, a town on the outskirts of the provincial capital of Petén, where fugitive Belizean Blacks escaped from slavery in British territory in 1795. Like many other enslaved inhabitants in the British territory that bordered Spain's expansive holdings, the pueblo's first settlers secured their permission to stay on the Spanish side by requesting conversion to Catholicism. From 1693 until 1790, Spain's sanctuary policy granted refuge to enslaved peoples fleeing Protestant-ruled lands for Spanish territories if they sought baptism. Yet the policy ended in Florida definitively in 1790. By 1800, neighboring Yucatán no longer recognized the claims of Belizeans seeking freedom. By contrast, hundreds of slaves from Belize continued to cross the imperial borderlands until 1825, bolstering San Benitos' numbers. Their persistence in the face of an uncertain future ensured that the practice of accepting fugitives from Belize remained in effect through the early independence period, long after Spain had revoked the guarantee of refuge. This chapter examines the legal strategies of these former slaves and how they kept a policy alive locally after its demise at the imperial level. In doing so, they exploited the uncertainty and variability of law on the ground and entrenched practices that prevailed in border regions.

In the sixth chapter, Robert Schwaller returns to a comparative analysis of island and mainland maroon independence, comparing Spanish-maroon conflict on Hispaniola and in Panama. For most of the sixteenth century, Spaniards struggled to control sizable numbers of Africans who had fled enslavement and established themselves as *cimarrones* (maroons). This chapter will argue that differences in local economies and geopolitical significance of these two regions resulted in different outcomes. Despite similar patterns of conflict, Spanish officials in Panama chose to negotiate with maroons and establish the first two free-Black communities in the Americas. In Hispaniola, only limited negotiation occurred, and officials instead opted for a radical reorganization of Spanish settlement on the island as a means to limit conflict with maroons and foreign interlopers. Ultimately, these cases reveal the multiple forces that mediated the response of Spaniards to maroons in different parts of the circum-Caribbean.

The seventh chapter moves the narrative to South America, as Juliet Wiersema's chapter explores cases of African autonomy and opportunity in New Granada's Chocó. By the mid-eighteenth century in this remote mining region, some Africans and their descendants had acquired their freedom, owned their own mines and enslaved workers, and operated in niche markets that addressed local demands, including money lending and canoe transport. These same individuals successfully navigated the complex Spanish legal system, gained *vecindad* (citizenship), and created strong multigenerational communities with other free-Black mining families.

Charles Beatty-Medina's essay in chapter eight considers African and Native American marronage on the Pacific coast borderland of sixteenth- and seventeenth-century Quito. The coast of northern Ecuador formed both a hard barrier to colonization and conquest as well as a porous border for escaping African slaves and native peoples. Therefore, it created an autonomous society of independent communities of African and indigenous peoples who held significant power and authority over commerce, labor, and physical control of the region. The coastal borderland, rather than simply a desolated husk of conquest, became a significant focal point of activity for maroon-centered processes of colonization, trade, and social interactions. Understanding the centrality of Esmeraldas in the larger Atlantic world underlines the importance of Africans and Afro-descendants in the development of Spanish America.

Rachel Sarah O'Toole underlines how African and Afro-descendant fugitives, especially those sold from Angola, Congo, and Cabinda, engaged in oppositional strategies to enslavers and colonial authorities in provincial, northern Peru. This ninth chapter explores how primarily fugitive men confronted the rural guard, intent on their capture, calling attention to their masculine qualities that made them equal to enslavers. By examining the ritual language of fugitive communities surrounding coastal sugar and wheat estates of the Peruvian northern coast, this chapter illuminates how West Central African fugitive communities were in dialogue with surrounding indigenous and Spanish sovereignties. Specifically, the gendered politics of fugitive communities reveals how African and Afro-descendant men employed their military skills to claim positions of patriarchal patronage.

In the tenth and final chapter, Alex Borucki examines the range of divergent frontier and borderland experiences of Africans and their descendants in late colonial Buenos Aires, Montevideo, and the countryside surrounding these two towns. The Río de la Plata constituted different types of borderlands for Africans and their descendants. Some of this population had relations with Native peoples who lived outside Spanish control both in the pampas south of Buenos Aires and between the Portuguese and Spanish territorial claims in what is today Uruguay and Southern Brazil. In these borderlands, Africans served as mediators and translators between Spanish colonial interests and the native population. Other Africans and their descendants played an important role in the Spanish-Portuguese colonial borderlands in relation with the imperial politics of this region. Particularly in the maritime region around the Río de la Plata, Africans and their descendants were integral to life on ships connecting Brazilian ports, most prominently Rio de Janeiro, with Buenos Aires and Montevideo in a time of peaking trans-imperial traffic in the South Atlantic. Africans and their descendants used these borderlands to shape their own strategies to gain freedom, autonomy, and subjecthood.

Representation of Communities in Scholarly Production

This volume, like so many other academic products, is one written by experts in the regions and periods that made up the Spanish American imperial project in the Americas writ large. That said, it is a product of the academic milieu in which it was produced and does not include direct representation in terms of authorship by the descendants of the peoples addressed throughout its chapters. Our authors have exercised great care in their use of language to express, as accurately as they can, the lived experiences of the peoples who are their subjects on the pages that follow. Representation of a people's stories by their descendants is a laudable goal and one we hope to see in the places and spaces addressed in the volume, in future scholarship on Africans and their descendants in the Spanish American Borderlands.

Notes

1. The editors used as a language guide to talk about slavery P. Gabrielle Foreman et al., CMS 14.32 "Writing about Slavery/Teaching About Slavery: This Might Help," community-sourced document, June 28, 2021, https://docs.google.com/document/d/1A4TEdDgYs-lX-hlKezLodMIM71My3KTN0zxRv0IQTOQs/mobilebasic. This was to ensure that this volume did not perpetuate language that normalizes the inequalities of slavery and the racist institutions Africans and their descendants faced in the Americas in general.

2. Critical Race Theory emerged from a group of American legal scholars in the 1970s and '80s, including Derrick Bell, Alan Freeman, Kimberlé Crenshaw, Richard Delgado, Cheryl Harris, Charles R. Lawrence III, Mari Matsuda, and Patricia J. Williams. See Amy Ansell, "Critical Race Theory," 344–46.

3. Probably the most famous examples of this line of thinking from where this quote was taken is Domingo Faustino Sarmiento's *Facundo: Civilización y barbarie*, first published in 1845. The most recent English version is Domingo Faustino Sarmiento, *Facundo: Civilization and Barbarism* (Berkeley: University of California Press, 2004).

4. Lewis, "Negros, Negros-indios, Afromexicanos," 49–73.

5. Vasconcelos, *La Raza Cósmica: Misión de la raza iberoamericana*.

6. Martínez Montiel, "Our Third Root," 165–85.

7. Peter Wade, *Degrees of Mixture, Degrees of Freedom*, 99–100.

8. See the introduction to Bannon, ed., *Bolton and the Spanish Borderlands*. See also Hurtado, *Herbert Eugene Bolton*.

AT THE HEART

OF THE

BORDERLANDS

CHAPTER ONE

"SE LLAMAN GENTE DE RAZÓN"

Afro-Descendants in Early Spanish California, 1769–1821

Cameron D. Jones

SCHOLARS READILY accept that Afro-descendants populated early Spanish California. Though little work has been done on the topic, often cited is the census of 1790, which includes California's four presidios, San Diego, Santa Barbara, Monterey, and San Francisco, along with its two struggling towns, San Jose and Los Angeles, that identifies roughly 19 percent of their populations as being of African descent.[1] The extent of the impact of Afro-descendants in early California, however, has been little understood and little examined. This is because many Spanish Californians of African descent hid their origins in church and state records, often just referring to themselves as "gente de razón" or people of reason. This ethnic designation was prevalent among frontier areas in Northern Mexico (now the Southwest of the United States) and generally meant people who lived in or near the missions that spoke Spanish were Catholics, but not subject to the missionaries.

Furthermore, resistance to understanding the racial makeup of early Californian settlers has come from local traditional narratives in the nineteenth, twentieth, and even into the twenty-first centuries that perpetuate popular racist notions. Local histories tend to portray populations of color in a negative light without any evidence for their allegations except their race, for example, calling the forty-four inhabitants of Los Angeles, who were mostly of color, "half-criminals," or the "off-scourings of colonial Mexico." People's own internalized racism also tends to cause an obsession with the few actual Spaniards living in early California. Some go as far as searching archives for spurious claims of nobility when in reality only the highest, nonpermanent government officials held such titles. The more public manifestation of these Eurocentric historical revisions remains in things like Santa Barbara's "Old Spanish Days," where Spanish tradition and history are emphasized rather than the Mexican (or even African) traditions of its settlers.[2]

This chapter will look both at the number of Afro-descendants and the challenges they faced as soldiers and colonists in California. It will argue that the known estimates of Afro-descendants in California are low at best, given the incentive that hiding one's identity brought. Just as in the case of María Faustina Trejo (chapter 4) and Africans in the Río de la Plata region (chapter 10), Afro-descendants in California used the ambiguities created by their distance from colonial centers of power and Spain's desire for Catholic, Spanish-speaking settlers as a vehicle for social advancement. This, of course, did not come without its challenges as the racial hierarchy ran deep within Spanish colonial society. In the case of Afro-descendants, however, at least some did overcome such structural racism to form part of the early California elite and had an important impact on the development of the mission and rancho systems.

Identifying the African Presence in California

The presence of Afro-descendants in California is unsurprising given the larger trends in race demographics in Spanish America. Africans had been present in Mexico since Cortez in 1519. In the early eighteenth century, however, the number of Africans arriving in Mexico exploded, due principally to the British receiving the *asiento* (or monopoly) over the slave trade to Spanish America. As compared to British and French colonies, a larger percentage of these Africans were manumitted. These higher rates of manumission were due to Spain's long legal tradition with slavery, which unlike their northern European counterparts had been continuously practiced in the Iberian Peninsula through the medieval period. The Spanish medieval law code, *Las Siete Partidas*, established the principal that all slaves had a right to manumission if they could pay their enslavers the cost of buying another enslaved person of a similar age and sex to replace them. Courts regulated this process forcing enslavers to accept fair market value no matter if the enslaved person possessed specialized skills valuable to their enslavers. Such high rates of manumission led to growing and economically viable communities of free Blacks and people of mixed African ancestry throughout Latin America. Enforcement of the laws regarding manumission were, of course, inconsistent, prone to corruption, and more carefully adhered to in urban areas where civil and ecclesiastic authorities had more sway over enslavers. Furthermore, while legally free, these Afro-descendants were still subject to both the legal restrictions and limitations imposed by the socioracial hierarchy of Hispanic society. Many moved to frontier regions where social distinctions were more blurred, and people of color could hope to achieve a higher socioeconomic status. Indeed, it was probably for this reason that many Afro-descendants in frontier areas, such as California, chose to conceal their racial heritage. They hoped that the Crown's desire for Hispanicized settlers could overcome their perceived inferior origin that elsewhere barred them from passing in the higher echelons of society.[3]

Identifying Afro-descendants in the colonial Spanish context, even in the colonial center, can be difficult. The language used to describe different racial groups reflected in many ways the complicated relationship colonial Spanish society had with race. While this is not to say that a racial hierarchy did not exist, racial categories could be more fluid, reflecting the chaotic formation of colonial Latin America itself. As three racial groups came together, European, Native, and African, identifying one's race became almost impossible. By the late eighteen century, Spanish intellectuals had drawn up complicated lists of how certain racial categories were created, such as specifying that the union of a mestizo and a Spaniard begat a *castizo* (someone who is one quarter indigenous and three-fourths Spaniard). While such terms were used in colonial documents, such care to determine the exact racial makeup was rarely taken. Race, as a social construct, was determined by appearance both physical and social. Race, therefore, could change depending on the perception of one's social standing. For example, even a person's style of dress or clear Spanish diction could allow them to pass as a supposedly superior racial category, or *casta*.[4]

In referring to people of African descent, several words were commonly used. While English generally uses *Black* to describe someone of mostly or completely African descent and *mulatto* to describe anyone of mixed African ancestry, colonial Spanish used several words. Documents used *Negro* to describe Blacks and *Mulato* to describe mulattos, but also used interchangeably *Moreno* and *Pardo*, respectfully, to mean the same thing. Afro-descendants seemed to have preferred the latter terms rather than the former in referring to themselves and they seem to have had a more positive connotation particularly in the late eighteenth and early nineteenth centuries. Though less common, however, terms like *color quebrado* (broken color) and *morizco* (Moor) were also used to describe people of African descent. In California, no fewer than eleven designations are used to describe race in the historical record. To further complicate the matter, at least in California's colonial documents, there is no category for a person of mixed mestizo and mulatto heritage. Generally, they are just called mestizos, further downplaying the African influence in early California.[5]

In California's historical documents, not surprisingly, the description of people's race changed over time. The reasons for this could be multiple: from the social standing of an individual affecting how their race was perceived by the community to simply the judgement of the census taker on the color of their skin. William Marvin Mason in his study of the 1790 California census has identified dozens of examples of people's race changing over time. José María Pico, for example, is listed in 1790 as being a Spaniard, even though his four brothers and mother, María Jacinta de la Bastida, are listed as being mulattos. Pico was from a large family who later gained prominence in California and generally the family is acknowledged to be of African descent. Máximo Alanís had no less than four racial designations over his lifetime including mulatto, Indian, mestizo, and Spaniard. By the end of the colonial period, many of the colonists just began to use the title *gente de razón*, especially among the soldiers who by 1790 made up 73 percent of the non-indigenous adult male population.[6] Therefore, looking at census and church records gives an incomplete picture of the racial and ethnic makeup of early California.

Afro-descendants and the Military

The fact that many of the soldiers that came to California were of African descent also is in line with changes in the Spanish Colonial military during the late eighteenth century. Free people of color in Latin America had a long history of serving in colonial militias. While such service offered little or no pay, it did bestow social prestige, which many Afro-descendants desired. Furthermore, military legal exemptions, or *fueros*, not only gave Afro-descendants special legal protections but also allowed them to avoid many of the taxes typically imposed on nonwhite populations. Soldiers of color served in segregated militias, which, while giving them prestige in their own communities, did in more settled areas prevent them from being accepted into the highest socioeconomic circles that were generally reserved for people of principally European descent (or those who could pass as such).[7] Service in the regular army, however, was prohibited, as it was for all American-born Spanish subjects, for fear that it would create a force that could rebel against the Crown. This prohibition was lifted in 1763, after a humiliating defeat at the hands of the British a year before as part of the Seven Years' War, which resulted in the temporary loss of Havana. Crown authorities began to recruit American-born subjects into the army. Ideally, they sought Creoles or Peninsulars, but given the long tradition of militia service among Afro-descendants, and Spain's desperation, many soldiers of color filled the regular army ranks.[8]

The military presence in California was part of a push to take influence out of the hands of the missionaries while emphasizing cultural assimilation of indigenous populations. By the mid-eighteenth century, many in the Spanish government believed that while attempting to make converts dependent on the missions, frontier missionaries had failed to make them good Spanish subjects, occupied in "useful" European-style trades and taxable commerce. Starting in 1749 in the frontier region of Nuevo Santander, colonial officials enacted what they called the "New Method of Evangelization," a colonization effort led by the military rather than the Church. Soldiers were to escort settlers to frontier areas where they were to mix with the native population and thereby convert and acculturate them to Spanish Catholicism.

In California the New Method met with fierce resistance from the missionaries who had a free hand in administering the missions. In 1772, the viceroy tried to limit the missionaries' activities to just preaching and saying mass, to which Friar Francisco Palóu responded, "If it must be that way, better that we retire to the College." Knowing that the colony would not survive without the friars' support, the Crown acquiesced and allowed the missions to continue to be administered by the friars. The problem was attracting colonists to far off California. With the exception of the Juan Batista de Anza and the Fernando Rivera y Moncada expeditions (1775–1777), very few Hispanicized peoples wanted to come. As a result, the nonnative population never exceeded two thousand during the entire Spanish period with most of it coming from the natural increase of these early colonists. Most of those who did not already come as soldiers incorporated into the presidial force anyway as their few numbers necessitated a strong military presence to repel rebellion and gave those who joined social prestige in the new colony. Most of the labor for agricultural production and building came from the indigenous population attached to the missions, making the nonnative population beholden to the native, and by extension the influence of the friars. Of course, it was a symbiotic relationship since the missionaries had to depend on the soldiers for protection against rebellions, of which there were several.[9]

Of the military companies that entered California during the initial expansion, only one was an all-European unit, the Catalan Volunteers. They, however, numbered only twenty-five, and twelve of them died even before they reached San Diego. Furthermore, only five stayed after the initial Portolá expedition that was the first to colonize California (1768–1770). Ninety-five Catalans did then return in 1796, sent there out of fear of a British invasion, but their presence was temporary and most were withdrawn by 1804–1805. Due to the deployment of the companies, the Catalans were mainly concentrated in the northern regions of Alta California around the presidio of San Francisco.[10]

The other companies mentioned in the historical record, the Company of Loreto and Company of Cuera (the leatherjacket company), as well as the colonists of the Anza and Rivera expeditions, were drawn from frontier areas, such as Sonora, Sinaloa, and Baja California, which all had sizable Afro-descendant populations. Records from third-party observers suggest that indeed while most of the commissioned officers in these units were Creoles, noncommissioned officers and private soldiers were mostly mulattos and mestizos. Soldiers were distributed throughout the mission system with a squad of six in each mission under the command of a corporal. Larger numbers of troops were of course stationed at the five California presidios in San Diego, Santa Barbara, Monterrey, San Francisco, and later Sonoma. Many of these soldiers and settlers also brought their families, suggesting they had always considered service in California to be permanent.[11] For example, after the Portolá expedition fifty of the men in these companies decided to stay (as opposed to just five Catalans).[12] As many of these soldiers in early California sought to hide their race, uncovering it from census records has proved difficult, but other records remain that help to show the extent of the African influence in California.

The Cádiz Questionnaire

One of the most revealing sources of the racial makeup of the gente de razón in California was a result of conflicts on the other side of the globe. After the Napoleonic invasion of the Iberian Peninsula in 1808, many of Spain's most liberal-minded politicians gathered in one of the few remaining Spanish strongholds, Cádiz. In 1812, this rump of Spain's political elite, under the watchful eye of the British, promulgated probably one of the most liberal constitutions of the nineteenth century. The Spanish Constitution of 1812 created a limited monarchy, which shared power with a unicameral legislative body, the Cortes. What is remarkable about this document was that it extended nearly universal male suffrage to all of Spain's possessions. The one exception was those of African or mixed African origins. The constitution did not, for example, abolish slavery, and enslaved individuals were, of course, barred from voting. Furthermore, voting rights for people of African descent were, according to the Constitution, only given to those who had proven themselves in military service.[13] Keeping the need to understand these demographics in mind, Dr. Ciniaro Gonzales Carvajal, internal overseas secretary for the Cádiz government, issued a questionnaire in October 1812 aimed at inventorying the cultural and ethnic makeup of the California missions. While most of the questions regarded specifically the native inhabitants, who had been given voting rights, much to the terror of the Creoles, the first two questions sought to understand the nonnative population: "1. Express how many castes the people are divided into, that is American, Europeans, Indians, Mestizos, Blacks, etc. without omission." The second question then focused on the Black populations: "2. What is the origin of these castes with exception of the first two (American, which probably assumes Creoles, and Europeans)." "This [you] will relate," the question continued, "with respects to (the fact that) Blacks are not of the same origin everywhere, while in general it is Africans that have come to America, in the Philippines there are [Blacks] that are natural to that land, hiding in the jungle since the Malaysians dominated that island" (which is referring to the so-called Moros of the Southern Philippines). The questionnaire was first sent to the Bishop of Sonora, who remitted it to the Franciscan College of San Fernando, which administered the California missions. Finally, in late 1813, just a few months before the restoration of the Spanish monarchy and consequently the fall of the Cádiz government, it was distributed to the California missions for the friars stationed there to respond.[14]

As alluded to earlier, most of the priests identified the inhabitants that were not themselves or the indigenous Californians as gente de razón, using the phrase precisely in fourteen of the nineteen responses. Most of these were the soldiers stationed at the missions and their families. Several friars struggled to define what they meant by gente de razón. Friar Juan Amerés of Monterrey stated, "[They] call themselves *gente de Razón* without distinction of class or caste; and with passable Spanish, they think of themselves as the heroes of these new lands; so thus I will be excused from making a distinction between caste or class of these people, because they do not understand themselves that way, just as *gente de razón*."[15] As Friar Amerés's quote suggested the *gente de razón* did not want to be given racial labels, probably because they fell short of elite categories. They did want to be known for their participation in the annexation of California into the sphere of Spanish influence, essentially as conquistadors. Such service could earn them rewards from Crown officials, many of whom were in far-off Mexico City, therefore making racial anonymity important for their strategy of social advancement.

Fortunately for modern historians, though perhaps not for the gente de razón, some missionaries were more explicit about their racial makeup. Whether the missionaries' openness on this matter was simply an insensitivity to the desire of these people to hide their racial heritage or a conscious attempt to reinforce racial hierarchy is unclear. The best example were the missionaries of San Luis Obispo who stated: "Of the Gente de Razon there are six men and their families of which five are Mulattos or Mestizos, [or in other words] the offspring of Mulattos and Indians, [and] one is European . . . the offspring of a European and Neophyte woman from Monterrey."[16] Of the nineteen responses to this questionnaire, twelve made reference to people who were neither white Creoles nor Peninsulars nor Native Californians and six specified that some of these people were of African origin. Treating these responses as a census and simply counting the number of people identified in each category, however, gives a false impression of what was really happening demographically.[17]

Indeed, in many ways the manner in which the missionaries failed to respond to these very specific questions can be just as revealing as those who were more forthright. Some missionaries, for example, simply dodged the questions. The missionaries of San Luis Rey simply said in response to the origin of the soldiers garrisoned there that they were from the Presidio of San Diego.[18] The friars at Santa Cruz waxed more philosophic, stating, "To tell the truth, [we] ministers ignore the diversity of bloods and mixing that there is in the Indies; because until now our attention since we came from Spain has only been the caring of Souls."[19] The mission priest at San Jose gave just as cryptic of an answer but perhaps a more revealing one: "[The soldiers] repute themselves to be all Spaniards, although perhaps there is the same diversity among them as there are in other parts of America."[20] The friar at Santa Barbara, possibly explaining the reluctance of the missionaries to publicly state the race of the soldiers, admitted that while most likely not all of them were Peninsular or Creole Spaniards, "it would seem to give them great offense to suggest that they were not and thus we cannot respond any other way."[21] Certainly one can understand the reluctance of this missionary to out the racial identity in a way that may be prejudicial to the socioeconomic advancement of the only men in the mission with guns.

José and Juan José

The probability that many of the private soldiers were of African descent sheds light on events that occurred in Santa Cruz in 1824. One evening in late August, Juan José, a native living in the mission , was at home with his wife when a "*negro*," or Black man, named José seemingly burst into his home. José's status of servitude is unclear, given that he was identified as a *negro*, as opposed to a *moreno*, suggests that he might currently or had at one time been enslaved. He was accompanied by sixteen-year-old Francisco Rochin, the son of a soldier stationed at the mission, Miguel Rochin. Both father and son are listed in church records as gente de razón. After entering the abode, "*el negro*" José then demanded that Juan José give them meat. When he refused, José called the indigenous man a "whore's wart" and then emitted flatus at him in an insulting manner (he farted in his general direction). Such rudeness so enraged Juan José that he threw a stick at "*el negro*" José who retreated outside. Juan José then pursued José, but by the time he got outside, José had grabbed the stick just thrown at him and beat Juan José "until his head split open." The indigenous man, Juan José, later claimed that he had not previously known his assailant.[22] The corporal commanding the mission detail put José in a cell and almost immediately had him punished, most likely publicly flogged, without first getting authorization, because he feared that if the natives in the mission saw that "no one does anything for them, and they being vengeful, it will come upon all of us."[23]

While certainly the corporal would want to dissuade indigenous rebellion and punish anybody associated with the mission for such a crime, the urgency with which he punished José suggests deeper concerns. Colonial officials could be and were often punished themselves for overstepping their authority in matters of justice even in frontier areas. The corporal, therefore, was taking some risk in his expediency. Perhaps the fact that the "*negro*" José looked like many of the soldiers under his command made it essential that he act quickly. Further evidence of the association between José and the corporal's men lies in the fact that the assailant was accompanied by Francisco Rochin, a gente de razón, and the son of one of his soldiers. Even in the socially ambiguous setting of frontier California, a Peninsular or even Creole so freely associating with a Black man, especially during such a nefarious act, would have been in itself scandalous. The fact that no comment was made about this suggests that the corporal understood that the socioracial standing, and perhaps the appearance, of the two men was not so different. The indigenous people of the village, therefore, would make little distinction between the gente de razón and this Black man.

The Limits of Racial Ambiguities

While racial ambiguities in some parts of California allowed for at least some form of informal racial passing, race and one's status in society did matter. Take the story of an enslaved twelve-year-old African boy named Máximo in the Presidio of San Francisco. The fort was garrisoned by the only all-Spanish company in California, the Catalan volunteers. San Francisco had just been reinforced in 1796 by ninety-five new troops. Spanish officials feared a British invasion after the Spanish switched sides in the French Revolutionary War enveloping all of Europe. Spain's flip-flop occurred as a result of their humiliating defeat in the War of the Pyrenees a year before. Included in that reinforcement was a new commandant of the presidio, Lieutenant Colonel Pedro Alberni. In June 1798, Alberni claimed that he noticed the chest that held the garrison's funds was open. Swearing that he had last seen it locked, he counted the money to find seventy-seven pesos missing. He immediately focused his inquiry on his personal servant, an enslaved "11 or 12-year-old" boy named Máximo. The boy admitted that he had seen one of the soldiers of the garrison, Faustino Hoseguera, taking coins from the box during prayers a few evenings earlier. Alberni commanded that Sargent Joaquin Tico arrest Hosequera and search his house where he found six pesos in the thatch of his roof above his bed. Having been the victim of the crime, Alberni ordered his second-in-command, Captain Josef Aguellos, to judge the case. During the testimonies, Máximo held to his story that he had seen Hosequera enter the room where the chest was held and, seeing that it was open, grabbed two large handfuls of pesos. While other witnesses could collaborate that they saw Máximo and Hosequera together, they could not substantiate the boy's claim. When Hosequera was finally interrogated, he claimed that Máximo had actually come to him with thirty pesos and gave them to him. He claimed that he did not know they were from the garrison's chest but still spent most of the money.[24]

Given this clear contradiction in the story, Aguellos questioned Máximo again. During the interrogation, however, Aguellos had his enslaver, Alberni, removed because he felt the boy was being timid in his responses. Nonetheless, Máximo stuck to his story, saying that Hosequera had taken the pesos. When asked whether Máximo had a good relationship with his enslaver, he responded that he did. Captain Aguellos ultimately seemed to side with Hosequera, placing the majority of the blame on Máximo. Since the boy was so young, the captain felt that capital punishment was too extreme and sentenced the twelve-year-old to eight years' service on a Spanish warship, mercifully "with rations," but of course without pay. Hosequera did not escape all punishment either since he had taken and spent the money. He was also sentenced to five years' service on a warship. Despite the contradiction, Aguellos felt that his conclusions were just and considered the case settled in his report to the governor of California who was required to ratify the sentences.[25]

One of the company sergeants, Josef Roca, however, sent along a differing account. Roca pointed out that there was no other evidence that Hosequera had stolen the money other than Máximo's story. He also questioned whether such a young boy would have had the wherewithal to steal the money himself. Furthermore only fourteen of the supposed seventy-seven pesos had been recovered from Hosequera (counting both money in his possession and the cost of the goods he had just bought) and nothing had been recovered from Máximo. Roca's alternative explanation was that the new comandante himself, Lieutenant Colonel Alberni, had stolen the money and forced the enslaved boy to take the blame, knowing that his age would mitigate any punishment. Such corruption was typical of Spanish officials, particularly far away from the prying eyes of high-ranking colonial officials such as in California, but perhaps Alberni feared that such an accusation would ruin his chances for advancement and ordered Máximo to take the fall. This story seems more plausible given the contradicting testimonies and Máximo's apparent timid behavior while Alberni was present during his interrogation. Máximo would have been an easy patsy, since the word of an enslaved Black boy would have carried little weight against his European officer enslaver. Though the final resolution of the case is unclear, Alberni wanted to expedite the ratification of the sentence since a ship waited in the bay that would allow Hosequera and Máximo to immediately start their sentences.[26]

As the story of Máximo demonstrates, race, and to a certain extent status, did matter in Alta California. The more powerful Alberni was able to blame his own crimes on his enslaved servant. While imperial needs allowed Afro-descendant soldiers and settlers that came to California opportunities for social mobility, a young, enslaved boy like Máximo had no such chance. The social and racial hierarchies were still deeply entrenched in the Spanish imperial system. Even a Spaniard like Hosequera was swept up in the affair and potentially served time. Hosequera was only a foot soldier and, judging by the fact that he could only sign his name with a crude cross, was most likely illiterate, and his arrest and prosecution on seemingly false charges caused little scandal.

Even Afro-descendant soldiers who achieved a measure of prominence had limitations in their ability to climb the social hierarchy during the Spanish period. A survey of the 1814 service reviews of the cavalry officers serving in Alta California bears out these disparities. Most of the commissioned officers list their *quality*, a term sometimes used as an approximation of race that incorporated someone's perceived social standing, as either being "Spanish" or "noble." The term *noble* here is seemingly used to describe someone of Spanish or European descent rather than connote a rank of nobility given that no other evidence for such status is given. Many of the noncommissioned officers, mainly sergeants, have their "quality" listed as "honored," including a well-known soldier of African descent, José María Pico. Though it is not a perfect stand-in for race, it does have a connotation that this person had earned his position rather than being born to it. In colonial Latin America two terms were used to describe the English word *honor*. The first was *honor*, which was a quality that was passed through birth rather than earned. A person with honor generally was of legitimate birth and of European descent. *Honra*, however, was used to describe the type of honor that is earned by one's actions. In the service reviews, the word used to describe these sergeants' "quality" is *honrrado*, the past participle of *honra*.[27] These were men who had earned their positions and despite their racial background not being of pure European descent, they were granted rank due to their service. There, however, seemed to be a limit to the honrrados rise in the ranks, with only two of them being listed as a lieutenant (a commissioned officer), while the rest were sergeants (noncommissioned officers). Also, those officers listed as honrrados were much older than their "Spanish" or "noble" counterparts. The ages of the honrrado commissioned officers were forty-nine and sixty, while most of the other lieutenants were in their thirties. Furthermore these honrrado officers had to rise through the ranks starting as a private soldier and work their way up to become an officer, while the "noble" officers started their careers as cadets. There were some "nobles" that did work their way up, including the inspector himself, Captain José Aguellos. However, it seems clear that nepotism was at play in receiving advancement since many of the youngest cadets shared the same last name as Aguellos.[28]

The Afro-descendent Population and the Native Californians: Godparents, Marriages, and Rebellions

While tracking the influence Afro-descendants had on the native populations is difficult at best, not just because Afro-descendants tended to not want to be identified but also because neither group left many records, there are windows into this relation if one looks at the ethnicity of gente de razón. Again, this is not a perfect stand-in for Afro-descendants, but probably most in this category were at least people of color (or those who could not pass as being of primarily European descent). Probably the three best ways to demonstrate this relationship is by looking at godparentage of indigenous baptisms, marriages between gente de razón and natives, and the gente de razón's suppression of native rebellions.

Throughout the Hispanic world, ties of *padrinazgo* (or godparentage) were essential relationships that bound communities together. Godparents are assigned to all Catholic converts at the time of their baptism, whether adults or children. Godparents share the responsibility for both the temporal and spiritual wellbeing of their godchildren and, in the case of legal minors, take responsibility for the children in case of the parents' untimely deaths. This was not to say that a godchild was equal to one of the godparents' own biological children, the status of the godchild within society would be taken into consideration. In many cases, parents sought to tie their children (or in the case of their own baptism themselves) to a more powerful figure who could watch out for their interests or at the very least prevent them from starving to death by giving them employment. Godparents and their godchildren were therefore not matched haphazardly and taking on such a responsibility usually assumed a preexisting relationship. In the Early California Population Project (ECPP) database, which is a survey of most of the known sacramental records in California from 1768 to 1848, the godparents' ethnicity is listed 1,314 times, of which 827 are categorized as gente de razón. This represents 62 percent of the total godparents where ethnicity is listed. Only 56 Spaniards or Europeans are listed as godparents where the rest were listed as *Indios* (most likely native Californians). While ethnicity is only listed in a fraction of the 101,000 baptisms in the database, if these ratios are a good sample, then they demonstrate the gente de razón's important contribution to the colony. The numbers get even more substantial when you look at the numbers of soldiers and noncommissioned officers, the group that most consistently identified as gente de razón. These servicemen served as godparents for 5,235 of the 6,016 baptisms where military status is listed. This is proportional to the number of soldiers and noncommissioned officers to that of commissioned officers, if not favoring commissioned officers given that there were so few in comparison to the former group, but still demonstrates the importance of this group serving as godparents.[29]

Another way in which the gente de razón population could have influenced native Californians is through marriage. Again, though the ethnicity of gente de razón is not a perfect stand-in for race, given the evidence previously stated, it can be assumed that at least a few were Afro-descendants. There was a long-standing tradition of Africans and Afro-descendants marrying native women. In his work on Africans in the Yucatán, an area not well-known for its African or Afro-descendant population, Mathew Restall demonstrates that marriages between Africans and native Mayan women were not only frequent but outnumbered those of African or Afro-descendant men choosing women of African descent. This may of course be due to the sex ratios among enslaved Africans brought over from Africa that tended to favor men two to one, but it certainly shows a pattern to watch. In the frontier this pattern was probably even more pronounced as few women of African or even European ancestry were available for coupling.[30]

This does not seem to have been the case in California, but probably more for the reason that the missionaries resented the Spanish military presence, of which most gente de razón belonged, rather than any sort of racist logic. Further impeding such marriages were changes in the late-eighteenth-century environment of the Spanish empire that at least tried to crack down on the wide-spread practice of miscegenation. The 1776 Royal Pragmatic on Marriage forced couples to get their parents' permission to wed if they were considered minors (age twenty-five for men and twenty-three for women). Parents could reject these marriages if they, and by extension the courts, judged the marriage to be an unequal match, which was often cited in cases when one member of the couple was of an "inferior" race, among other "undesirable" traits.[31] This was further reinforced by royal orders in 1803 and 1812, though the reissuing of the Pragmatic does suggest that it was not necessarily being followed. By the early nineteenth century in California, the enforcement of "unequal" marriage fell to an ecclesiastical tribunal popularly known as the *Diligencias Matrimoniales*. Probably for this reason, it seems very few marriages were recorded between gente de razón and natives (27 out of approximately 28,000 in the ECPP). No marriages, however, between a person of Spanish and mestizo descent and a native Californian are listed at all. In fact, the only other native/nonnative marriage in the ECPP is between a mulatto man and an indigenous woman. This not to say that they did not occur, but that there was perhaps an incentive to hide them. In the early years (1768–1800), marriages between gente de razón appear to be more frequent, with the vast majority of these 27 occurring within this range. This is logical given that at least some of the private soldiers that came to California were young, unwed males. Indeed, anecdotal evidence suggests that relationships with native women were quite desirable.

One of the most compelling examples of the desirability of native brides (or at least sexual partners) is found in the 1779 murder case of Corporal Alexo Antonio Duarte. Corporal Duarte was married to Gertrudis María, a native of "la cañada de Robles" (most likely modern-day Paso Robles, California). She was baptized at Mission San Antonio de Padua. Given her origin she was most likely from the Salinan Tribe, though it is not stated in the records.[32] Alexo Antonio Duarte is listed as a "Razón" in only one of the records in which he appears, though the record extractor noted that it seems that "Razón" was written sometime after the initial record. By 1779 they had at least two living daughters, though they had lost another shortly after her birth in 1778.[33]

On September 3, 1779, Corporal Duarte entered the courtyard of the barracks of the Presidio of Monterrey and, according to several witnesses, approached from behind a soldier named Antonio Espinosa, a native of Sinaloa and a gente de razón. After yelling "there's the dog," Duarte stabbed Espinosa in the back on the right side, sliding his knife two inches beneath the ribs, possibly penetrating Espinosa's liver and/or kidneys. According to Espinosa, at this he turned and ran from Duarte, who was now wielding his sword. Duarte, however, eventually cornered Espinosa, and in the struggle that ensued, Espinosa, though mortally wounded, was able to pry the sword out of Duarte's hands and stab him on his left side through the ribs, lacerating both Duarte's heart and lungs. Though his death record would later state that Duarte "died a violent death but gave signs of repentance" according to the presidio surgeon, he most likely was killed instantly by the wound. As the commandant questioned Espinosa on his deathbed whether there was a motive behind the initial attack, Espinosa at first said recently there had not been a problem between them, but finally admitted that three or four months previous he had had an argument with Duarte regarding his wife, Gertrudis María. Though he does not state the nature of the conflict, Duarte had ordered Espinosa to have no contact with his wife, which Espinosa claimed to have observed. Such a defense was unnecessary, however, since Espinosa joined Duarte in death, succumbing to his wounds at four in the morning the next day. Gertrudis María, of course, was not consulted on the matter, though perhaps the shock of her husband's death affected her in other ways. She gave birth to two twin girls four months later, both of whom died shortly after their births. Mother would follow her daughters four years later, dying at Mission San Antonio in 1784.[34]

While the case of Duarte and Espinoza may seem on the surface as a petty conflict between soldiers that turned fatal, it demonstrates the ways in which native women were important sexual and marriage partners. The soldiers had little choice in the matter. There were few nonnative women in California, particularly in those early years. If these men wanted to start a family, native Californian women were in most cases their only option. The case, however, also shows how jealously Duarte guarded this relationship. He was willing to kill (and ultimately be killed) to protect the exclusivity of his relationship with his wife. Though historical records may never give a complete insight into their relationship, at the very least it is clear that Duarte valued it, or the honor he would lose at not protecting it. What effect these relationships ultimately had on the native population is still relatively unclear, but given the intimacy they created, it must have been significant.

Finally, probably one of the most common ways gente de razón interacted with the native population is through suppressing rebellions and otherwise maintaining order in the missions. Since most of these individuals were soldiers their mandate was to maintain order in the colony. Though it challenges the romantic (or perhaps not so romantic) image of relationships such as Alexo Duarte and Gertrudis María's as described above, the hard truth is that many of these soldiers, even those of color, were there to subdue the native population.

One of the most famous examples of an Afro-descendant soldier aiding the suppression of a native revolt is that of José María Pico's role in Toypurina's Revolt. Fed up by the harsh work requirements put upon them, the Tongva of Mission San Gabriel plotted an uprising against the friars. Led by a runaway convert named Nicolas José, the rebels claimed that a woman named Toypurina had magical power sufficient to lull the mission guards to sleep, so that the Tongva could slaughter soldier and friar alike. Pico, who seemingly understood the Tongva language, overheard their plans and informed the garrison who suppressed the rebellion by arresting its leaders.[35] The story of the revolt underlines both the connection Afro-descendent soldiers had with the native population and their defense of the empire. Pico had had enough contact with the Tongva to have learned their language, but ultimately decided to inform his superiors in the Spanish army rather than aid the revolt. While Afro-descendants used their service in California as a vehicle of social prestige, it was still within the context of an oppressive empire.

Social Climbing

Despite the preexisting socioracial hierarchy, many Afro-descendants, particularly soldiers, were able to rise to great prominence in the chaotic transition from Spanish to Mexican control. They were able to get large land grants in the process of secularizing the California missions after Mexico declared independence (1821). These land grants formed the now-famous ranchos that came to dominate the economic life of California up until the transfer of power to the United States after 1848. Prominent Afro-descendants include Manuel Nieto, a soldier from the Portola expedition. He later acquired 158,000 acres in Southern California, which included the area encompassing the modern cities of Long Beach, Huntington Beach, Norwalk, and Downey. At his death in 1804, he was the wealthiest man in California. Tiburcio Tapia, a soldier stationed at Santa Barbara who later commanded the military detail at Lompoc, acquired Rancho Cucamonga, became a judge, served in the California provincial legislature, and was three-time mayor of Los Angeles.[36]

One of the most prominent Afro-descendant families in early California was the Pico family. The patriarch of the family, Santiago Pico, was a mestizo soldier who accompanied the Juan Bautista de Anza expedition in 1775. Pico's wife, however, was a mulatta. Their five sons, including José María Pico, rose to great prominence in and around Los Angeles. José María's son, Pío Pico became one of the most important players in Mexican- and later US- controlled California. In 1831, Pío led a rebellion against the Mexico City–appointed governor of California, Manuel Victoria. After defeating the governor, he was briefly elected territorial governor in 1832. Though his tenure was short, Pico oversaw the transition of mission lands to prominent families of California, including many of African descent. When the Mexican American War broke out (1846–1848), he was again governor and favored an independent California but later became involved in Republican politics during the 1850s and 1860s. Pío Pico continued to push for the rights of Californios until his death at ninety-three years old in 1894.[37]

○ ○ ○ ○ ○

Afro-descendants played an important role in the establishment of California as a colony during the Spanish period. They were the settlers and soldiers who helped to extend Spanish hegemony into this new territory. They also used the ambiguities of the frontier to socially advance in ways that they could not in the colonial center. While it is still unclear what exact impact the fact that they were African had on their influence in California, their presence was significant, as many rose to prominence throughout the Spanish and Mexican periods.

The presence of Afro-descendants in California also challenges two narratives within the larger discussion of westward expansion and the California missions. The first is a white nationalist, Eurocentric narrative of the development of the American West that sees the establishment of "civilization" by white settlers of European descent over the native peoples. While this narrative is problematic for many reasons, it assumes that settlers were indeed white and of European descent. This chapter joins a growing body of scholarship that demonstrates that settlers in the American West were from multicultural, multiracial, and multiethnic backgrounds.

Perhaps on the other end of the spectrum, the presence of Afro-descendants pushes back against another popular and scholarly narrative of the California missions. Many have portrayed the missions as one-dimensional spaces that only existed for Europeans to enforce their racial, ethnic, and cultural superiority on the native population. While the presence of Afro-descendants does not refute or diminish the suffering that native Californians experienced, it does complicate the mission space as a multiethnic, multiracial space where groups and individuals vied to survive and even thrive under the socioracial hegemony of the Spanish imperial system. By moving away from such facile arguments, scholars, and hopefully the public at large, can begin to understand the actual factors, political, social, and ecological, that led to the native demographic collapse. The story of the California missions was certainly one of imperialism but also of unintended consequences as different groups vied to raise their respective social standings in a frontier colonial society.

Notes

1. Goode, *California's Black Pioneers*, 11.

2. Mason, *The Census of 1790*, 45–47.

3. Ibid., 10.

4. For an excellent discussion of these ambiguities see Vinson III, *Before Mestizaje*, 1–17.

5. Mason, *The Census of 1790*, 47–73.

6. Ibid., 73.

7. Vinson III, *Bearing Arms for His Majesty*, 7–45.

8. Kuethe and Andrien, *The Spanish Atlantic World in the Eighteenth Century*, 236–47.

9. Weber, *Bárbaros Spaniards and Their Savages in the Age of Enlightenment*, 122–23.

10. Mason, *Census of 1790*, 40–44.

11. Wheeler, *Black California*, 19–31.

12. Mason, *Census of 1790*, 22.

13. Reid-Vazquez, *The Year of the Lash*, 117–45.

14. Dr. Don Ciniaro Gonzales Carvajal, Secratario interino de la gobierno del Reyno de Ultramar, "Preguntas y Respuestas," October 6, 1812, Cádiz, SBMAL.

15. Friar Juan Amerés, "Preguntas y Respuestas," February 3, 1814, San Carlos Borromeo (Monterrey), SBMAL.

16. Friars Antonio Rodriquez and Antonio Muñoz, "Preguntas y Respuestas," February 20, 1814, San Luis Obispo, SBMAL.

17. This survey was done of all nineteen responses in "Preguntas y Respuestas," SBMAL.

18. Friars Francisco Suñer and Antonio Peyri, "Preguntas y Respuestas," December 12, 1814, San Luis Rey, SBMAL.

19. Friars Marcelino Marquinez and Jayme Escudi, "Preguntas y Respuestas," June 30, 1814, Santa Cruz, SBMAL.

20. Friars Narciso Duran and Buenaventurada Fortuni, "Preguntas y Respuestas," November 7, 1814, San José, SBMAL.

21. Friar Ramon Olber, "Preguntas y Respuestas," December 31, 1813, Santa Barbara, SBMAL.

22. CMD 2643 Santa Cruz, August 23, 1824, SBMAL.

23. CMD 2645 Santa Cruz, August 27, 1824, SBMAL.

24. Causa criminal contra del soldado Faustino Orsequera y del menor Máximo, 1798, AGN-Mexico, Instituciones coloniales, Californias, Vol. 73, 689/5, Exp. 5, 86r–120v.

25. Ibid.

26. Ibid., 121r–130v.

27. Johnson and Lipsett-Rivera, eds., *The Faces of Honor*, 3–6.

28. Hojas de Servicio de Oficiales de las Compañías de California, 1814, AGN-Mexico, Instituciones Coloniales, Indiferente de Guerra, 1747, Vol. 216ª, s/f.

29. The Early California Population Project (from now on ECPP). Also see Hackle, "Early California Population Project Report," 73–76.

30. Restall, *The Black Middle*, 257–65.

31. For more on the Pragmatic see Shumway, *The Case of the Ugly Suitor & Other Histories of Love, Gender, & Nation in Buenos Aires, 1776–1870*.

32. This information is found in Alexo Antonio Duarte's death record, September 4, 1779, ECPP, record # 00129.

33. ECPP records # 00174, 00272, 00488.

34. Causa criminal que comprueba la violente muerte que se dieron al cabo Alexo Antonio Duarte, el soldado José Antonio Espinosa, ambos de la compañía de presidio de Monterrey, AGN-Mexico, Instituciones coloniales, Californias, vol. I, 2ª parte, 611/14, exp. 14, ff. 328r–369v; Alexo Antonio Duarte's death record, September 4, 1779, ECPP, record # 00129; the birth and death of the twins on January 6, 1780, is recorded in ECPP record # 606 and 607; Gertrudis María's death record, November 19, 1784, ECPP record # 00324.

35. Sandos, "Toypurina's Revolt Religious Conflict at Mission San Gabriel In 1785," 4–7.

36. Fisher, *Discovering Early California Afro-Latino Presence*, 1.

37. Wheeler, *Black California*, 31–36; Salomon, *Pío Pico*.

CHAPTER TWO

BLACK FUGITIVE STRATEGIES

Slavery and Self-Emancipation in the Spanish Gulf Coast Borderlands

Christina Marie Villarreal

Introduction

IN THE 1720s, Francisco Menéndez escaped enslavement among the English in South Carolina by fleeing to the Yamasee and then to the Spanish in St. Augustine, Florida. In 1758, an unnamed Black fugitive pursued sanctuary in Los Adaes, the Spanish capital of Texas, after running away from French enslavers in Natchitoches, Louisiana. During the American Revolution, enslaved men and women abandoned West Floridian plantations in search of refuge among Spanish sailors in the Mississippi River Valley. Others ran in the opposite direction, looking for a haven in Mobile to elude enslavers in New Orleans. All the while, a countless number fled to the *monte*, or wilderness, to free themselves from the growing system of plantation slavery developing along the Gulf Coast of Mexico.[1]

Throughout the eighteenth century, Black fugitives escaping slavery navigated an ever-shifting geopolitical terrain on the northern Gulf Coast of Mexico to achieve liberation. The Spanish, one political power vying for control of the region, often received Black fugitives from French and British colonies searching for asylum. After 1783, when Spain claimed all coastal territory from Florida to Texas, the enslaved continued seeking refuge by moving among these coastal colonies and escaping to areas outside of imperial control. Hence, fugitivity offers a unique view into one Black experience of the Spanish borderland: the act of self-emancipation through flight.

Though historians have explored legal and illicit avenues to freedom in the Gulf Coast, specifically in Louisiana, few have studied the strategies involved in fugitivity as a means of understanding African and Afro-descendant perspectives of the region's shifting geopolitical and social realities.[2] While understanding Black fugitivity alone is valuable, it also reveals how acts of self-emancipation affected the Spanish

Borderlands. By examining fugitives from enslavement—their strategies and itinerar-ies—historians can more easily see the limitations of colonial claims and authority. Successful and failed maroon communities, networks of information, and supposed alliances between Black and indigenous communities all reveal where imperial terri-tory ended and where *rival geographies*, as historian Stephanie Camp describes them, began.[3] Black fugitives exposed the fictive territorial claims of distant empires. The proliferation of rival geographies—which maroons reinforced through repetition and persistence—influenced how the Spanish exercised control over their territory, implemented religious sanctuary, and regulated slavery. When colonial officials could not stop fugitives, they changed their laws and adjusted their territorial claims. In other words, Black freedom seekers helped shape the imperial contours and colonial realities of the Spanish Gulf Coast. They stood at the heart of the borderlands.[4]

This chapter explores Black fugitive strategies for pursuing emancipation in the late eighteenth-century Spanish Gulf Coast, with a particular focus on Spanish Louisiana, to expose what freedom seekers knew, how they used that knowledge, and how their actions impacted the Spanish borderlands. First, it lays out the shift-ing geopolitical situation that made the Gulf Coast territories a dynamic site for fugitives. Then, focusing on two escape methods—sanctuary and marronage—this chapter examines how enslaved Africans and Afro-descendants attained information regarding freedom opportunities, pursued them, developed aid networks to support them, and ultimately persisted until such channels bore liberation.

Africans in the Spanish Gulf Coast Borderlands

The Gulf Coast held a unique position within the Spanish Borderlands. It was home to several indigenous societies and the site of a century-long imperial com-petition between European powers. Karankawa tribes lined the Texas Coast; the Atakapa resided along the Louisiana shoreline, while the Caddo, Natchez, Choctaw, Chickasaw, Mobile, Creek, and Apalachee lived along the coastline and within the lands extending east and west from the Mississippi River. In the centuries preceding European intrusion, indigenous people had complex geopolitical connections to territory and trade that colonists did not often understand or respect.[5]

Spanish, French, and English converged upon the region by the end of the seventeenth century. They mounted permanent settlements in Florida, Louisiana, and Texas by the early 1700s, with critical posts at St. Augustine, Biloxi, Mobile, New Orleans, Natchitoches, Los Adaes, and San Antonio.[6] Although the English did not claim territory along the coast, they allied themselves with indigenous peo-ple who carried their trade goods and influence into the region. After 1763, the British gained coastal lands when they acquired La Florida, which stretched from current-day Mississippi to Florida. They divided the province in two. Following the American Revolution, East and West Florida fell to Spain (1783). The Spanish maintained nominal control of the entire coast until 1803 when France recovered Louisiana and sold it to the United States of America.[7]

Africans and Afro-descendants entered this contested territory along the Gulf Coast in different ways. As Cameron David Jones explains for California, Afro-descendants of mixed racial ancestry constituted a portion of the free colonial population in Spain's northern borderlands.[8] These trends were present in the Gulf Coast colonies. In Texas, for example, African descendants with mixed ancestry constituted approximately 15 percent of the colonial population when the Spanish began to collect census material in the 1770s.[9] In time, Louisiana, the site with the largest Black population, had a growing population of *libres*, or free people of color.[10]

Most Africans and African descendants, however, arrived in the Gulf Coast colonies by force. White settlers carried enslaved Africans to the lands that constitute present-day Texas, Louisiana, Mississippi, Alabama, and Florida. The Spanish and British introduced Africans to the region but the French were the first to do so in large numbers starting in the 1710s. Landing in New Orleans, slave ships established Louisiana's initial Black population, leaving approximately 5,987 enslaved Africans in the colony by the end of the French period.[11] This early Black population surpassed the white population, 4.6 to 3.7.[12]

When Spain acquired the colony in 1763 following the Seven Years' War, the slave population of Louisiana distinguished the province from other Spanish territories.[13] Whereas those enslaved comprised more than 50 percent of Louisiana's population, New Spain's slave population was shrinking by the mid-eighteenth century.[14] Few new slaveholders from Spain's territories entered the region, leaving French settlers to constitute Spanish Louisiana's slaveholding class.

With few alternatives, Spanish officials needed to please their adopted French subjects. In 1769, demonstrating the intention to maintain the status quo, Governor Alejandro O'Reilly upheld the spirit of the Code Noir, the French regulations for slavery.[15] The Spanish governor maintained the portions of the legal code that endowed the planter class with the power to brand, maim, and execute enslaved people for significant offenses.[16] In 1777, Spain relaxed mercantilist regulations for Louisiana by allowing trade between the colony and Caribbean ports. The change demonstrated that the government had no intention of dismantling the plantation economy.[17] Thus, everyday life for the enslaved in Louisiana did not change dramatically under the Spanish government.

In fact, Spain redoubled efforts to supply colonists with enslaved laborers. In 1782, the Spanish made it easier to import enslaved Africans by lifting the duties on captives entering via the French West Indies.[18] Although a small free-Black population emerged through *coartación* (self-purchase), natural growth, and manumission, most Blacks in Spanish Louisiana remained enslaved.[19] The growing slave population led to greater incidents of marronage. The new government quickly realized that large swaths of territory across the province fell outside of colonial control, forming ideal hiding spots for fugitives from slavery. These factors compelled Louisiana authorities to alter and/or enforce slave laws in the colony. For example, the New Orleans *cabildo*, or town council, imposed stricter curfews on Blacks, restricted gatherings, prohibited unions between Blacks and whites, and organized runaway slave patrols and police units.[20] These changes affected the options of potential freedom-seekers, leading some to flee to Texas.

Texas, the western-most Spanish territory along the Gulf Coast, was an underpopulated province with a small enslaved population. Although colonists subjugated Africans and indigenous people to establish Hispanic communities, ease diplomatic trade, and promote economic profit, the slave population remained small. Perpetually short of laborers, Texas officials often kept Louisiana runaways—as free people or captives—to benefit from their labor.[21] Even when Spain governed both Texas and Louisiana, Texas officials rejected their neighbor's requests to return Black fugitives, often citing jurisdictional conflicts or engaging traditions of ecclesiastical sanctuary to deny the appeals. That Black fugitives fled toward Texas despite the uncertainty of freedom there underscores the cruel realities experienced in Louisiana.

Altogether, the eighteenth-century Gulf Coast was an uneven, shifting, and often unpredictable terrain for Africans and Afro-descendants, enslaved and free. Within this contested territory, host to competing and growing slave societies, those seeking liberation from enslavement had to develop a keen understanding of the competing imperial systems, the surrounding indigenous societies, and the physical environment. Some found freedom through legal recourse, like *coartación* and manumission. In this way, the population of free people of color grew.[22] However, most enslaved Blacks lacked access to capital and explored other ways to set themselves free. Two prevalent avenues were ecclesiastical sanctuary and marronage.

Sanctuary, Asylum Precedents, and Florida's Connection to the Caribbean

While *coartación* and manumission were legally recognized processes, religious sanctuary—wherein the church or state would offer refuge to individuals seeking Catholic conversion—was possible for some Black fugitives in the Spanish Gulf Coast. This route to liberation had legal precedents but, unlike self-purchase, "seeking the waters of baptism" began with a subversive act.[23] Enslaved people had to run away from their enslavers to request refuge. In turn, Spanish officials might offer the refugees asylum upon their conversion to Catholicism and expressions of loyalty to the Most Catholic monarchs.[24] These instances typically occurred at *inter*-imperial borders, where Spanish rivals with slave-based economies—like the French in Louisiana— stood in contrast to Spain's mission-based approach, which prioritized evangelization and Hispanization of Native populations to advance colonial agendas.[25] It was not uncommon, however, for the enslaved to search for religious sanctuary across *intra*-imperial borders—moving from one Spanish colony to another in search of asylum. Indeed, given the shifting geopolitics of the eighteenth-century Gulf Coast, officials enforced sanctuary in an ad hoc fashion.

For example, in Florida, officials did not always grant sanctuary to asylum seekers, despite the 1693 *cedula*, or royal edict, that called for the protection of all enslaved runaways seeking Catholic conversion in Florida.[26] The policy was meant to weaken Spain's English rivals in Carolina by denying them access to absconding bondmen. At the local level, however, promoting peace was safer than instigating aggression, so officials often returned fugitives. When the choice between obeying royal edicts and aggravating neighbors proved fraught, officials returned fugitives to Cuba, temporarily relieving themselves of the diplomatic dilemma.[27] This political strategy had precedents in the Caribbean, where enslaved people from French-controlled Saint Domingue fled to Spanish-controlled Santo Domingo starting in the seventeenth century. Officials there responded to fugitive arrivals based on the state of relations with the neighboring colony.[28] It also occurred in Guatemala, as Mark Lentz describes in chapter 5 on fugitives from Belize.

Despite the lack of uniform enforcement of religious sanctuary, enough Black fugitives from the Carolinas successfully reached Florida by 1738 to establish Fort Mose—the first free-Black settlement in what is today the United States. Because neither empire could stop the fugitives, Spanish officials used them to supplement colonial populations and defenses. The English responded by creating the colony of Georgia, which was to function as a buffer zone and reduce renegade activity.[29] The establishment of Georgia offers a clear example of how Black fugitive activity altered the geopolitical maps. Persistent slave flight forced colonial officials to acknowledge the limits of their territorial claims and adjust their settlements accordingly.

Europeans also reacted to Black fugitivity by adjusting their relationships with indigenous communities. In both the Caribbean and North America, colonial officials urged indigenous allies to capture runaways from slavery. The strategy was meant to cause division between Native Americans and Blacks.[30] For their part, indigenous communities only cooperated with requests to capture runaways when it benefitted their larger political or economic goals. The contingent circumstances meant that sometimes native allies returned runaways, such as when the Cadaudakious and Yatassés agreed to return Blacks fugitives to Athanase de Mézières, lieutenant governor of Natchitoches in Louisiana.[31] When there was no advantage to returning runaways, they sometimes helped Blacks reach their destinations, providing critical guidance through difficult terrains.[32] On occasion, they even acted as sites of refuge, embracing Black refugees as kin.[33] At other times, native agents enslaved Black freedom seekers.[34] In sum, indigenous communities were not reliable havens, leading many Black fugitives to seek sanctuary among the Spanish.

If not reliable, religious sanctuary was at least formulaic for fugitives. Fugitives could present themselves to an official in a foreign territory or in a church and request ecclesiastical asylum. This type of refuge first appeared in Spanish Texas when Louisiana pertained to France. In 1753, Texas Governor Don Jacinto de Barrios y Jáuregui was investigating French encroachment into the Red River district.[35] Observing their large slave populations, Barrios y Jáuregui concluded that the French posed a real threat to Spain's tentative hold on the region. He needed to weaken these neighbors lest they overtake New Spain's frontier settlements. Hoping to undermine their labor force, the Texas governor made a bold proposal to liberate the enslaved of French Louisiana by offering them asylum if they deserted to Texas.[36]

While Barrios y Jáuregui's superiors took his suggestion seriously, the Council of the Indies deemed the policy inappropriate for New Spain's northern frontier.[37] They could not risk foreign retaliation so close to their vulnerable silver mines. Nonetheless, the proposal and the hope it generated among the enslaved sparked an emancipatory route between Texas and Louisiana.[38] Despite the plan's rejection, runaways from slavery appeared in East Texas throughout the eighteenth century. Many of the fugitive arrivals requested sanctuary explicitly, hiding in churches and missions to demonstrate their intentions. Even after Spain acquired Louisiana, Black fugitives pursued the possibility of asylum in Texas, reinforcing the southwestward route into the Mexican period.[39]

The trajectories of runaways suggest a continued association of the west with emancipation. Archives preserve few clear cases of fugitives from slavery arriving at Spanish posts in colonial Texas, and even scarcer are records documenting instances of formal asylum.[40] However, late-eighteenth-century records from Texas and Louisiana contain consistent references to Black runaways heading toward Texas. Correspondences, council proceedings, royal decrees, and census records attest to this elusive experience. These sources, read collectively, reveal the continued western movement of freedom seekers. Indeed, colonial agents typically found runaways west of their enslaver's property. This evidence suggests that enslaved people, at the very least, headed toward Texas to inquire of possible sanctuary.

A few examples demonstrate this point. In 1775, Antonio Gil Y'Barbo of Nacogdoches captured Michel, an enslaved man from Bayou Manchac (below Baton Rouge), who had arrived from a maroon settlement in the Attakapas region.[41] He made it to Texas after seven years on the run. Again on May 20, 1789, an unnamed woman enslaved by Luis de Blanc of Louisiana arrived at Nacogdoches with her child in the company of a Spanish fugitive.[42] In 1795, a group escaped slavery in Opelousas and headed for Nacogdoches. The group had not coordinated beforehand but crossed paths in the Louisiana woods as they individually moved west toward Texas.[43]

Black fugitives fled toward the supposed sanctuary of Texas even when they did not reside close to the frontier. For example, in 1771, Louis Charles de Blanc St. Denis captured a group of Black fugitives from New Orleans in Natchitoches. The runaways—Marie Anne, Alexander, Charlot, and an unnamed pregnant woman—had different owners back in New Orleans but had traveled west together for eighteen months. They testified to having been on their way to Los Adaes, the Texas capital—presumably to request asylum.[44]

These fugitive itineraries, which included starting points in the colonial metropole and periphery, reveal that enslaved people navigated shifting political, legal, and religious traditions in pursuit of liberation. As in Florida, Texas authorities returned runaways, kept them enslaved, or sent them to the Caribbean. Although freedom through sanctuary remained elusive, the occasional success of these cases across the Gulf Coast bolstered this fugitive strategy.

Marronage in an Increasingly Hostile Environment

Not all fugitives from slavery sought emancipation through religious sanctuary. Most elected to abandon colonial society and live as maroons, or runaways, beyond the control of European institutions. *Grand* and *petit marronage*, permanent and temporary truancy, were common occurrences in French Louisiana.[45] Slave flight reached a high point in the late 1740s in an episode that one historian calls "The Panic of 1748." Hundreds of maroons had gathered in dispersed camps in the Bas du Fleuve, the intricate estuary south of New Orleans.[46] During the Spanish period, the geographical distribution of maroons remained the same: most Black fugitives remained near the cities and towns in which they were enslaved.[47] Moreover, the growing slave population ensured continued incidents of slave flight to these hideouts.

How did these Black fugitives survive? Who did they rely on for aid and information? What impact did their maroon communities—de facto rival geographies—have on the Spanish borderlands? Mapping out these emancipatory strategies and sites reveals how fugitive and colonial spaces shaped each other.

Louisiana Case Studies and Criminal Records

Criminal records include invaluable insight into Black fugitive strategies. Historians must read Black fugitive depositions from these documents with a critical eye, not because their declarations are false but because colonial officials framed, directed, and transcribed the interviews. Conflicting responses allow the researcher to imagine the survival strategies and priorities of the interviewees.[48] For example, the declarations of Bobo and Jacobo expose an elaborate and diffuse network of fugitive spaces that ran from the backyards of the plantation elite into the swamps and woodlands beyond colonial reach.[49]

According to Bobo, a forty-year-old man escaping a punitive enslaver, he had lived for a year as a fugitive in a small maroon community behind the plantation of Mr. LaCose by 1772. In the forests surrounding the settler's estate, a small band of at least five runaways had built two *chosas*, or shacks. Bobo resided in one of the structures with two men. In the other abode lived a man and a woman. Bobo suggested that these fugitives knew each other, having constructed their homes only "half a fanega" apart. While the tiny community survived on the margins of colonial society, it also interacted with fugitives residing far away from European settlements—stretching the parameters of the fugitive space into the *monte*, or unsettled wilderness.

The distribution of this maroon community suggests that fugitive geographies overlaid diverse and challenging topographies to remain separated from planter and state violence. Although the state could attempt to inflict violence and demonstrate sovereignty, fugitives had the upper hand in the *monte*. For example, when Spanish forces captured Jacobo, a Black fugitive who lived near Bobo, they found him "among the reeds," likely in a swampy area.[50] When he gave his deposition, he revealed that his hunting range took him toward Bobo's territory, near the woods that lined New Orleans plantations. His movements highlight the diverse landscapes fugitives traversed. These spaces were in contact with the colonial world and set apart entirely. Interactions between these peripheral and interior landscapes—the *monte* and the plantation's periphery—suggest that rival geographies were symbiotic.

This criminal record also suggests that the interior and peripheral maroon communities worked in tandem. Consider the use of guns. Bobo's experience confirms that firearms were a ready currency in the fugitive landscape, tools that connected the peripheral fugitive territories to the interior. He owned a gun and ammunition that he used to hunt. Bobo claimed to have stolen the gun and said he relied on other fugitive Blacks for ammunition and gunpowder. His suppliers accepted game in exchange. It is unclear how widespread these arms dealers were, but Bobo alleged that "various *negros*" participated in this exchange.[51] Who were these Black agents who assisted runaways?

The experiences of Bobo and Jacobo highlight the active role enslaved people played in supporting maroon communities. Enslaved people readily helped runaways by selling the wares of fugitives in local markets, sheltering them in their times of need, and helping them steal from enslavers. The fact that most absconders carried stolen goods in their possession at the time of their capture confirmed this final method of enslaved-fugitive thefts. For instance, upon capture, Bobo had three stolen sacks of rice and a barrel of green beans that had gone missing from a nearby estate.[52] Such conspiratorial possibilities rattled colonial officials.

Perhaps aware of these suspicions, Jacobo claimed that he did not own a gun, nor did he know how to shoot one. Hunting with a firearm was common by the late eighteenth century. Many enslaved Blacks, Bobo included, owned and used guns to hunt. Hence, the revelation that Jacobo did not own a weapon suggests two possibilities: he was hunting with different methods, or he was lying.[53] The first possibility reveals new points of inquiry regarding the hunting practices of fugitives; the second points to Jacobo's awareness of colonial fears. Given the loss of crops and cattle from nearby plantations, perhaps Jacobo hoped to distance himself from possible culpability. The capture of Bobo and Jacobo reveals that fugitive strategies depended on knowledge of allies and resources; they were dependent on diffuse networks that were built on trust.

The fugitive-enslaved network was personal. Fugitives and the enslaved were in communication as friends. For example, Jacobo had risked several visits to the estate of Monsieur Tijiran. Upon capture, he was having dinner with Julia, an enslaved woman. Prior to this dinner, he was in the cabin of Simon, an enslaved laborer on the same plantation.[54] Jacobo's pattern of visitation is evidence of sustained contact with Simon and Julia, suggesting long-term cooperation. It also uncovers a source of information. Jacobo surely received regular updates and the latest news when he ventured out from the monte and into colonial terrain. Maintaining these networks was critical to survival as they furnished fugitives with precious resources and intelligence. Similar networks persevered in South America, as described by Alex Borucki in chapter 10 on the Río de la Plata.

Magdelon and Family Feuds

While fugitives relied on Black networks for resources and information, relations among white settlers also offered critical information to those determined to escape enslavement. The way they treated, leased, and/or sold their enslaved laborers provided invaluable intel to aspiring fugitives. The decades-long family feuds between the Chaperon and Dupart families demonstrate a prime example of the types of intelligence the enslaved could gather from settler drama.

In the early 1770s, Magdelon, a forty-five-year-old Black *criollo* (Creole, born in the Americas), escaped the New Orleans plantation of Jaques Chaperon. She found shelter with Leveille, a Black freedman living on Francoise Julia Larche Delile et Dupart's estate. Chaperon alleged that Larche had stolen Magdelon to take advantage of her labor. Indeed, he sued Larche and found three witnesses to give testimony against her. The three men claimed to have spotted Magdelon on Larche's property during the previous months. One witness, Santiago Porte, claimed to have confronted Larche about the fugitive but claimed that the woman "had hurled such vicious insults" at him that "he was forced to retreat."[55]

However, Francisco Broutin, Larche's counsel, painted a different picture. Broutin claimed that Julia was feeble-minded, a "person unable and incapable of being in a trial."[56] She did "not know what it is to hide a fugitive black nor take service from [him]." Julia's lawyer claimed that her intellectual disability absolved her of any crime. Conversely, Broutin claimed that Chaperon's history of violence implicated him.[57] Magdelon, after all, had traveled to the plantation in search of medical aid. She found assistance in the cabin of Leveille, who "helped cure her of her sickness." Upon recovery, Leveille returned her to Chaperon with the recommendation that she need only to rest and avoid overwork. By including the freedman's assessment in the record, Broutin suggested that Chaperon's poor treatment of Magdelon had caused her to flee in the first place.

The textual evidence points to Magdelon's presence on the Larche property, but conflicting colonial descriptions point to two possibilities for what Magdelon was thinking. Was she an unlucky fugitive, captured by a neighboring slaveholder when en route to a more liberating space? Was she seeking medical aid from a known healer or refuge among a less perilous household, albeit a slaveholding one? What of Julia? Was she an opportunistic enslaver capturing runaways? Or was she an oblivious slaveowner who did not realize that her enslaved laborers were hosting fugitives? Was she somehow involved in a fugitive network herself? Were Julia's vicious insults to nosy neighbors meant to defend Magdelon? Did Magdelon know of these possibilities before leaving Chaperon's estate?

Evidence suggests that Magdelon knew much about the disputes between Santiago Chaperon and Julia Larche Delile et Dupart, a family entangled in feuds for more than five decades. First, Chaperon was married to Larche's aunt and had raised the young girl after the death of her parents. A cruel uncle, Chaperon's abuse sent Larche to the hospital on at least one occasion.[58] In 1776, after the passing of her conservator, her cousin Francisco Larche requested a new guardian to manage her estate because the French council had previously declared Julia "feeble and incapable of administrating her assets."[59] It may be that Magdelon saw an opportunity to hide in plain sight under the protection of "simple-minded" Julia.

Magdelon would have had access to the inner workings of the Dupart household from Marianne, a woman formerly enslaved by Larche. She had also served Chaperon alongside Magdelon for several years before the latter made her escape. Chaperon had purchased her from Julia Larche on July 30, 1765, approximately eight years before Magdelon appeared on the Larche-Dupart estate.[60] Magdelon and Marianne knew each other well. Perhaps Marianne shared stories of the Larche estate that inspired Magdelon to seek refuge there. She would have learned from Marianne about the extent of Julia's illness and the trustworthiness of Leveille, the Black medical practitioner. Maybe the work Magdelon did on Julia's plantation was not for the estate but for herself.[61]

At the very least, Magdelon's experience highlights the networks of information available to runaways. Enslaved people who remained within white families knew of vulnerabilities and blind spots. The drawn-out quarrels between Chaperon and Larche would have made Magdelon privy to the ongoings in the Dupart home. Beyond these plantation hinterlands and *petite marronage*, larger maroon communities in the *monte*—out of sight of colonial officials—posed a bigger threat to colonial society across the Gulf Coast.

Black fugitives who wished to remain autonomous found effective ways to ward off colonial encroachment. Consider the material conditions of the maroon community of San Maló.[62] Jean Saint Malo or Juan San Maló escaped from his enslavers in the early 1780s and began helping others flee captivity. Like other Black fugitives, he embraced the natural barriers and harsh landscapes that limited colonial expansion—such as swamps and heavily canopied areas—to create a defensible maroon community in Louisiana by 1783.[63] Geographer Willie Jamaal Wright argues that such "unruly environments . . . were and remain essential to the practice of marronage." Further, "without the existence of challenging, unoccupied, and unruly environments, fugitive slaves might have never become maroons."[64] Accordingly, San Maló's maroon community was well hidden and set apart in the marshlands. From a Spanish perspective, this was an undesirable landscape without a need for surveillance.

San Maló established clear boundaries around his claimed territory using visible and audible symbols. Most apparent were the visual warnings San Maló etched into the landscape, such as the tree trunk that read, "woe to the white who crosses these limits," threatening all white people who would trespass into this territory.[65] The community also used auditory markers to outline their land. Black fugitives surrounded their hamlets with dried leaves and twigs that would break when someone approached.[66]

Besides visual and audible markers, San Maló used violence to enforce his boundaries. His men always carried weapons and, when able, traded goods for guns and shot.[67] San Maló beckoned men and women, young and old, to his self-emancipated communities, promising protection as a brother-in-arms.

This rival geography was so well established and well protected that Spanish authorities had to rely on individuals who knew or had access to the "wilderness" (an implicit admission that it was not under colonial control) to capture runaways. In 1783, Louisiana governor Esteban Rodríguez Miró enlisted soldiers and Black spies to enter the marshlands and learn about San Maló's community. These efforts were fruitless. It was not until a wealthy planter offered the services of his trusted slave, Bastien, did the government experience any success. Bastien infiltrated the maroon community and returned to New Orleans with San Maló's whereabouts.[68] With the enslaved spy's information, Spanish soldiers captured and executed the principal maroon leaders late in 1784.[69]

The limitations of colonial authority are clearly visible in this example: the maroon community found, established, and defended a space outside of colonial control. Even colonial exposure of such spaces did not make them subject to imperial authority. The downfall of San Maló's band and the subsequent measures of Miró did not dissuade future runaways. In 1789, the Louisiana Regiment pursued another maroon community in the reeds of Lake Pontchartrain. They killed fourteen maroons. Nonetheless, enslaved people continued to flee bondage in Louisiana and establish secure emancipatory sites as maroons.[70]

Moreover, despite their elusive nature, these rival geographies produced a colonial transformation. Governor Miró's experience with San Maló's maroon community inspired more slave regulations. In 1784, Miró announced an eleven-article proclamation that restricted the movement of enslaved individuals within the colonial dominion. The advisory prohibited bondservants from wandering beyond their enslaver's property without written permission, and from gathering together either during the day or at night. These provisions reduced the mobility of enslaved people within colonial society.[71]

Conclusion

Imperial rivalries, indigenous politics, colonial courts, and most important, Black initiative made self-liberation possible in the Gulf Coast, from Florida to Texas. While Spanish colonial legal codes made emancipation, manumission, and self-purchase possible, many of the enslaved chose to evade local institutions when seeking freedom. Instead, they decided to pursue liberation via fugitivity and escape. Black fugitives imagined, found, and created places where they could become free.

For the enslaved, successful marronage informed their understanding of the space in which they lived. The methods of escape the enslaved used suggest a broad knowledge of the terrain and an adaptive aid network. They understood the laws that governed the competing colonies, the indigenous polities that controlled the surrounding areas, and the white planters who enslaved them. Successful liberation, permanent or temporary, reified possible routes to freedom and reinforced their rival geographies. Black fugitives and maroon communities revealed the physical and political limits of colonial power.

For colonial officials, the potential existence of fugitive communities or maroon communities both threatened and circumscribed their power in a given territory, forcing them to ignore, reinforce, or create a new spatial imagination or understanding of their land claims. When colonial officials could not control the subsequent rival geographies, they created new laws and established new colonies to restrain fugitive territory. Runaways, then, shaped both colonial space and colonial authority.

Black fugitives forged landscapes and routes of emancipation in the Gulf Coast, transforming the Spanish borderlands at the same time. Some of these landscapes found concrete recognition and codification among the Spanish, as with the Florida case. Others remained recognized but challenged among colonial officials such as the cases around the swamps that surrounded New Orleans and the Texas-Louisiana border. Historians have established that Spaniards controlled very little territory in their northern frontier. Studying Black fugitivity not only supports these findings, exposing where exactly those limitations stood, but it also reveals rival geographies that competed with and contested colonial space. Testing Spanish-claimed territories with their movements, fugitives from slavery drew new and challenging landscapes in which they could escape oppression and find liberation. Black fugitivity—slave flight in particular—contributed to geopolitical processes of legal and social border construction in the northern fringes of colonial Latin America and at the heart of the Spanish borderlands.

Notes

1. The Spaniards first re-enslaved Menéndez and sent him to Havana before returning him as a free man to Florida. See Landers, "The Atlantic Transformation of Francisco Menéndez." For reference to fugitives at Los Adaes, see Bexar Archive (henceforth BA), April 5, 1758. For reference to fugitives during the American Revolution, see Chester to Galvez, January 1778, in Kinnaird, *Spain in the Mississippi Valley* (henceforth SMV),1:247; Declaration on Stephen Shakspear, May 6, 1778, SMV, 1:274. The *Louisiana Historical Quarterly* (henceforth LHQ) is filled with examples of local marronage.

2. Several works focus on the African and Afro-descendant populations of colonial Louisiana and Florida. Most of these works focus on the institution of slavery, legal avenues to freedom, and European reactions to fugitives. See Hall, *Africans in Colonial Louisiana*; Hanger, *Bounded Lives, Bounded Places*; Din, *Spaniards, Planters, and Slaves*; Ingersoll, *Mammon and Manon in Early New Orleans*; Johnson, *Slavery's Metropolis*; Landers, *Black Society in Spanish Florida*.

3. Historians of slavery in the antebellum US South have theorized about this, speculating on how slaves perceived geography. Camp, "The Pleasures of Resistance," 535.

4. The author is excluding the coastal territory south of the Rio Grande because of its disconnect from the political, economic, and social dynamics of the Mississippi River Valley (e.g., plantation slavery and imperial competition).

5. Barr, *Peace Came in the Form of a Woman*; Barr, "Geographies of Power," 5–46; Dubcovsky, *Informed Power*.

6. Even in these areas, which remained sparsely populated by Europeans for a century following contact, Spanish explorers used enslaved Africans and indigenous people to explore and establish their first permanent settlement at St. Augustine. See Landers, *Black Society*, 14–15.

7. Historians have considered the experiences of Africans in colonial Louisiana and, to a lesser extent, Black life in early Florida and Texas. Studies on Louisiana overwhelmingly focus on French Louisiana, leaving a gap in historical investigation on the impact of Spain's acquisition of the colony in 1763 and, after 1783, control of the entire northern Gulf Coast of Mexico. This region demands examination for the questions that it allows researchers to ask regarding how enslaved people experienced the changes, the state of the Spanish empire in the region, the development of local culture and governance, as well as the role of Africans and African descendants in shaping the Spanish borderlands. To begin to understand the fertile ground of this framing, studies must consider the complicated social and political terrain of the first half of the eighteenth century. Notwithstanding this gap, there are a few critical studies on Africans in Spanish Louisiana, see endnote 2. There is no full-length monograph on African descendants in colonial Texas. For works that briefly speak to Black experiences in Spanish Texas, see de la Teja, *Faces of Béxar: Early San Antonio and Texas*.

8. See Cameron David Jones, chapter 1, in this volume.

9. For population of enslaved persons, see Meacham, "The Population of Spanish and Mexican Texas 1716–1836," 172–75. A dozen families from the Canary Islands supplemented the initial population; however, subsequent frontier migrants reified the community's mixed-race character. Tjarks, "Comparative Demographic Analysis of Texas, 1777–1793," 139; De la Teja, "Why Urbano and María Trinidad Can't Get Married," 121–46. For a fuller conversation of Afro-descendants and demographics in Texas, see Richmond, "Africa's Initial Encounter with Texas," 200–221; Tjarks, "Comparative Demographic," 291–338.

10. Hanger, *Bounded Lives*. The *libre* population was growing naturally and through legal channels by the end of the eighteenth century.

11. While the French government terminated the trade in 1731–1743, the clandestine delivery of captive Africans continued throughout the French period. Hall, *Africans in Colonial Louisiana*, 34, 279.

12. Hall, *Africans in Colonial Louisiana*, 10; Burton and Smith, "Slavery in the Louisiana Backcountry: Natchitoches, 1714–1803," 151; Taylor, *Negro Slavery in Louisiana*.

13. Ingersoll, "Free Blacks in a Slave Society: New Orleans, 1718–1812," 173–200. For slave society versus society with slaves, see Berlin, *Many Thousands Gone: The First Two Centuries of Slavery in North America*.

14. Valdés, "The Decline of Slavery in Mexico," 167–94.

15. Decree, Alejandro O'Reilly, August 27, 1769, Archives Nationales d'Outre-Mer (hereafter ANOM) C/13ª/49, f.69; "Sobre el comercio," New Orleans, 1776, Archivo General de las Indias, Sevilla (hereafter AGI), Santo Domingo (hereafter SD) 2586. For information on O'Reilly's tenure, see Texada, *Alejandro O'Reilly and the New Orleans Rebels*. For a treatment on Indian Slavery, see Spear, *Race, Sex and Social Order in Early New Orleans*, 166–72. For an overview of changes made after the Spanish acquisition, see Ingersoll, *Mammon and Manon*, 233; Hall, *Africans in Colonial Louisiana*, 276–315; Hanger, *Bounded Lives*, 7–11.

16. French vassals could legally enslave indigenous people with whom they were at war. O'Reilly outlawed Indian slavery. Zitomersky, "The Form and function of French-Native American Relations in Early Eighteenth-Century French Colonial Louisiana," 154–77. Vidal, "Private and State Violence Against African Slaves in Lower Louisiana During the French Period, 1699–1769," 92–110. Din argues that it was more nuanced that the simple affirmation of the Code Noir. See Din, *Spaniards, Planters, and Slaves*, 222.

17. On Spanish slave imports, see Hall, *Africans in Colonial Louisiana*, 276.

18. Hanger, *Bounded Lives*, 10–11.

19. There is some debate regarding the *libre* population. Whereas Hanger originally argued that this population developed a "group consciousness," subsequent historians disputed this claim and the suggestion that free Blacks achieved a valued or respected place in colonial New Orleans. Ingersoll found that "colonists were basically hostile toward the free black population," and argued that their presence hindered the emergence of a white artisanal class. See Ingersoll, *Mammon and Mamon*, 232.

20. Ingersoll, *Mammon*, 233–37

21. Villarreal, "Colonial Border Control: Reconsidering Migrants and the Making of New Spain's Northern Borderlands, 1714–1820"; Hoonhout and Mareite, "Freedom at the Fringes?," 61–86.

22. *Coartación* was a recognized practice in Spanish courts by the eighteenth century. Although some of these laws were reflected in French legal codes, Louisiana slaveowners were not accustomed to their enforcement. Nonetheless, at least 1,330 cases of *coartación* were successful in Louisiana during the Spanish period. Between 1763 and 1803, there were between thirty and forty successful self-purchases a year, with a few significant spikes in the 1790s. Hanger, *Bounded Lives*; Hanger, "Avenues to Freedom Open to New Orleans' Black Population, 1769–1779," 257. Estimates from Ingersoll, *Mammon and Manon*, 222–23.

23. Rupert, "Seeking the Water of Baptism: Fugitive Slaves and Imperial Jurisdiction in the Early Modern Caribbean," 199–231.

24. Most historians who work on sanctuary for fugitives from slavery have focused on Florida or the Caribbean. Their research confirms that the practice shaped routes of escape by encouraging more slave flight. Historians have come to discuss these decrees that offered liberation to the enslaved as "sanctuary laws"; however, this was not their official title. And, despite the religious elements of the decrees, it did not fall under the jurisdiction of the Church. This author discusses the issue below. For the purposes of this chapter, the terms *sanctuary* and *asylum* are used interchangeably.

25. Native Americans who lived in Spanish missions, sometimes referred to as "mission Indians," did not always reside in missions permanently or by choice. Many indigenous communities used Spanish missions for trade and as a seasonal lodging. See Barr, *Peace Came in the Form of a Woman*, 119.

26. Landers, "Spanish Sanctuary: Fugitives in Florida, 1687–1790," 296; Landers, "Gracia Real de Santa Teresa de Mose: A Free Black Town in Spanish Colonial Florida," 9–30; Clavin, *Aiming for Pensacola*, 7–38.

27. See G. Hall, *Africans in Colonial Louisiana*; Din, *Spaniards, Planters, and Slaves*.

28. For references to the Caribbean, see Rupert, "Seeking the Water of Baptism," 199–231. For Spanish use of sanctuary laws for political means, see Landers, "Spanish Sanctuary," 296; Landers, "Gracia Real de Santa Teresa de Mose." See also Scott, *The Common Wind*.

29. Dubcovsky, *Informed Power*, 187–88. Georgia was established in 1732 in part to hinder slave flight.

30. Usner, *Indians, Settlers, & Slaves in a Frontier Exchange Economy*, 72–76; Dubcovsky, *Informed Power*, 167–69.

31. Agreement made with Indian Nations, Natchitoches, April 21, 1770, in Bolton, *Athanase de Mézières and the Louisiana-Texas Frontier, 1768–1780*, 157.

32. Dubcovsky, *Informed Power*, 167–69.

33. The topic of fugitives from slavery escaping to indigenous territories requires greater examination. Indeed, indigenous communities often traded with fugitives and enslaved Blacks alike. See SMV, V1–V3.

34. SMV, 2:90; 3:360.

35. Certified Copy of Proceedings, February 10, 1751, Los Adaes, BA, microfilm (mf), 9:225–73; Certified Copy of Proceedings, September 25, 1752, Los Adaes, BA, mf, 9: 422–38; Certified Copy of Proceedings, January 21, 1754, Mexico City, BA, mf, 9:461–82; Proceedings, September 20, 1754, *BA*, mf, 9:509–30.

36. For quotation, see Hackett, ed., *Pichardo's Treatise on the Limits of Louisiana and Texas*, 4:66.

37. The Spanish Crown had issued similar *cedulas*, or decrees, for other provinces in the Indies since the seventeenth century.

38. A prelude to the Southern underground railroad. However, the author finds that these policies were not explicitly connected to the subsequent slave flight to Mexico. The Mexican War of Independence set the foundation for Texas existing as a byway toward actual "free soil." The association of liberty in Spanish territory, the issue explored in the author's forthcoming manuscript, may have been related to subsequent journeys south. For literature on nineteenth-century flight to Mexico, see Kelley, *Los Brazos de Dios*; Cornell, "Citizens of Nowhere," 351–74; Torget, *Seeds of Empire*; Nichols, *The Limits of Liberty*.

39. Kelley, *Los Brazos de Dios*; Kelley, "'Mexico in His Head,'" 709–23.

40. To the author's knowledge, slavery appears as the main subject of colonial correspondence fewer than thirty times in the Bexar Archive during the period covered. This does not mean that slavery was rare or absent in Spanish Texas.

41. Antoine Bernard and Gil Yarbaro, sold on October 20, 1776. See Hall, *Louisiana Slave Database*. It was not uncommon for Santo Domingo settlers to hold on to fugitives from slavery that presented themselves in the Spanish colony. Governor Azlor and French Governor Roan on restitution of enslaved fugitives, AGI, IG 2787, December 15, 1766.

42. Proceedings in case against Juan José Peña, May 7, 1792, BA.

43. The four men were enslaved by different Louisiana planters. Together the five runaway cases are in Hall, *Louisiana Slave Database*, Slave Testimony: November 16, 1795.

44. Slave Testimony, July 29, 1771, St. Denis Diary at Natchitoches in Hall, *Louisiana Slave Database*. The group of fugitives had not escaped with a concrete plan or even at the same time. It seems that a network of knowledge and assistance pulled freedom seekers west, into the woods and toward Attakapas.

45. Price, ed., *Maroon Societies, Rebel Slave Communities in the Americas*, 3, 107. *Petit* and *gran marronage* describe the size and permanency of slave flight. Scholars define *petit marronage* as short-term slave escapes that typically occurred at the individual level. Whereas *gran marronage* describes permanent absconsion.

46. For "the Panic of 1748," see Brasseaux, "The Administration of Slave Regulations in French Louisiana, 1724–1766," 155–56; G. Hall, *Africans in Colonial Louisiana*, 202–36.

47. The historiography on marronage in Louisiana confirms that most slaves in the colonial capital kept to the familiar marshland and Black networks surrounding the lower bayous of the delta. G. Hall, *Africans in Colonial Louisiana*, 202–36; Diouf, *Slavery's Exiles*, 160–61.

48. Example from Louisiana Historical Center, Spanish Judicial Records (hereafter SJR), February 20, 1770.

49. For the criminal case examined in the following paragraphs, see SJR, March 10, 1772. There is also a summary of this document in the *Louisiana Historical Quarterly* (hereafter LHQ), 8, no. 727.

50. SJR, March 10, 1772, f. 100, 111–12.

51. Ibid. Summary in LHQ 8, no. 727.

52. Ibid. Colonial officials also feared that the enslaved helped fugitives kill domestic cattle. A string of incidents involving runaways killing cows also made officials suspicious. There were known incidents of Black fugitives leading cows to the margins of their enslaver's property so that fugitives could have easy access to them.

53. This testimony also presents an opportunity to explore the hunting strategies of fugitives. Was Jacobo using traps and/or other weapons to hunt? What game did he hunt?

54. SJR, March 10, 1772, f. 100–12.

55. SJR, February 4, 1775, f. 3. There is also a summary of this entire criminal case in LHQ 11, no. 1: 155.

56. Ibid., f. 22.

57. For more on Jaques Chaperon, see Vidal, "Private and State Violence," 100.

58. SJR, May 5, 1768.

59. SJR, December 11, 1776.

60. SJR, July 30, 1765. Marianne was twenty years old at the time of her sale, an adult with a deep understanding of the places from which she came.

61. In the end, the Spanish Judge Odoardo required Larche to cover the damages suffered by Santiago Chaperon due to her hosting the fugitive on her property for up to 427 days. SJR, February 4, 1775.

62. Jean Saint Malo, or Juan San Maló, is a heroic figure in many Louisiana histories and folklore. Today, the New Orleans voodoo community honors San Maló as a religious icon and as the patron saint of fugitives from slavery in the New Orleans Voodoo tradition. See Voison, "Saint Malo Remembered." Scholars of Spanish Louisiana have discussed his attempts to establish communities of freedmen in some detail. See Din, "'Cimarrones' and the San Malo Band in Spanish Louisiana"; Hall, *Africans in Colonial Louisiana*; Usner, *Indians, Settlers, & Slaves*. These historians have uncovered several important details about this man's life and efforts. The author has decided to start with his story because it captures the energy and creativity shared among the growing slave population to forge areas of possible liberation around colonized territories.

63. Gilbert Din argues that the Black fugitive settlements in Louisiana should not be considered *palanques* because they were not fortified. Moreover, the majority of flight in Louisiana was *petit marronage*, or short-term flight. I contend that constant short-term flight from a planter's supervisor and constant interaction with an alternative community gave these settlements a permanency or reliability. See Din, *Spaniards, Planters, and Slaves*.

64. Wright, "The Morphology of Marronage," 1137.

65. Miró to Gálvez, New Orleans, 1783, AGI, Santo Domingo 2549, N. 127.

66. Ibid. Diouf has also analyzed these alarm systems. See Diouf, *Slavery's Exiles*, 157–86.

67. Miró to Gálvez, New Orleans, 1783, AGI, Santo Domingo 2549, N. 127. Hall, *Africans in Colonial Louisiana*, 212–36; Din, "'Cimarrones' and the San Malo Band in Spanish Louisiana," 237–62.

68. The author has not found the second Black spy's name in her own collection of primary source material. Din mentioned this person in "'Cimarrones.'"

69. SJR, March 1, 1783.

70. Details on this campaign appear in the muster rolls for the Louisiana Regiment, New Orleans, June 30, 1792/93, AGI, PPC.

71. Quote from Gilbert Din's examination of this bando, "'Cimarrones,'" 246–47.

CHAPTER THREE

THE MOVING BORDER

Black Experiences in Caribbean Frontiers and North American Borderlands in the Late Seventeenth Century

Joseph M. H. Clark

ON APRIL 29, 1685, a Spanish admiral named Gaspar de Palacios departed the South American port of Cartagena on a mission to find a "mysterious island" in the far southwestern corner of the Caribbean Sea, where there were rumored to be plentiful silver deposits. Three weeks after setting sail, an early summer storm forced him to abandon his search. He first attempted to put in at the Cape of San Anton, the westernmost extent of Cuba, but when the storm developed into a hurricane, his ship was forced westward to the Yucatán peninsula. As he rounded the peninsula, Palacios and his crew observed a fleet of eight corsair vessels cruising southwest, in the direction of the Mexican port of San Francisco de Campeche. Evading the corsairs, Palacios hastened his way to Veracruz, where he arrived on June 2, immediately sending warnings to Viceroy Tomás de la Cerda in Mexico City. By the time word of the enemy fleet reached la Cerda, however, the raid of Campeche was well underway. On July 6, a landed force of at least 750 men attacked the port, overwhelming its defenses "without resistance."[1] Led by French buccaneer Michel de Grammont, the corsairs proceeded to occupy the city for fifty-seven days, holding 350 hostages in wait of ransom. When Spanish officials decided not to meet the corsair's demands, the invaders executed some of the hostages, released others, and fled the port carrying 243 hostages as captives, most of whom were of African descent.[2]

A week later, on September 10, Spain's Caribbean war fleet apprehended two foreign vessels suspected of having participated in the raid. They escorted the captured ships to Veracruz, where their 120 passengers and crew were imprisoned in the fortress of San Juan de Ulúa and subjected to extensive interrogation. In November, these interviews bore fruit in the testimony of a twenty-two-year-old native of Normandy named Denis Thomas. Asked to recount his activities in the Americas, Thomas divulged that he had come from France a year before as member of an expedition led by the explorer René-Robert Cavalier de la Salle, which aimed to establish a colony on the American mainland. Although Thomas had abandoned the expedition when it reached the port of Petit-Goâve, in French Saint-Domingue, he claimed that other would-be colonists had traveled on to a location that he called the "Bay of Misipipi . . . on the coast of Apalache y Pachicola"—a location that his interrogators assumed to be the Bay of Espíritu Santo, "between Apalache and Tampico, on the coast of the Mexican Sea," in the province of Texas.[3]

The revelation of a possible French colonizing mission in Texas set off a whirlwind of activity among officials in Veracruz and other nerve centers of the Spanish empire. A naval expedition was launched from Havana, working north and west along the Gulf Coast, to discover the precise location of the French settlement.[4] Subsequent overland and naval expeditions were also prepared, and towns and cities throughout New Spain were warned to be alert for any sign of French activity, whether connected to the expedition or not. When the news reached Spain, officials in Madrid commissioned secret reports from Spanish diplomats and merchants in Paris and London for information on the expedition's logistics and intentions, and in Seville, the Council of the Indies began protracted discussions on how to best insulate Spain's American possessions from the growing French threat.[5]

○ ○ ○ ○ ○

The end of the seventeenth century brought sweeping changes to the landscape of European colonization in the Americas. In the Caribbean, for the first time in two hundred years, Spain could no longer claim a clear naval or territorial advantage over its European rivals. Large and strategically important islands like Jamaica, Curaçao, and Hispaniola were now occupied by Dutch, English, French, or Danish colonists, who oversaw dramatic expansions of plantation slavery, commodity production, and regional contraband trade.[6] At the same time, even as Spanish power—and especially naval power—declined in the Caribbean and the Atlantic world, Spanish officials in Mexico increasingly turned their attention northward, to the frontiers of New Mexico, Texas, Louisiana, and Florida. Responding in part to indigenous revolts in New Mexico and in part to the La Salle expedition, between 1680 and 1701, officials in Mexico organized more than a dozen expeditions to survey northern territories, dispatched a series of Franciscan and Dominican missions, and redirected a significant quantity of military resources from coastal defenses to northern expansion.[7]

Taken together, heightened interest in New Spain's northern frontier and the recession of Spanish power elsewhere in the Atlantic portend the emergence of two discrete paths of American colonial history at the start of the eighteenth century: one in the Caribbean, where plantation slavery dominates the eighteenth-century narrative, and another in the North American borderlands, where boundary disputes and cultural exchanges between multiple European and Amerindian polities reign supreme.[8] While these two narratives share many common themes—creolization and ethnogenesis, for instance, or resistance and accommodation—their commonalities tend to be understood in a comparative sense rather than as interlocking parts of the same narrative.

What were the implications of late-seventeenth-century political developments in the Caribbean and Gulf Coast for Africans and their American descendants? While the story of the La Salle expedition and subsequent Spanish search for a French colony has been told innumerable times, Africans and their descendants often play a relatively quiet role in its retelling. A small but growing number of studies have begun to correct this omission, demonstrating the vital roles played by Africans and their descendants not only as captives but also as informants, soldiers, brokers, and colonizers.[9] This literature has done much to elucidate the previously unknown lives of Afro-descended people and their contributions to early borderlands history. Work remains, however, to fully explicate how enslaved and free people of African descent helped shape the social and cultural worlds of early borderland societies and were in turn transformed by their experiences in borderland settlements.

Revising the story of the La Salle expedition from the perspective of the Spanish Caribbean and Mexico can help us begin to understand not only the involvement of African diasporans in early phases of North American borderland history but also the distinctive social and cultural backgrounds they brought to the region. In particular, to the extent that Afro-descended individuals and communities have been written into early borderlands narratives, there is a tendency to understand them in the context of borderland societies, emphasizing the way Afro-descended people navigated "frontier" conditions, the competitive spaces between European empires, and interactions with indigenous communities. These perspectives are extremely important, but they do not always recognize that Afro-descended people brought with them to the borderland—to French, English, and Spanish settlements—existing understandings of race, ethnicity, status, and religion that were often formed not on the fringe of the colonial world but in the core of the Spanish American empire.

At the same time, following La Salle, imperial competition for territory migrated from Caribbean islands like Hispaniola and Jamaica to the North American mainland. The movement of the borderland from the maritime spaces of the Caribbean and Gulf of Mexico to the mainland not only involved people of African descent as agents and victims of colonial expansion, but it also transformed an existing set of material and political relationships that had mediated Black community formation in the wider Caribbean. Trade networks established in the course of European colonial expansion would lay the foundation of new regional systems and interimperial relationships that influenced Black experiences not only in the borderlands but in the heart of the colonial American world as well.

The sack of Campeche and subsequent naval engagement that led to the Spanish discovery of the La Salle expedition was not the only buccaneer raid in the Mexican mainland in the 1680s with long-range implications for the development of early European outposts in the North American continent. Two years before the Campeche raid swept more than 200 Black and indigenous Mexicans into an uncertain captivity, another raid in Veracruz resulted in a much larger forced migration of 1,500 Afro-Mexicans. In May 1683, a multinational coalition of corsair captains—including two of the same who later organized the Campeche raid, Michel de Grammont and Laurens de Graaf—attacked and occupied the larger and wealthier port city of Veracruz. After overwhelming the city's defenses, plundering its treasury, and desecrating its cathedral, the invaders took as many as 4,000 of the city's residents hostage and decamped to the barren island of Sacrificios just south of the port. When ransom arrived a week later the invaders freed some of the surviving hostages (others had already perished of hunger and thirst), but they took approximately 1,500 as captives—all of whom were Afro-descended and many of whom were free people—to be sold as slaves elsewhere in the Americas.[10]

The subsequent fate of the Afro-Mexican captives has long been a matter of speculation. Some were probably resold in the Mexican port of Coatzacoalcos one month later, while others were rescued by the Armada de Barlovento off the coast of Cuba.[11] Recently, the pathbreaking work of Pablo Miguel Sierra Silva has begun to provide more definitive answers. According to Sierra Silva, the majority of the captives were taken directly to Petit-Goâve. Sierra Silva has turned up multiple references to Afro-Mexican women of Veracruz in Saint-Domingue's parish records in the succeeding two decades.[12] While many remained in Saint-Domingue, it is clear that others were taken on to other destinations. For example, Sierra Silva has shown that at least two hundred of the Afro-Mexican captives were sold as slaves in the markets of Charles Town, South Carolina.[13] While Jamaican governor Thomas Lynch reported a rumor in July 1683 that the buccaneer known as Jacob Hall had taken Veracruz captives to Carolina, for Sierra Silva, the definitive evidence comes in the testimony of two English-speaking indentured servants who escaped their captivity in Carolina and were later questioned by Spanish authorities in Saint Augustine.[14]

It is important that the corsairs who raided Veracruz in 1683 did not make distinctions of caste or status among the Afro-descended people they took captive, instead seeing all hostages of dark complexion as potential slaves. Given what we know of seventeenth-century Veracruz, it is certain not only that many of the captives were and always had been free but also that some held relatively high status. It is likely, for example, that the Afro-Mexicans taken captive in the Veracruz raid included both enslaved people and, in some cases, the people who enslaved them, to be sold alongside one another in Saint-Domingue or Charles Town. The difference between Afro-Mexican perspectives on caste and those of their captors is articulated in a description appended to the journal of Henri Joutel, one of the La Salle expedition's few survivors. Although Joutel's journal has long been a core source of information about the expedition, it is in a comment made by the journal's editor, Sieur de Mitchell (who prepared it for its initial publication in 1715), that the divergence of attitudes is made clear. Describing Veracruz, Mitchell writes, "Most of the inhabitants are Mulattoes, that is of a tawny dark Colour . . . If those Mulattoes call themselves white, it is only to honour themselves and by Way of Distinction from their Slaves, who are all Black."[15] At once this description testifies both to the value that some Afro-descended Mexicans placed in distinctions of caste and color and to the disregard with which white European observers often treated such distinctions.

Almost precisely one year after the corsairs who sacked Veracruz returned to Petit-Goâve with more than one thousand Afro-Mexican captives, the La Salle expedition stopped there on its way, they believed, to the Mississippi River. Most accounts of the expedition refer to the large number of would-be colonists who abandoned La Salle in Saint-Domingue—as Denis Thomas had—and it is possible some people, including Afro-Mexican captives, may have joined the expedition there before it proceeded to the Texas coast.[16] In fact, some accounts suggest that La Salle's mission was to act as a vanguard for a more widespread French invasion of Texas. The subsequent French invasion was to be carried out by the same companies of privateers who had organized the Veracruz raid, led by Michel de Grammont. The plan was devised by Diego de Peñalosa, the former Spanish governor of New Mexico then in exile in Paris, and had the backing of Abbé Claude Bernou, an influential figure in the French court and formerly La Salle's agent in Paris. The goal of such an invasion would be the conquest of the Spanish province of Nueva Vizcaya where, Peñalosa promised, there were excellent silver mines.[17]

While Peñalosa's scheme was not realized and subsequent contingents of French invaders from Saint-Domingue did not follow La Salle, one person who did claim to have joined La Salle's Texas colony in the Americas was an Englishman named Ralph Wilkinson (Raphael Guilquinsen in Spanish documents). Wilkinson was arrested in Havana, allegedly on his way to London, and gave testimony in Veracruz and Mexico City about a French settlement in Texas that he called San Juan (Saint-Jean). In his long and elaborate testimony, Wilkinson recounted a life spent traveling "around the world," though he spent most of his adult life plying his trade as a maritime carpenter in Barbados, Jamaica, and Petit-Goâve. Hoping to settle down, he claimed to have joined "400 French families" in a fortified colony around the thirtieth parallel north on an islet in a large river that connected the Gulf Coast to Canada. There, he claimed, he had married a French-speaking woman from the English island of Jersey who owned a plantation in the colony.[18]

Wilkinson's testimony contained several inconsistencies and conspicuously omitted important details. Most glaringly, when asked who the leader of the expedition was, he claimed that he could not remember but that it might have been La Salle. Nevertheless, Wilkinson's recollection was enough to set in motion another naval expedition to locate La Salle's colony. The search failed, leading Spanish officials to deem Wilkinson as nothing but a "great liar" (*gran embustero*), and subsequent historians have likewise dismissed Wilkinson's testimony as the work of a fabulist. One detail of his testimony that has received little attention, however, is his suggestion that the French colony included multiple large plantations (*haciendas*) that were worked by enslaved Africans.

Given Wilkinson's history in Jamaica, Barbados, and Saint-Domingue, his description of Black captives in La Salle's colony is unsurprising—elsewhere in the Caribbean, new European colonies meant quick expansion of plantation agriculture and racial slavery. Nevertheless, the fact that Wilkinson may not have had any actual contact with the La Salle expedition deprives his description of tangible meaning. What role, if any, did Black captives play in La Salle's expedition, and where did they join it? Neither Wilkinson's testimony nor other evidence have given us a clear answer to these questions. Symbolically, however, Wilkinson's testimony speaks to an expectation of colonizing missions like La Salle's that both Spanish officials and common people around the Caribbean shared: La Salle's colony in Texas, had it succeeded, might well have become a hub of plantation slavery as other French and English colonies had.

At least one other source attested to a Black population within a French settlement on the Gulf Coast. In December 1687, twenty months after two English-speaking deponents gave Spanish officials in Saint Augustine their account of the arrival of Veracruz captives to Charles Town, a *mulatto* man named Thomas de la Torre testified to the same officials both about his experiences as a captive in Carolina and his subsequent visit to a French settlement in the Gulf Coast.[19] According to his testimony, Torre had embarked on a Spanish expedition to attack the English colony of Carolina but was captured by Chiloquin Indians who turned him and other survivors over to the English. Torre's English captors imprisoned him in Charles Town for three weeks. While in prison, Torre was questioned by the Dutch privateer Jan Willems (also known as Janke or Yankey), who had participated in both the Veracruz and Campeche raids and was present in Petit-Goâve when the La Salle expedition was there, about Saint Augustine's defenses.[20] In exchange for information, Willems helped secure Torre's release. Once free, Torre claimed that he joined Willems, sailing from Charles Town to Jamaica in 1686. In Jamaica, Torre joined two ships on an expedition ostensibly to raid for indigenous captives along the Gulf Coast. Claiming to know where to find plentiful potential captives, Torre guided the ships to a place he called the Bahia del Espíritu Santo—the location that Spanish officials suspected to be the home of La Salle's Texas colony. Upon entering the bay and sailing upriver, Torre claimed that he and his cohort encountered a French settlement numbering two hundred inhabitants, including an unspecified number of Black slaves.

Like Wilkinson, Torre's declaration lacks important details and contains some geographic inconsistencies. In particular, the location of the French settlement as he described it appears to have been nowhere near Texas; instead it was somewhere along the Apalachee coast. This has again led historians to doubt the veracity of his testimony, suggesting instead that he fabricated the French settlement as a way of offering valuable information that might lead to his release. Again, however, Torre's testimony speaks to both the expectation and fear that competing European settlements, if they were to be viable, would draw on enslaved Black labor. This sentiment was expressed again thirty years later, in Sieur de Mitchell's comment on Henri Joutel's journal. Remarking on the French colonization of Louisiana under the proprietorship of Antoine Crozat, Mitchell observes, "Such a Grant cannot subsist without Blacks."[21] Subsequent French colonists, hoping to succeed where La Salle had failed, sought the labor of the enslaved, only this time delivered from West Africa rather than stolen from the enslaved and unenslaved residents of Spanish territories.

While African and Afro-descended captives taken from Spanish American colonies entered fledging English and French outposts, Afro-descended people from the same places were often recruited or impressed into service in competing Spanish settlements. For example, according to Jane Landers, in the 1670s St. Augustine's governor Pablo de Hita y Salazar complained that soldiers assigned to the Florida garrison were overwhelmingly the "sons of blacks, *chinos*, and mulattoes" of Mexico. In September 1683, four months after the sack of Veracruz, Hita y Salazar's successor in St. Augustin, Juan Márquez Cabrera, mustered the colony's first company of free-Black militiamen. Although demographic details about the forty-eight *pardo* and *moreno* men who formed St. Augustine's militia are lacking, their names likewise indicate that many were likely born in the mainland colonies.[22]

As Landers and others have noted, the free-Black militia had a long history in the Spanish Americas, going back more than one hundred years by 1683.[23] It was in the context of increasing attacks of Spain's European rivals in the late seventeenth century, however, that the militia and its members would be incorporated into Spanish polities as a chief mediator of free-Black social status. In 1669—eleven years after an expedition of free-Black fighters had been sent from Veracruz to aid the Spanish resistance to the English invasion of Jamaica—Veracruz's free-Black militia petitioned New Spain's viceroy and the *junta de guerra* for tribute relief, citing mounting foreign threats and their deployment to guard the colony's coasts.[24] Subsequent petitions followed throughout Mexico's Gulf Coast, including a significant cluster filed in the aftermath of the Veracruz disaster of 1683—an event during which free-Black militiamen as far away as Mexico City were mustered.[25] In other words, at the same time that free-Black militiamen in mainland centers of the Spanish American empire were calling upon their service to negotiate for things like tribute relief—in effect changing the material meanings of Blackness in the Spanish Americas—militia companies including members from those same colonies were being mustered to guard the Spanish frontier. What ideas about status and strategies for attaining it did they bring with them? While the answer may not always be evident in the particular cases of borderland societies, the precedents being set at the same time in mainland centers offer us a useful guide.

Fifteen years after the raid on Veracruz touched off the embrace—from Mexico to Saint Augustine—of free-Black militias as a formalized corporate institution, another group of Afro-Mexicans prepared to supplement Spanish defense of the Gulf Coast. After years of searching, in 1689 a Spanish overland expedition finally located the abandoned ruins of La Salle's colony in Matagorda Bay.[26] Although the immediate threat had extinguished, fear of further French designs upon the coast persisted, and the Council of the Indies devised plans to better secure the entire Gulf Coast. After much debate, the Council authorized the establishment of a fortress in Pensacola Bay, in Florida, west of the Apalachicola River.[27] In 1698, the Council appointed Andres de Arriola, the *sargento mayor* of the fortress of San Juan de Ulúa, as the new governor of Pensacola. In the late summer of that year, Arriola organized 350 settlers and three ships for a colonizing expedition. The colonists were recruited or impressed among soldiers stationed in Veracruz; convicts conscripted from prisons in Mexico City, Puebla de los Ángeles, and Veracruz (*forzados*); and tradesmen from the port city of Veracruz. The Mexican recruits were joined in Pensacola by a separate expedition of fifty colonists from Havana.[28]

Like the populations of the cities that they came from, a substantial proportion of the Pensacola colonists were undoubtedly of African descent.[29] Although the identities of the initial colonists are almost entirely unknown, a report of 1708—ten years after the settlement's founding and after several ensuing rounds of migrants from Mexico had arrived to supplement and replace those who had died or deserted—indicated that a quarter of the residents at the presidio Santa María de Galve were Afro-descended, while as many as two-fifths were recorded as indigenous or *mestizo* natives of New Spain. Later reports similarly indicated that subsequent colonists arrived from New Spain were predominantly Afro-Mexican and *mestizo*.[30]

On the Texas side of the Gulf Coast, other Spanish settlements of the late seventeenth century also bore the presence of Spanish-speaking people of African descent. During his second voyage to the Mississippi River in 1700, Pierre Le Moyne d'Iberville reported an encounter with the Nabedache Indians of the southern Caddo confederacy in which he was informed of a "Spanish settlement . . . [where] there are a number of men, women, and children, whites, and mulattoes and blacks, and they till the soil." This settlement, which the informant called Yayecha, was reportedly five-and-a-half days to the west of Kadohadacho, in the vicinity of Texas. The same informant claimed to have lived in this Spanish settlement for one year, occasionally visiting a second settlement, which he called Connessi, a further five days by horseback to the west-northwest, where "there were only Negroes with their families . . . [who] did not welcome any white Spaniard."[31] Failing further evidence, it is difficult to say precisely where in Texas the Spanish settlement of Yayecha or the Maroon settlement of Connessi were or how accurate their description was. Afro-Mexicans did participate in the Spanish colonization of east Texas in the 1690s, at Mission San Francisco de Tejas and elsewhere, and Iberville's informant may have referred to these establishments.[32] If so, the informant suggested larger numbers of Afro-Mexican settlers than other accounts indicate.

While Afro-Mexicans were taken into captivity in places like Charles Town, Petit-Goâve, and later French settlements on the mainland, they also formed a core part of the Spanish outposts in Saint Augustin, Pensacola, and Texas. Their experiences, the communities and relationships they built, and their negotiations for categorical status in these spaces are often frustratingly opaque. At the same time, archaeological studies on some of these settlements have demonstrated aspects of material culture and techniques that captives and colonists brought with them from their homelands in Mexico.[33] For example, in a comparative study of pottery production in the port of Veracruz and Pensacola, archaeologist Krista Eschbach found that one-fifth of pottery samples drawn from Spanish settlements in northwest Florida in the early eighteenth century drew on methods used by *castas* (caste system) in Veracruz.[34]

What else did early Black borderlanders bring with them from their experiences in the wider Mexican Caribbean world? Unlike many borderland settlements, early colonial Mexico and parts of the Spanish Caribbean have a vast archival record brimming with rich evidence about Afro-descended individuals and communities. Using this record, in the past thirty years, Mexicanist and Caribbeanist scholars have produced exquisitely detailed narratives showing processes of community formation, ethnogenesis, social mobility, religious syncretism, status negotiation, resistance, and much more.[35] Rather than begin a search for Black lives in the borderlands *in media res*, we should take this literature as a starting point. As we have seen, the Black colonists and captives who populated early borderland establishments came from Spanish American societies where distinctions among *negro, mulato, pardo,* and *moreno* defined social opportunities and obligations. They came from places where social mobility could be found in the service of the Crown, as in the case of the free-Black militia. It is perhaps not surprising, then, that when the founding governor of Pensacola, Andres de Arriola, sought to stop unpaid *forzados* from deserting the colony, he did so by offering them a wage and uniform.[36]

Black settlers in the borderlands came from a world, too, in which dispersed communities of African diasporans were connected along lines of material exchange and migration, creating a regional unity of Black experience. The formal and informal commercial networks that connected New Spain, South America, and the Spanish Caribbean islands bore people and ideas as well as goods, allowing free-Black residents of Spanish American cities and towns surprising mobility and opportunities to create common understandings of race, caste, and religion. The expansion of European colonial ambitions from the Caribbean to the North American mainland destabilized established systems of trade and migration, introducing existing diasporic networks to environments, people, languages, and spaces that had not previously factored in Black community formation. If looking to colonial Mexico and the Caribbean can help us understand early Black settlers in the borderlands, then the transformation of material networks precipitated by colonial expansion can help us understand what came after.

Changing Material Relationships in the Late Seventeenth Century

The urgency of Spain's search for La Salle was driven as much by the threat the expedition posed to the security of commercial routes in the Caribbean world as it was by the threat to Spain's territorial claims in North America. In April 1686, for example, Spain's war council (*junta de guerra*) argued that extinguishing the French threat in Texas should take precedence over similar threats in Panama, Tierra Firme, and the Pacific Ocean. They reasoned that if the French were able to establish a settlement in Texas it would do "irreparable damage to commerce," as French settlers would "become the owners of a principal port on the Gulf of Mexico," from which they could "infest the ports and coasts of the Gulf, and all of the Indies, as proxies of a site so suitable for it, and the fleets and galleons will suffer the risks that they are enabled to inflict."[37] Elsewhere, the council compared the French threat in Texas to rumored Scottish and English colonies in Central America and the western Caribbean.[38] Other officials worried that foreign presence in Texas would upset commerce in the Gulf just as it had in the Caribbean's South American littoral, where "Cartagena is made into a borderland (*frontera*) of France, England and Holland, as these Nations are as close as Matalino [Martinique], Jamaica, and Curaçao."[39]

In particular, like similar challenges in the southern Caribbean, the French presence in Texas and the northern Gulf Coast threatened to introduce Spanish and indigenous settlements to the perdition of foreign smuggling. Although contraband and informal trade had long been a central part of the Caribbean's commercial world, in the early seventeenth century, imperial boundaries were loosely defined and somewhat fluid. In the late seventeenth century, the territorial advance of Spain's European competitors resulted by definition in the demarcation of space. As a result, foreign smuggling gained new political meanings, as proceeds of contraband not only funded European wars but also aided the disintegration of Spanish colonies. Spanish officials had always seen contraband not only as a threat to the royal treasury but as a potent force of moral corruption and political subversion as well. That force was amplified as new European colonies threatened the propagation of the Catholic faith as well as Spanish coffers.

Fear that illicit material networks might carry more than commodities were not unfounded, though perhaps not always in the way Spanish officials anticipated. Recently, historians of the early modern Caribbean have described informal trade and interimperial commerce as a formative of regional identities that diverged from the ascriptive categories of the metropole.[40] This applied both to Spanish subjects as well as to African diasporans, who formed a substantial, and in many cases majority, portion of Caribbean populations. Free and enslaved Africans were active participants in the Caribbean's informal trade networks as traders, mariners, consumers, and in a variety of ancillary industries, like local service economies.

While informal networks often included non-Spanish Europeans as carriers and merchants, before the middle of the seventeenth century, these networks primarily connected populations *within* the wider Spanish American world rather than connecting Spanish and non-Spanish territories. For example, in the early seventeenth century, informal trade connected larger ports like Veracruz and Cartagena to smaller Spanish ports like Campeche and Maracaibo. These relationships carried goods and, often, people across colonial jurisdictions within the Spanish empire, often connecting Black communities in disparate colonies. Networks of informal trade then predicated social and cultural similarities, including the development of corporate institutions like the free-Black militia and Black confraternities.[41]

When the search for La Salle finally led to the ruins of a French fort in Bahía del Espíritu Santo, Spanish officials worried that, in finding Espíritu Santo, the French had discovered a bay that was potentially better situated to control commerce in the Gulf than Veracruz was itself. A Spanish naval officer named Martín de Echegaray, who had participated in the search for La Salle, even recommended that Veracruz should be relocated from San Juan de Ulúa to Texas to prevent the French from returning. He argued that stationing Mexico's primary port in Texas would not only quell French ambitions over the territory but would also provide better defense of shipping lanes in the Bahama Channel and would open more direct overland routes to northern silver mining regions. His proposal received serious consideration from officials in both Mexico and Spain, who suggested that, unlike Veracruz, Espíritu Santo was "fit in all seasons of the year to give sustenance."[42]

By founding a new settlement at Pensacola, the council hoped to achieve the goal of securing shipping lanes in the northern Gulf without uprooting one of the oldest and largest ports in Spanish America. Ever aware of the expense involved in maintaining outposts like Pensacola, the council also reasoned that locating a fortified settlement at Pensacola could deter French interest in the northern Gulf as well as English interests in Georgia and the Carolinas. In a cedula of 1694, the crown reasoned that, if the new settlement were to be positioned any further west than Pensacola, then it would result in the "dismantling and reduction of our forces in the presidios of La Florida [Saint Augustine], which, because of its proximity to the land called San Jorge, possessed by the English, would diminish the maintenance and preservation of our Holy Catholic Faith among the Indians [of that land]."[43]

One year after the Pensacola colony was founded, however, it became clear that holding a single port on the northern Gulf would not be enough to deter foreign contraband traders from taking advantage of New Spain's maritime frontier. In January and February 1699, three French vessels under the command of Pierre le Moyne d'Iberville established a trading base in Mobile Bay. From Mobile and later Biloxi, French traders used a combination of maritime and overland routes to import goods like tobacco, coffee, and furs from the Caribbean and Canada to cities in northern New Spain, including Zacatecas, San Luis de Potosí, and Monterrey.[44]

Although these goods entered New Spain by land, the border was still understood as a maritime construction: French traders accessed New Spain from the land via Texas, but Spanish officials perceived their ability to enter the land as the failure to maintain control over the coast. A 1719 report, for instance, described that, in order to "extend themselves to the innermost part of [the northern] provinces, to spread prejudice throughout the Continental domain of New Spain, and to penetrate to the heart of it, [the French] seek to establish ports and anchorages."[45] At the same time, contraband traders in Mobile also conducted an active maritime trade with Veracruz. Though in 1699 royal officials in San Juan de Ulúa noted that "no ships of [the French nation] are allowed to enter besides those that bring *negros*," just nine years later in 1708, Andrés de Pez—the commander the Armada de Barlovento who was one of the earliest supporters of placing a colony in Pensacola—reported that eighty French ships had illegally sold goods in Veracruz in the preceding three years, most conducting this traffic from Mobile.[46]

What were the repercussions of the transformation of Caribbean commerce for African diasporans, both in new borderland societies and in older cities like Veracruz? In the short-term, it is hard to disentangle the gradual transformation of material networks from more immediate crises like the captivity of 1,500 Afro-Mexicans taken from Veracruz, or the formalization of the free-Black militias that followed. In the long term, the port cities and towns of New Spain's Gulf Coast maintained close trade ties with French settlements in the northern Gulf.[47] Precisely how new relationships between Veracruz, Tampico, and Matamoros on one side and New Orleans, Biloxi, and Mobile on the other affected Black communities on either side of the Gulf is a question that will need to be answered elsewhere. What we can say is that the material relationships that shaped Black communities in New Spain and the Spanish Caribbean in the early seventeenth century were changed in the expansion of European empires to the northern Gulf. Elaborating the resulting commercial networks will be central to understanding not only how Africans and their descendants shaped the borderlands but also how the borderlands transformed Black communities far beyond.

Conclusion

"Neither Florida nor New Mexico immediately grew into full-blown Spanish colonies," the eminent borderlands historian David Weber once wrote. "To the contrary," he continued, "both initially skidded into decline as their limited opportunities became evident to the pioneers who founded them."[48] With this, borderland settlements of the late seventeenth century are consigned to an inferior status, blips on the way to more important and more lasting settlements in the eighteenth century. As subsequent scholars have begun to write Africans and their descendants into this narrative moment, however, we have an opportunity to assign early frontier establishments importance not based on what they did or did not represent in the broad sweep of European colonialism but for how they mark a turning point in the history of African diaspora. In the plunder of Black bodies to provide labor for English and French frontier settlements in 1683 and 1685, we see the sudden and violent insistence on a status tied not to language or ethnicity or religion or wealth, but skin color. In Spanish reliance on the same Black labor in Pensacola, Saint Augustine, and Texas, we see a delicate balance of coerced labor alongside the promise of social mobility channeled through cohesive corporate units. And in the rearrangement of material networks, we see the breakup of older regional systems in the Caribbean and the emergence of new interimperial relationships that would set the context of Black communities in the frontier in the eighteenth century.

Notes

1. See Moreno, *Corsarios y piratas en Veracruz y Campeche*, 331–66.

2. AGI-México 616, Gaspar de Palacios to Pedro de Oreytia, November 17, 1685. See also AGI-Indiferente Virreinal 1879, Junta de Guerra to VM, April 2, 1686.

3. AGI-México 616, Gaspar de Palacios to Pedro de Oreytia, November 17, 1685.

4. See the series of correspondence in AGI-México 616, Andres de Munibe to VM, December 31, 1685; AGI-México 616, Andres de Munibe to VM, July 9, 1686. See also AGI-México 616, Antonio de Astina to VM, April 13, 1686.

5. AGI-México 616, Pedro de Ronquillo to Consejo de Indias, October 28, 1686; AGI-México 616, Junta de Gerra to VM, June 18, 1686.

6. On the Dutch, see Sluiter, "Dutch-Spanish Rivalry in the Caribbean Area, 1594–1609," 165–96. On the British capture of Jamaica, see Wright, "The Spanish Resistance to the English Occupation of Jamaica, 1655–1660," 117–47. On the French settlement of western Hispaniola, see Boucher, *France and the American Tropics to 1700: Tropics of Discontent?*, 88–111.

7. On the Pueblo Revolt, see Knaut, *The Pueblo Revolt of 1680*. On the La Salle expedition to Texas, see Chipman and Joseph, *Spanish Texas, 1519–1821*, 60–82. On Spanish expeditions to survey northern territories and Dominican and Franciscan missions, see AGI-México 311, Cartas y expedientes de personas eclesiásticas, March 30, 1686; AGI-México 617, Andrés de Pez to Consejo de Indias, February 22, 1690; AGI-México 633, Manuel de Aperregui to VM, August 3, 1701. The redirection of military resources northward is evident both in funding and in supplies like gunpowder. On funding, see Sluiter, *The Gold and Silver of Spanish America, c. 1572–1648*, 137–51. On supplies, see Villar Ortiz, *La renta de la pólvora en Nueva España, 1569–1767*, 115–17.

8. On the eighteenth-century Caribbean historiography, see Cromwell, "More than Slaves and Sugar," 770–83. On the eighteenth-century borderlands, see Adelman and Aron, "From Borderlands to Borders," 815–16.

9. See Dubcovsky, *Informed Power: Communication in the Early American South*; Landers, *Black Society in Spanish Florida*; Dawdy, *Building the Devil's Empire*.

10. AGI-Patronato Real 243, r. 3, "Peligro de Nueva España por la invasión de Veracruz," August 18, 1683, f. 1r–1v

11. On those resold in Coatzocoalcos, see Robles and Leal, eds., *Diario de sucesos notables (1665–1703)*, 380–83; on those rescued, see AGN-IV, Marina, caja 2748, exp. 4, August 9, 1683, fs. 7r–8r.

12. Sierra Silva, "Afro-Mexican Women in Saint-Domingue," 3–34.

13. I am indebted to Sierra Silva for sharing with me his unpublished work on this case. See Sierra Silvas, "The Pirate Link: Rethinking Early Charleston, Blackness and the 1683 Raid on Veracruz." Cited with author's permission.

14. See *British Calendar of State Papers Colonial, America and West Indies*, vol. 11, 1681–1685, pp. 486–95.

15. Joutel, *Joutel's Journal of La Salle's Last Voyage*, 189–90.

16. See Laprise, "The Privateers of Saint-Domingue and Louis XVI's Designs on Spanish America, 1683–1685," 75.

17. See Laprise, 68–71. See also Weddle, *The Wreck of the Belle, the Ruin of La Salle*, 83–103; Chipman and Joseph, *Spanish Texas*, 60–69.

18. AGI-México 616, "El virrey conde de la Monclova a VM," July 25, 1687. See also Dunn, "The Spanish Search for La Salle's Colony on the Bay of Espiritu Santo," 352–53.

19. AGI-Mexico 616, "Carta de Don Fernandez Marmolejo," May 7, 1688. See also Dubcovsky, "The Testimony of Thomás de la Torre," 559–80.

20. Laprise, "The Privateers of Saint-Domingue," 74–75.

21. Joutel, *Joutel's Journal of La Salle's Last Voyage*, 187.

22. Landers, *Black Society in Spanish Florida*, 22–23.

23. See Vinson III, *Bearing Arms for His Majesty*; Klein, "The Colored Militia of Cuba: 1568–1868," 17–27; Kuethe, "The Status of the Free Pardo in the Disciplined Militia of New Granada," 105–17; Andrews, "The Afro-Argentine Officers of Buenos Aires Province, 1800–1860," 85–100; Landers, "Gracia Real de Santa Teresa de Mose," 9–30; Hanger, *Bounded Lives, Bounded Places*, 109–35; Vinson III, "Race and Badge," 471–96; Sartorius, "My Vassals: Free-Colored Militias in Cuba and the Ends of Spanish Empire."

24. In 1658, three years after the English invasion of Jamaica began, New Spain's viceroy authorized the deployment of 558 infantrymen, most of whom were of African descent, from Veracruz. A combined force of Mexican, Spanish Jamaican, and maroon fighters were routed by English combatants at the battle of Rio Nuevo in the summer of 1658. The battle proved to be decisive, inspiring one of the island's chief Maroon commanders, Juan Lubolo (known to the English as Juan de Bolas) to switch allegiances to the English side. Meanwhile, survivors of

the broken Spanish resistance returned to Mexico via Santiago de Cuba, likely including some Afro-Jamaicans. Nine years later, there appeared in Veracruz a confraternity constituted of the *"negros lobolo,"* which may have referred to Afro-Jamaicans. In this, we see how the movement of Black fighting forces across the Gulf-Caribbean can result in meaningful social changes. If the deployment of Afro-Mexicans to Jamaica resulted in new social and cultural institutions in Veracruz, then we might expect similar exchanges to follow from subsequent deployments and migrations to and from the later North American borderlands. See Clark, *Veracruz and the Caribbean in the Seventeenth Century*, 172–73; Wright, "The Spanish Resistance," 135.

25. Vinson III, *Bearing Arms*, 33, 246, n84.

26. Chipman and Joseph, *Spanish Texas*, 75–76.

27. See AGI-México 617, "Real cédula al virrey de la Nueva España que en vista de lo que ha escripto y ordenes que le estan dadas fortifique luego la vahia nombrada Santa María de Galve," 1694. See also AGI-México 616, "Expediente sobre el reconocimiento y fortificación de la Bahía del Espíritu Santo, en la costa septentrional del Seno Mexicano," April 2, 1686.

28. AGI-México 618, "Expediente de fortificación de la Bahía del Espíritu Santo," 1698.

29. According to the 1681 census of the archdiocese of Puebla, precisely half of the free population of the city of Veracruz was either *"negros y mulatos."* The same census found that more than sixty percent of the free residents of Puebla were *"indios, negros, mestizos y mulatos,"* without differentiating further. Neither figure included enslaved people, who would have constituted a considerable portion of the populations of both cities and would have been entirely of African descent. See Gerhard, "Un censo de la diócesis de Puebla en 1681," 530–60.

30. Clune, Childers, Coker, and Swan, "Settlement, Settlers, and Survival," 25–82.

31. Iberville, *Iberville's Gulf Journals*, 154–55.

32. See Richmond, "Africa's Initial Encounter with Texas," 203.

33. See, for example, Bense, *Archaeology of Colonial Pensacola*; Bense, "Presidio Santa María de Galve (1698–1719)," 47–65; Deagan, "Eliciting Contraband Through Archaeology," 98–116; Worth, "Forging a New Identity in Florida's Refugee Missions."

34. Eschbach, "Mechanisms of Colonial Transformation at the Port of Veracruz and the Northwest Florida Presidios," 493.

35. On Afro-Mexico, see Carroll, *Blacks in Colonial Veracruz*; Chávez-Hita, *Esclavos negros en las haciendas azucares de Córdoba*; García de León, *Tierra adentro, mar en fuera: el puerto de Veracruz y su litoral sotavento, 1519–1821*; Bennett, *Africans in Colonial Mexico: Absolutism, Christianity, and Afro-Creole Consciousness, 1570–1640*; Germeten, *Black Blood Brothers*; Bristol, *Christians, Blasphemers, and Witches*; Proctor, *Damned Notions of Liberty*; Sierra Silva, *Urban Slavery in Colonial Mexico*; Terrazas-Williams, *Capital of Free Women*. On the Caribbean, see Wheat, *Atlantic Africa and the Spanish Caribbean, 1570–1640*; Ponce-Vázquez, *Islanders and Empire*; Gómez, *The Experiential Caribbean*; Block, *Ordinary Lives in the Early Caribbean*.

36. Clune et al., 27.

37. See AGI-México 616, "Expediente sobre el reconocimiento y fortificación de la Bahía del Espíritu Santo, en la costa septentrional del Seno Mexicano," April 2, 1686.

38. AGI-México 617, Council of the Indies to VM, March 22, 1691.

39. AGI-Indiferente General 789, Melchor de Navarra to VM, April 21, 1684.

40. See Ponce-Vázquez, *Islanders and Empire*, 56–97 and passim; Cromwell, *The Smuggler's World*, 271–308, passim; Rupert, "Contraband Trade and the Shaping of Colonial Societies in Curaçao and Tierra Firme," 35–54.

41. See Clark, *Veracruz and the Caribbean*, chap. 3.

42. AGI-Contratación 5460, n. 5, r. 6, "Expediente de información y licencia de pasajero a Indias del capitán Martín de Echagaray, corregidor de Chietla, a Nueva España," July 5, 1704.

43. See AGI-México 616, Declaracion de Andrés de Pez al el virrey Conde de la Monclova, May 27, 1688; AGI-México 617, "Real cédula al virrey de la Nueva España que en vista de lo que ha escripto y ordenes que le estan dadas fortifique luego la vahia nombrada Santa Maria de Galve," 1694. See also AGI-México 616, "Expediente sobre el reconocimiento y fortificación de la Bahía del Espíritu Santo, en la costa septentrional del Seno Mexicano," April 2, 1686.

44. AGI-Guadalajara 134, "Extracto de la acaescido en las entradas y Poblaciones de Franceses en el Seno Mexico desde año de 1684 hasta el de 1719," January 13, 1720.

45. AGI-Guadalajara 134, "Extracto de la acaescido en las entradas y Poblaciones de Franceses en el Seno Mexico desde año de 1684 hasta el de 1719," January 13, 1720, sf.

46. AGN-IV, Marina, caja 6242, exp. 006, "Autos sobre la llegada a Veracruz, del navío frances Conde de Plovert, siendo capitán Comandante Monsiur de Beauveais, al cual no se le dejó entrar al puerto de San Juan de Ulúa," 1699, f. 8v; AGI-México 377, Andrés de Pez to Gaspar de Pinedo, December 10, 1708, sf.

47. See Galván, "From Contraband Capital to Border City: Matamoros, 1746–1848," 15–90.

48. Weber, *The Spanish Frontier in North America*, 89.

CHAPTER FOUR

THE CASE OF MARÍA FAUSTINA TREJO

Fluid Racial Categories in Jalisco's Highlands, 1781–1815

Anne M. Reid

IN THE parish of San Felipe in Cuquío, Nueva Galicia, María Faustina Trejo was identified as *mulata* in her baptism record of February 1781. By 1802, when she appeared again in the same parish to receive the sacrament of marriage, she was labeled as *mestiza*. By the time she passed away in 1815, she was documented as *española*. This case of racial (mis)identification speaks to the larger practice of sometimes arbitrary ascriptive racial and ethnic categories. Yet this curious case also demands more scrutiny because it suggests that other factors may have also influenced how persons of African descent, like *mulatas*, could birth Spanish children, despite the supposed rigidity of the *sistema de castas*.

Students of colonial Latin American history know that there is extensive debate on race and class. Scholarship on the *sistema de castas* falls into that larger historiography. The *sistema de castas* functioned as a hierarchy of racial or ethnic classification, rooted in an individual's degree of African, indigenous, and/or European lineage. The *castas* refer to the mixed-race products of these three main groups. Regardless of where these mixed individuals existed in the social hierarchy, the *sistema* routinely favored those who could confirm European lineage or at least visibly present as European. As historian María Elena Martínez notes, the *sistema de castas* "disenfranchised people of mixed ancestry [by] limiting their political and economic claims" and reserved the greatest number of privileges for Spaniards.[1]

Yet the life history of María Faustina Trejo and the history of the area in which she resided demonstrates that non-elite persons could potentially undermine the *sistema* through changing their racial and ethnic classifications. As Cameron D. Jones notes in chapter 1 of this volume, individuals potentially had much to gain by taking advantage of such racial fluidity. While Jones's essay focuses on Afro-descendant military personnel in California, this work primarily examines malleable racial categories among civilians in the highlands of Jalisco. Building on the scholarly literature on New Spain's *sistema de casta*, this essay uses sacramental records to illustrate the ambiguity and fluidity of racial categories. Contrary to the dominant narrative that eighteenth-century persons of African ancestry and their descendants had few chances to achieve social mobility, the phenomenon of transcending racial categories from Black to indigenous and to white was much more common in practice than the rigid *casta* system hierarchies admitted. Additionally, other factors, such as Cuquío's frontier status in relation to the city of Guadalajara, may have also played a role in the fluidity of these categories. Environmental and social factors that shaped this particular borderland area led to conditions in which racial-ethnic classification became elastic and potentially manipulable for the benefit of its racially mixed denizens.

As fellow volume contributor Robert C. Schwaller observes, the definition of *mulato* "placed individuals of European-African descent and African-Indigenous descent within the same socio-racial category."[2] This racial and ethnic slipperiness poses a challenge for historians studying persons of African descent in colonial Mexico. A secondary aim of this essay is to illustrate the ambiguity inherent in such terms as *mulato* or *mestiza*. Yet determining the racial or ethnic classification of past rural populations is problematic. While most archival documentation does not contain specific racial or ethnic information about non-elite persons, sacramental records, however imperfect they may be as we shall see in this essay, yield some understanding of the popular usage of such terms.

This essay principally draws on remarkably complete records from San Felipe Church in Cuquío and secondarily from other sacramental registers in the immediate area of Cuquío. While these records have been photographed and made electronically available to researchers, these eighteenth-century records have been minimally indexed so that the only information that is usefully searchable is a name and date of sacrament. A relational database would make it possible to search for and longitudinally track individuals whose names are correlated among three (baptism, marriage, and burial) record sets, but the San Felipe Church records are not contained in such a database. As such, locating specific individuals and their offspring presents a challenge for those of us who study this particular parish. The familial genealogies presented in this essay had to be reconstructed manually by searching for individuals within the pages of the registers. It is entirely possible that during the process of family reconstruction there are omissions among these familial histories. Nonetheless, there is more than sufficient evidence from the sacramental registers to demonstrate the persistent fluidity of these racial and ethnic categories among these parishioners.

This study is necessarily speculative in its findings, presenting various scenarios to explain how and why individuals repeatedly transcended racial and ethnic classifications over their lifetimes. Studying non-elite peoples in borderland areas usually means contending with a thin historical archive. The scribal agents of the Spanish empire—royal, legal, and clerical officials—often did not interact with ordinary peoples unless those individuals came under scrutiny for criminal acts. Therefore, one must be attentive to clues contained in such existing official documents. But before we delve into the details of racial and ethnic vagueness, we should acquaint ourselves with the geographic region.

Lying seventy-nine kilometers (forty-nine miles) northeast of the city of Guadalajara, Cuquío and the surrounding towns and villages form part of the Los Altos region, otherwise known as the Jaliscan highlands. Even before European settlement in the 1530s, the region had been a borderland situated on the furthest northern edge of Mesoamerica, where nomadic indigenous peoples intermittently subsisted on the area's natural resources.[3] Even though the highlands can be divided into two distinct ecological regions, they do share some unifying characteristics. First, this is an environmental transition zone where the arid north meets the tropical south and the Pacific littoral nudges the desert plains. Second, higher elevations tend to dominate this region, usually from 1,600 to 2,100 meters (5,249 to 6,890 feet), even though isolated mountain ranges reach 2,700 meters (8,858 feet) above sea level. Together, these characteristics coalesce to create a semi-humid and semi-arid prairie and mountainous landscape.[4]

When European settlers expropriated these lands in the mid-sixteenth century, they transformed the landscape for agricultural use, ranching and husbandry, despite limited arable land and water sources. Initially reliant on Native labor for agricultural production, European settlers soon imported African, and to a lesser extent Asian, peoples to fulfill increased labor demands.[5] While most historical literature tends to focus on the African presence along the Atlantic Gulf area or the various mining districts throughout New Spain, African peoples could be found in significant numbers along the Pacific coastal region and in Nueva Galicia specifically. By the middle of the seventeenth century, Nueva Galicia was home to at least 5,180 African persons and 13,778 Afro-mestizos and Afro-Spaniards.[6]

While eighteenth-century demographic data are harder to come by for the Los Altos region, we know that fluctuations in population occurred due to environmental and social factors. Part of the reason for this is due to Los Altos's critical role in facilitating the urban growth of Guadalajara. By the end of the eighteenth century, Guadalajara's urban core numbered 28,000 persons, making it the fourth largest city in New Spain. The city's urban center plus its immediate surrounding areas amassed a population of more than 64,000 persons. In the second half of the eighteenth century, its populace and geographic boundaries grew in large part due to its agriculturally productive hinterlands, which sustained the city's denizens with maize, wheat, and livestock. But a decade of drought, early frost, crop failure, rising food prices, and famine in the mid-1780s forced destitute families of the highlands into the city of Guadalajara, a phenomenon that also contributed to outmigration from Los Altos's communities and high death rates.[7]

In terms of late eighteenth-century population counts for Cuquío, where María Faustina was born and baptized, the best estimates that scholars have for its population are derived from compilations of various census records. The subdelegation of Cuquío, which included the town itself and the constellation of villages around it, numbered 17,241 persons.[8] More detailed demographic data, such as the exact number of indigenous, Spanish, and Afro-descendant persons are more difficult to ascertain. A review of the community's 1770 *padrón* (census) is partially helpful, though the number of individuals listed in this registry is likely an undercount. The *padrón* lists 317 Cuquío residents by name and their racial-ethnic classification. Of these, 150 of these residents were labeled as *mulatos*, meaning that of all the Cuquío residents whose names appear on the census about 47 percent of them were of African descent. As for the number of enslaved persons, 40 individuals were unfree and almost all of them—excepting one person—were also labeled as *mulatos*. About 13 percent of Cuquío's residents listed in the 1770 *padrón* were enslaved.[9]

It took more than thirty years for the next census of Cuquío to be conducted. By the time of the 1800–1801 *padrón*, population levels had stabilized after the crisis of the 1780s. Of the approximately 500 individuals—which constituted only half of all residents of the town—listed by name in the later *padrón*, 36 individuals were unfree. Of these, 15 were specifically labeled as enslaved *mulatos*. The remaining 21 persons were labeled as enslaved but did not have racial-ethnic classifications ascribed to them. Furthermore, the total number of *mulatos* declined from 150 in 1770 to 30 by 1800, though this likely represents a gross undercount.[10] Nevertheless, the number of Cuquío's residents described as *mulatos* and/or enslaved declined considerably over three decades.

Assessing the demographic shifts that occurred during the intervening years requires examination of different types of documents other than the *padrón*. One way to better understand the demographics of María Faustina's community during the 1780s is to examine the sacramental records of Cuquío. During the eighteenth century, priests routinely noted the racial and/or ethnic categories of those receiving the sacraments. These baptism, marriage, and burial records yield a rich yet problematic trove of demographic information. For instance, we know that María Faustina was part of a larger cohort of *mulatos* born in 1781. Of the total 446 baptisms that were recorded in 1781, 62 free and unfree *mulatos* received the sacrament. Cumulatively, they represent nearly 14 percent of all baptisms performed in that year. With respect to sex ratio, there were slightly more females (34) than males (29). And the majority of these *mulato* children were free. Aside from enslaved persons, there were three orphans (*expuestos*) who did not have a racial or ethnic category ascribed to them, even though other foundlings baptized that same year were identified by their race or ethnicity. There was one child whose race or ethnicity was simply missing. Overall, only 12 of the 446 individuals did not have a racial or ethnic category ascribed to them. The assignation of race mattered to these recorders, even if clerical officials applied those racial categories arbitrarily, as we shall see.

Complicating the demographic picture somewhat is the designation of *esclavo*, or enslaved. Of the total number of baptisms performed in 1781, officiants recorded a total of ten enslaved individuals. Yet only two—one male and one female—were specifically designated as *mulatos esclavos*. The other eight had no racial or ethnic category ascribed to them. This was not wholly unusual. A review of the earliest sacramental records for the main parish church of San Felipe in Cuquío show that on the first page of its baptism register in 1666, the fourth entry describes an enslaved woman named Tereca from the village of Tacotlán (also known as Tlacotán). Other than the names of her enslaver and godmother, we have no additional details about Tereca, such as her age, her mother's name, or her racial-ethnic category.[11] This demonstrates two factors. First, the institution of slavery in Cuquío has a much longer history, stretching back to the last third of the seventeenth century. Second, the practice of omitting the racial or ethnic designation, particularly for enslaved persons, dates back to the same period, though there are more examples that contradict this pattern. Perhaps officiants assumed that *esclavo* was a surrogate term for an enslaved person of African heritage. From the time of the sixteenth century, colonial elites—including those who officiated the sacraments—strongly associated slave status with persons of African descent.[12] This was also the case in Cuquío where the African presence in the area can be traced to individuals labeled as *mulatos esclavos*, who received baptism in the church's earliest years of operation in the 1660s.[13] Also, the enslavement of indigenous persons was technically illegal, at least on paper, so references to *esclavos* likely denoted peoples of African descent. On the other hand, it is also possible that *esclavo* was a catch-all classification for all nonwhite, unfree individuals, who, after generations of mixed racial unions, likely included indigenous persons.

The same ambiguity applies to the term *mulato*. When officiant José Antonio González described María Faustina as a *mulata*, what exactly did that term connote? The *sistema de castas* partly answers this question. Nearly all eighteenth-century caste classifications defined *mulatos* as the products of Spaniards and persons of African descent. It is tempting to assume that the 14 percent of all *mulatos* baptized in 1781 in Cuquío were children of Spaniards and African-descended peoples. Yet in its contemporary usage *mulato* connoted a vaguer and multivalent classification, a term capacious enough to include individuals of mixed Native and African ancestry. Etymologically speaking, the terms *mestizo* and *mulato* both refer to peoples of mixed ancestry. *Mestizo* derives from the Latin word *mixticius*, used to describe the offspring of couples from different lands or countries. The word *mulatto* derives from the Latin *mulus*, which refers to any descendant of two different species. In New Spain, *mulato* and *mestizo* became synonymous and conflated as early as the sixteenth century, used to label those who remained outside the supposedly separate republics of Spaniards and Native peoples.[14] Clearly, this conflation persisted into the late eighteenth century and not only in Cuquío's parish registers. In the distant province of New Mexico, for example, parish priests routinely used the term *mulato* to describe baptized individuals after 1744, even though no such evidence existed that these persons had any African ancestry.[15] In short, the term *mulato* could refer either to a person of mixed Native and Spanish heritage or a person of mixed African and Spanish descent.

It is worth noting that while the vast majority of baptized children in Cuquío had a racial or ethnic category ascribed to them, few, if any, of the parents were described by their racial or ethnic category in their children's baptism records. In other words, an officiant who described a baptized child as *mulato* usually did not indicate which parent had African ancestry. It is therefore impossible to determine from the baptism record alone if the designation of *mulato* indicated a child who was the union of Afro-Spanish or Afro-indigenous parentage. In order to determine the racial-ethnic parentage of the children, one must consult the parents' marriage or baptism records. And that is where racial-ethnic categorization begins to appear rather arbitrary.

An examination of María Faustina's genealogy reveals the arbitrariness of such categories. She was born to Francisco Trejo and Ana María (also known as Juana María) Morales. Her parents married in 1774 in the same church and community of Cuquío where their children received baptism. In their marriage record, Francisco was labeled as a mestizo while Ana [Juana] María was described as *española*.[16] María Faustina was the fourth of at least seven children born between the years 1775 through 1786. A survey of her six siblings' baptism records reveals a curious pattern: two were identified as *mestizos*, one as *español*, two as *mulatos*, and one as *morisca*.[17] In every case, the officiant who performed the baptism was different than the person who signed the baptismal record certifying its validity. Given that a different person baptized each of the seven Trejo children, it is likely that in each case the officiant guessed the children's racial status, applying his own criteria for assessing racial or ethnic status.

In May 1802, María Faustina married Juan Manuel Camacho in the church of nearby Tlacotán, situated about 30 kilometers (18.6 miles) west of the town of Cuquío but part of the same diocese. In that record, the officiant described Maria Faustina as *mestiza* and her husband as *español*.[18] As stated earlier, María Faustina was originally labeled as *mulata* when she was baptized as an infant, so the change in her racial category from *mulata* to *mestiza* represents an obvious difference in status since her baptism some twenty-one years earlier. Her husband, Juan Manuel Camacho, also underwent a change in his racial status. When he was baptized as an infant in 1777 in the same parish church at Cuquío, he was labeled as *indio*.[19] Juan Manuel's case demonstrates that the same vagueness could apply to the categories of or the difference between *indio* and *español*.

In May 1803, María Faustina and Juan Manuel had their daughter, María George, baptized in the same church of Tlacotán, where they married one year prior. The same three individuals—the scribe, lieutenant curate, and vicar—who signed the couple's marriage record also signed María George's baptism record in which the child was labeled as a *mulata libre*.[20] It is not clear how the same individuals who attested to María Faustina and Juan Manuel's indigeneity and Spanishness just one year earlier determined that their child was of African descent. To make matters more confusing, the couple's subsequent four children were labeled as *españoles*.[21] Even in their last child's baptism record in 1815, the child and parents were described as *españoles*.

After birthing her last child on August 3, 1815, María Faustina experienced complications that led to her untimely death at the age of thirty-four years, even though the priest inaccurately cited her age as twenty-four.[22] On August 18 of the same year, she was buried in the community of Ixtlahuacán del Río, which was closer to her home in Rancho de los Trejos, compared to the more distant town of Cuquío. In her burial record, the curate noted that she was *española*. Her final status as *española* extended to her first daughter, María George, who had originally been labeled as *mulata* in her baptism record. Only four years after María Faustina's death, María George married in the town of Ixtlahuacán del Río. In her marriage record, María George was described as *española*.[23]

What should we take away from these examples that underscore the complicated and confusing racial and ethnic categorization of individuals from this colonial outpost? Let's begin with that which has been implicit so far: the assignation of racial or ethnic categories by clerical representatives. As other studies of the greater region of Nueva Galicia have shown, the priest routinely ascribed a label to an individual receiving the sacrament.[24] There is no doubt that this happened at least part, if not most, of the time. If the arbitrary attribution of racial and ethnic categories demonstrates anything in Cuquío and its immediate environs, it is that church officials guessed at the categorization of persons based on phenotype. Given the relatively long presence of slavery of African peoples in and around Cuquío, it would make sense that multiethnic and multiracial households would form over time and that subsequent generations of these diverse households would ambiguously express themselves phenotypically. Yet there is some reason to believe that racial and ethnic assignation was not imposed, at least during the period of the 1780s when ecological devastation and social displacement struck the region.

As mentioned earlier, scarcity, crop failure, the soaring cost of food, and starvation plagued the 1780s. Sadly, the devastation was not localized in one province but became a widespread phenomenon that affected multiple agriculturally productive regions throughout the viceroyalty. The beginning of the crisis originated in 1784 when drought, frost, and untimely heavy rains persisted for more than a year, damaging subsistence and cash crops. Cycles of crop failures drove up the price of food and the impact of drought also increased the prevalence of disease among already hungry, nutritionally compromised rural communities. The worst years came in 1785–1786, which became known as the *año de hambre*, or the year of starvation, when a shortage of maize became endemic to nearly all of New Spain.[25] Agricultural areas, such as Los Altos, bore the brunt of the crisis. Juan Luis Argumaniz Tello's study of mortality rates in the greater Nueva Galicia region demonstrates that the number of deaths increased across almost all areas that supplied the city of Guadalajara. Cuquío, the place where María Faustina was born and raised, ranked in the top four places with the greatest number of deaths from 1784 through 1786, according to Argumaniz Tellos's study. In a three-year period, 854 people died in Cuquío alone.[26] During the *año de hambre*, the death rate more than doubled in Cuquío, from 241 to 481 deaths. For some context, the number of baptisms totaled 397 during that same period.[27] Recall that in 1781, the year of María Faustina's birth, that number was 446. Clearly, the birth rate was dropping while the death rate was climbing. Another town in Los Altos, Tepatitlán, took the lead as the community with the greatest number of deaths from 1784 to 1786, recording the loss of 1,925 people during this time.[28] The fact that settlements in Los Altos are overrepresented in these startling mortality rates demonstrates that the region was disproportionately affected by the crisis.

Given the dire levels of privation in Cuquío, it is reasonable to assume that individuals had a vested interest in retaining what they had or increasing their economic resources. One strategy that desperate families could employ to weather the crisis was migration. This is part of the reason why the city of Guadalajara grew substantially during the 1780s as individuals and families left the surrounding environs searching for food and better opportunities during the crisis. Nonetheless, the crisis did not leave the city unscathed. Despite Guadalajara's reputation for its thriving markets and commercial possibilities, the overcrowding of migrants in the city led to an increase in both disease and mortality rates. In the city, approximately one hundred persons died per day in May 1786. Between one-fifth and one-quarter of the population died during the *año de hambre*.[29] While outmigration from Los Altos could be used as a survival tactic, the cost of such a strategy for these highland fugitives was fraught with danger.

Another and arguably less dangerous strategy that could be used was changing one's racial or ethnic status in order to reduce or avoid the payment of tribute. Racial and ethnic categories such as *mulato*, *indio*, and *español* functioned as social signifiers of entitlements, indicators of who was eligible for certain privileges, obligations, and/or taxation.[30] The granting of privileges and the imposition of tribute varied widely across New Spain depending on local conditions. For example, in the eighteenth-century frontier area of San Felipe El Real de Chihuahua, *indios* wanted to be labeled as *mulatos* to avoid forced and possibly permanent relocation to estates where their labor served as payment of tribute. Conversely, in the eighteenth century, mulatos of Aguascalientes preferred to be labeled as *indios* because Native peoples paid lower taxes there compared to their racially mixed counterparts.[31] Despite these variable regional circumstances, the relationship between tribute payment and one's racial or ethnic-racial and ethnic classification was constant. Given this constancy, an individual could undermine the relationship between race and taxation by claiming membership in an exempt or privileged group to decrease or evade tribute. By doing so, the same individual could dictate some of the terms of his/her economic fortunes or those of his/her children.[32] Self-reporting one's racial or ethnic category to a priest or other official allowed the individual some input in the process of determining one's tax liability, thereby subverting an economic system that usually depended on the imposition of such categorization and allowing that individual's family to retain or increase resources, especially during times of scarcity.

In Nueva Galicia, those who paid tribute tended to be concentrated in six areas, including Cuquío. Yet even in Cuquío, tribute payers only constituted about 11 percent of the overall population.[33] For example, in 1789, Manuel de Saavedra y Alvarez, a regional subdelegate of the Royal Treasury, drew the ire and scrutiny of his superiors due to an absence of tributaries in Cuquío.[34] This occurred at the end of a very challenging decade, just a few years after the *año de hambre* devasted crops and livelihoods in the area. It would not be surprising if individuals and families from the community convinced their local pastors to alter their racial or ethnic categories in order to reduce or avoid tributary obligations. Alternatively, it is also possible that Cuquío's residents had a longer history of changing their racial or ethnic categorization to avoid tribute payment. For example, in 1762, royal officials based in Guadalajara committed themselves to improving tax collection in eight specific towns in Nueva Galicia. Cuquío was among them, along with three other towns in Los Altos.[35] More efficient tribute collection became a major goal of Bourbon-era officials, resulting in reforms that sought to maximize revenues throughout the viceroyalty. Yet it is safe to assume that collecting taxes in this particular corner of Los Altos had been a decades-long challenge for royal authorities. Frequently changing racial and ethnic categorizations undoubtedly made tribute collection more difficult.

Another important factor to consider is the relationship between racial and ethnic categorization and class status. María Faustina Trejo was part of the Trejo family that controlled its own ranch lands. As stated earlier, María Faustina lived her adult life in Rancho de los Trejos. This would imply that her racial or ethnic status whitened in proportion to her economic status or increased standing in the community. That there would be a relationship between racial categorization and economic or social mobility is not unusual. Indeed, numerous studies of eighteenth-century colonial Latin America attest to this as a fairly common phenomenon. Trejos had resided in the area since the sixteenth-century beginnings of Spanish settlement in Nueva Galicia. Even though generations and hundreds of years separated María Faustina from the earliest Spanish settlers in the region, her family and other Trejo descendants may have used their storied name to secure land, acquire social currency, or increase family honor.

If María Faustina's fluid racial classification and that of her children occurred due to enhanced social reputation or prestige, then we should ask if her experience was exceptional compared to other *mulatos* from Cuquío. If the answer is yes, then the argument that her changing racial classification had more to do with increased social status over time seems tenable. But if we investigate those in María Faustina's cohort—other individuals who were baptized at the same time and came of age in the same region—and look for patterns, we will see that the answer is not so straightforward.

As stated earlier, María Faustina was one of sixty-two free and unfree *mulatos* baptized in 1781. Unfortunately, efforts to definitively locate the whereabouts of the ten unfree individuals after 1781 have proven unsuccessful.[36] Of the fifty-two free *mulatos*, there are examples among them of individuals with siblings differently classified; persons whose children may or may not have had the same racial status; and individuals who retained their racial status in their adult years and passed on their status to their children. As an example of the first scenario, María Josefa Antonia, *mulata libre*, was born to Antonio Villareal and María Nazaria Nuñez and baptized on February 4, 1781. Two years earlier, María Josefa Antonia's sister, María Gertrudis de los Reyes, had been born to the same parents and classified as *mestiza*, despite the fact that the same officiant presided at both baptisms in same church at Cuquío.[37]

Another case for comparison is that of María Paula, baptized on June 24, 1781, the child of Anastacio Rocha and Joaquina Muñoz. In her baptism record, María Paula was described as a free *mulata*. She married on February 15, 1800, in the same church at Cuquío. In her marriage record, the recorder again noted that she was a *mulata libre* while her husband, José Simon Ramirez, was identified as an *Yndio lavorio* [sic], an indigenous estate laborer. From 1801 through 1822, the couple had at least seven children, five of whom assumed their mother's racial status of *mulato* or *mulata*. One assumed her father's condition of *Yndia lavoria* [sic]. But one conspicuous exception—Mamerto de la Trinidad—stands out for being described as *español*.[38] What differentiated his racial classification was the fact that his 1818 baptism was not performed at San Felipe Church in Cuquío where all his siblings had been baptized. Instead, his baptism occurred at the church at Ixtlahuacán del Río, the same location where María Faustina Trejo was identified as *española* and had received last rites about three years earlier.

It is possible that relocation to another community increased the odds of a child having a very different racial status than that of his parents, depending on the local officiant's criteria of racial categorization. Yet, as we have already seen, such variability existed within the same family who resided in the same parish over many years and whose members received sacraments from the same officiant. And even among those who physically relocated, there is evidence that an individual could retain her racial status from birth to marriage and pass on that same status to her children. For instance, María de San José, daughter of Christoval Gonzalez and Juana Petrona Hernandez, received baptism at San Felipe Church in Cuquío on

March 17, 1781. The recorder noted that she was a *mulata*. At some point, María de San José and her family relocated and settled in the nearby Los Altos community of Yahualica, about thirty-seven kilometers (approximately twenty-three miles) north of Cuquío. In the Yahualica church of San Miguel Arcángel, she married Antonio Rafael on June 4, 1794. In her marriage record, the recorder noted that she was a *mulata libre* while her husband was an enslaved *mulato*, who was also a transplant from another Los Altos town, Jalostotitlán. María de San José's case shows that she retained her racial status from the time she was born to the time of her marriage. As for her children, only two could definitively be located, and in each of those two records, the father was listed as unknown. One daughter was described as *mulata* while the other's racial status was omitted from her baptism record.

While such individualized cases confirm the variability of racial and/or ethnic categorization, it is also necessary to examine not only persons from María Faustina's cohort but also to take demographic snapshots of Cuquío over time to see how the overall population changed. Recall that in 1781, Cuquío's main church counted sixty-two baptized *mulatos*, free and unfree, who cumulatively represented about 14 percent of all baptisms that year. As for the other groups, Native peoples outnumbered them all, constituting about 46 percent of all baptized individuals. The next largest group was *españoles* who made up nearly 34 percent of all baptisms. There were only handful of other *castas* mentioned.

If we take another snapshot of this community in 1802, the year of María Faustina's marriage, we see that the number of *mulatos* who appeared in the baptism registers that year dropped to one unfree and forty free persons. Given that the overall number of baptisms was relatively small that year (353), *mulatos* constituted nearly 12 percent of the total. The number of *indios* and *españoles* was almost identical that year, each group constituting about 41 percent of the total. *Mestizos* made up 4 percent of all baptisms, followed by a handful of other *castas*.

Last, in 1813, which was the last year in which María Faustina's penultimate child was baptized at Cuquío, the demographic picture changed significantly. In that year, there were 558 total baptisms but the number of *mulatos* remained unchanged from eleven years earlier: they totaled 41 (free) individuals but only constituted 7 percent of the overall tally. In contrast, *españoles* comprised 45 percent of all baptisms, outnumbering all other groups. The next largest group was *indios*, who represented nearly 38 percent of baptisms. *Mestizos* accounted for a somewhat greater share of baptisms, totaling 6 percent.

Discerning patterns among such disparate evidence poses challenges. What these data do reveal is that any number of factors could determine racial or ethnic classification. Inconsistencies, whether intentional or unintentional, were rampant and potentially exploitable, especially during times of scarcity. Another conclusion that we could draw is the fact that over a thirty-two-year period, the people of Cuquío seemingly became whiter over time. The phenomenon of racially mixed communities becoming whiter over time is not exceptional. Historical demographer Carmen Paulina Torres Franco found a similar pattern in her analysis of sacramental records for the Los Altos community of Encarnación de Diaz during the same period of this study. In the case of Encarnación, Torres Franco found that persons of African descent intentionally married persons outside of their *casta* designation, resulting in mixed race families whose Africanness diminished over generations.[39]

Yet the case of Cuquío demonstrates a different path to a similar end. While the overall population became whiter as it had in the town of Encarnación according to its sacramental registers, Cuquío's histories of ecological crisis, social dislocation, avoidance of tribute payment, and inconsistent assignation of racial-ethnic classification paint a far richer and more complex picture of how African and indigenous peoples in this corner of Los Altos survived and overcame the constraints that the agents of empire placed on them.

Despite the general whitening of the people of Cuquío, the sacramental records also reveal that the persistence of the ambiguous racial-ethnic classifications continued throughout the same thirty-year period. If anything, the demographic snapshots of the community in 1802 and 1813 indicate a modest resurgence of dated *casta* terms that had been more widely used decades earlier. For example, among the nearly 450 baptisms that occurred in 1781, the year of María Faustina's baptism, the only racial-ethnic classifications specified were *indio, español, mestizo, mulato,* and *coyote.*[40] In 1802, the same categories remained in use among the 353 baptism records, but two additional categories resurfaced: *morisco* and *sambiago.*[41] By 1813, the categories of *coyote, morisco, lobo,* and *tresablo* could be found among the more typical categories of *indio, espanol, mestizo,* and *mulato* in the 558 baptisms recorded in that year.[42] *Morisco, lobo,* and *sambiago* were all predicated on degrees of Africanness. While the *mulato* population diminished by 1813, the terms that officiants used to describe Afro-descendant peoples did not. If anything, the number of categories increased.[43]

Mulatos did not disappear, nor did they relocate or succumb to disease in larger numbers than other groups. Instead, we should view these findings as proof that racially mixed individuals and families had become the norm by the end of the eighteenth and the beginning of the nineteenth centuries. As such, determining who was a *mulata* or *mestiza* likely proved to be a nearly impossible task. Individuals could potentially use the ambiguity of racial-ethnic classifications to their advantage, particularly during times of resource scarcity as seen in the dire years of the mid-1780s in Cuquío. Given the overall haphazard nature of racial and/or ethnic assignation, it may be tempting to posit that the subversion of racial-ethnic classification was more common in frontier areas. What this speculative study shows is that the social and environmental dynamics that affected this frontier community bred conditions in which such subversion could take place. Yet additional research is needed to investigate this question and to better understand the complexities of Nueva Galicia's unstudied highland communities.

Notes

1. Martínez, *Genealogical Fictions*, 167. In addition to Martínez's work, other works that address race and class specifically in New Spain include Chance and Taylor, "Estate and Class in a Colonial City: Oaxaca in 1792," 454–87; McCaa, "Calidad, Clase, and Marriage in Colonial Mexico," 477–501; Seed, "The Social Dimensions of Race," 569–606; Cope, *The Limits of Racial Domination*.

For works that specifically address the history of Afro-Mexican peoples during the colonial period, see Stern, "Gente de color quebrado:," 185–205; Vinson III, "Fading from Memory," 59–72; Carroll and Lamb, "Los mexicanos negros, el mestizaje y los fundamentos olvidados de la 'Raza Cósmica'," 403–38; and Althouse, "Contested Mestizos, Alleged Mulattos," 151–75.

2. Schwaller, "Mulata, Hija de Negro y India," 889.

3. Álvarez Macías, "Transformaciones de la identidad social en Los Altos de Jalisco (1926–1990)," 29.

4. Becerra Jiménez, *Indios, españoles, y africanos en los Altos de Jalisco: Jalostotitlán, 1650–1780;* and Jiménez Gonzalez, "Ecología de los Pastos Nativos de los Altos de Jalisco," 18–29. http://repositorio.cucba.udg.mx:8080/xmlui/bitstream/handle/123456789/1941/Jimenez_Gonzalez_Carlos_Alberto.pdf?sequence=1.

5. Although precise figures are difficult to come by, Deborah Oropeza Keresey has documented the presence of South Asian enslaved persons in Nueva Galicia and Guadalajara specifically. See Oropeza Keresey, "La esclavitud asiática en el virreinato de la Nueva España, 1565–1673," 5–57.

6. Bennett, *Colonial Blackness*, 59.

7. Van Young, *Hacienda and Market in Eighteenth-Century Mexico*, 29–37.

8. Van Young, *Hacienda and Market*, 37.

9. There are various inconsistencies in the 1770 *padrón*. For example, officials counted 75 families and a total of 246 persons in Cuquío alone. A manual count of all residents' names yields a tally of 317 individuals. It is not clear if the recorder intentionally excluded children from the tally. Furthermore, the recorder noted the presence of 75 families on page 4v, but five pages later a different recorder counted 62 families. See Archivo Histórico de la *Arquidiócesis* de Guadalajara, sección Gobierno; serie Padrones/Cuquío; ano 1770; Caja 22, exp. 1.

10. Like the 1770 *padrón*, the 1800–1801 *padrón* also contains significant inconsistencies. A manual count of all residents listed in the town Cuquío yields a tally of about 500 individuals. Yet in the final pages of the report, the recorder notes that there were 356 adults and 102 children plus 421 *indio* adults and 186 *indio* children, tallying 1,065 individuals. See Archivo Histórico de la *Arquidiócesis* de Guadalajara, sección Gobierno; serie Padrones/Cuquío; ano 1770; Caja 22, exp. 2.

11. See the fourth entry for Tereca of *Tacotlán* on October 4, 1666, on page 2v of the San Felipe Church baptism records, volume 1 of the Archivo de la Parroquia de Cuquío, Diócesis de Guadalajara, Jalisco, México.

12. Schwartz, "Colonial Identities and the Sociedad de Castas," 193.

13. Persons designated specifically as *mulatos esclavos* received baptism in the town's church of San Felipe in the late 1660s. See the following San Felipe Church baptism records, volume 1 of the Archivo de la Parroquia de Cuquío, Diócesis de Guadalajara, Jalisco, México: Juan, *mulato esclavo*, baptized on August 6, 1667, on page 6r; Gaspar, *mulato esclavo*, baptized on June 29, 1668, on page 7v; and Catarina, *mulata esclava*, baptized on December 17, 1668, on page 9r.

14. Vallet, "La Evolución del Mestizaje en la Nueva España," 59.

15. Gutiérrez, *When Jesus Came, the Corn Mothers Went Away*, 196.

16. See their July 6, 1774, marriage record on page 206r of the San Felipe Church marriage records, vol. 4 of the Archivo de la Parroquia de Cuquío, Diócesis de Guadalajara, Jalisco, México.

17. In the *sistema de castas*, a *morisco* was the product of a Spaniard and an individual of mixed African-European ancestry. Also, see the following baptism records of the San Felipe Church baptism records, volumes 10–11 of the Archivo de la Parroquia de Cuquío, Diócesis de Guadalajara, Jalisco, México: May 8, 1775, for Josef Alexandro Trexo (*mestizo*) on page 120v, vol. 10; September 25, 1776, for Josef María Trejo (*español*) on page 184r, vol. 10; January 13, 1778, for María Silveria Trejo (*mulata libre*) on page 249v, vol. 10; April 20, 1783, for Jose Teodoro Trexo (*mulato libre*) on page 144v, vol. 11; May 27, 1784, for María Pasquala Trexo (*mestiza*) on page 178r, vol. 11; and August 16, 1786, for María Siriaca Trexo (*morisca*) on page 251v, vol. 11.

18. See the couple's May 23, 1802, marriage record on page 39r of the San Felipe Church marriage records, volume 7 of the Archivo de la Parroquia de Cuquío, Diócesis de Guadalajara, Jalisco, México.

19. See his June 15, 1777, baptism record on page 222r of the San Felipe Church baptism records, volume 10 of the Archivo de la Parroquia de Cuquío, Diócesis de Guadalajara, Jalisco, México.

20. See the child's May 1, 1803, baptism record in the parish register of the Church of Santísima Virgen on page 26r of the baptism records, volume 1 of the Archivo de la Parroquia de Ixtlahuacán del Río, Diócesis de Guadalajara, Jalisco, México.

21. See the following baptism records of María Faustina Trejo's children: March 23, 1805, baptism record for Jose Pelagio Camacho (*español*) on pages 217v–218r, volume 17 of Archivo de la Parroquia de Cuquío, Diócesis de Guadalajara, Jalisco, México; July 8, 1806, baptism record for María Tranquilina (*española*) on pages 69r–69v of volume 1 of Archivo de la Parroquia de Ixtlahuacán del Río, Diócesis de Guadalajara, Jalisco, México; September 8, 1813, baptism record for María Luisa (*española*) on page 24r, volume 20 of the Archivo de la Parroquia de Cuquío, Diócesis de Guadalajara, Jalisco, México; and the August 7, 1815, baptism record for Estefania (*española*) on page 19r, volume 3 of Archivo de la Parroquia de Ixtlahuacán del Río, Diócesis de Guadalajara, Jalisco, México.

22. See her burial record in the parish register of the Church of Santísima Virgen on page 14v, volume 1 of Archivo de la Parroquia de Ixtlahuacán del Río, Diócesis de Guadalajara, Jalisco, México.

23. See María George Camacho's January 20, 1819, marriage record in the parish register of the Church of Santísima Virgen on page 66r, volume 2 of the Archivo de la Parroquia de Ixtlahuacán del Río, Diócesis de Guadalajara, Jalisco, México.

24. David Carbajal López's essay on colonial Bolaños, a remote community in northern Nueva Galicia, argues that priests assigned racial and ethnic categories to parishioners. See "Reflexiones metodológicas sobre el mestizaje en la Nueva España. Una propuesta a partir de las familias del Real de Bolaños, 1740–1822," 13–38.

25. Espinosa Cortes, "'El año del hambre' en Nueva España, 1785–1786," 161; and Florescano, *Los precios del maíz y crisis agrícolas en México, 1708–1810*, 75, 98.

26. Argumaniz Tello, "*El lapso de sobremortalidad* de 1785–1786 en Guadalajara y sus alrededores,"195.

27. The baptism totals for the years 1781 and 1785, respectively, were compiled through hand-counting the baptism records for the San Felipe Church, volume 11 of the Archivo de la Parroquia de Cuquío, Diócesis de Guadalajara, Jalisco, México.

28. Argumaniz Tello, "*El lapso de sobremortalidad* de 1785–1786 en Guadalajara," 195.

29. See Van Young, *Hacienda and Market*, 101; Hardin, *Household Mobility and Persistence in Guadalajara, Mexico, 1811–1842*, 26.

30. Schwartz, "Colonial Identities and the Sociedad de Castas," 186; and Castillo-Palma, "Calidad socio-racial, condición estamental, su variabilidad en el mestizaje novohispano," 174.

31. See Franco, "De Abuelos Maternos, Nietos Indios. La 'desaparición' de las familias mulatas en la parroquia de Encarnación, Los Altos de Jalisco, Nueva España, 1778–1822," 103.

32. Gharala's study of eighteenth-century Afromexican tributaries is the most exhaustive work on the subject of the crown's frustrated efforts to extract taxes from persons of African descent in New Spain. See *Taxing Blackness*.

33. See note 67 in chapter 2 of Ibarra, *La organización regional del mercado interno novohispano*, 55–56.

34. Archivo General de la Nación, México, Instituciones Coloniales, Indiferente Virreinal, Caja 6020, Expediente 53, Tributos Caja 6020.

35. Archivo General de la Nación, México, Instituciones Coloniales, Gobierno Virreinal, General de Parte (51), Volumen 44, Expediente 82, Fojas 78–78v.

36. While the sacramental records are quite complete for San Felipe Church in Cuquío, it should be noted that one of the burial registers is missing. The missing book covers the period from April 1763 to June 1783. It is possible that various *mulatos*—or other *castas*, for that matter—baptized in 1781 passed away between the time they were born and 1783, which would partly explain why efforts to locate them proved unsuccessful.

37. See María Gertrudis de los Reyes Villareal Nuñez's baptism record on page 301r, volume 10 and María Josefa Antonia Villareal Nuñez's baptism record on page 68v, volume 11 of San Felipe Church of the Archivo de la Parroquia de Cuquío, Diócesis de Guadalajara, Jalisco, México.

38. María Paula Rocha Muñoz's baptism record may be found on page 86r, volume 11 of San Felipe Church of the Archivo de la Parroquia de Cuquío; her marriage record is on page 128r, volume 6 of San Felipe Church of the Archivo de la Parroquia de Cuquío, Diócesis de Guadalajara, Jalisco, México.

The baptism record of Mamerto de la Trinidad can be found on page 24v, volume 4 of Santísima Virgen Church of the Archivo de la Parroquia de Ixtlahuacán del Río, Diócesis de Guadalajara, Jalisco, México.

39. The work of Carmen Paulina Torres Franco demonstrates that in the Los Altos community of Encarnación the number of *mulatos* also decreased over a twenty-year period in the beginning of the nineteenth century. Her findings indicate that those who considered themselves Spanish and, to a lesser extent, indigenous persons, actively adopted strategies, such as marrying equals or relatives, to guarantee that subsequent generations preserved Spanish or Native classification and lessened the incidence of African-descended categorizations. See Torres Franco, "De Abuelos Maternos, Nietos Indios," 93–113.

40. *Coyote* was usually reserved for individuals of mixed *mestizo* and indigenous heritage. See Earle, "The Pleasures of Taxonomy," 430.

41. Ben Vinson III examines the use of the terms *morisco* and *lobo* in New Spain as well as their connotations dating back to the sixteenth century. See Vinson, "Moriscos y lobos en la Nueva España," 159–76.

42. *Tresalbo* denoted a person who was born of a *mestizo* and someone with three-fourths indigenous heritage. See Katzew, *Casta Painting*, 213.

43. The number of individuals labeled as *sambiago* and *morisco* remained low. In 1802, there was one *sambiago* and three *moriscos*. In 1813, there were three *moriscos* and an equal number of *lobos*. For the 1802 baptism records, see pages 24–82, volume 17 of San Felipe Church of the Archivo de la Parroquia de Cuquío, Diócesis de Guadalajara, Jalisco, México. For the 1813 baptism records, see page 226v of volume 19 through page 53 of volume 20 of San Felipe Church of the Archivo de la Parroquia de Cuquío, Diócesis de Guadalajara, Jalisco, México.

CHAPTER FIVE

FROM SLAVERY TO CITIZENSHIP?

San Benito, Sanctuary Policy, and the Law on the Ground

Mark W. Lentz

". . . and these, though demanded back by our superintendent, were justly allowed the full protection of the statute which had proclaimed them free."[1]

THIS REPORT printed in the *Quarterly Review*, the more conservative, Tory-aligned of two leading journals circulating in early nineteenth century Britain, demonstrated the widespread nature of the knowledge of Guatemala's offer of refuge. Its approving tone regarding Guatemala's refusal to return escapees from bondage from a publication that usually gave voice to pro-slavery views showed that eventual abolition was a fait accompli. The same story appeared in an expanded account in a pro-abolitionist journal, *the African Observer*, edited by Enoch Lewis, a Quaker.[2] Published in Philadelphia, *the African Observer* provided a more celebratory version of events. It heralded the early decision granting freedom to fugitives from slavery and freed Guatemala's enslaved as the thirteenth article in the constitution of the new nation. It lauded the national founding document, stating that Guatemala's thirteenth article placed it "on a footing with the temples of the ancients, which served as an asylum to the fortunate."[3] The author, likely Lewis himself, wrote that the Assembly approved "the abolition of Slavery, which disgrace of civilized ages was annihilated by a decree of the 17th of April, 1824."[4]

News spread across the Atlantic Ocean quickly, bringing notice of the new Central American republic's abolition of slavery and the slave trade to an English-speaking readership.[5] Awareness of the illegality of slavery and a reiterated offer of freedom spread far more quickly across the frontier between a Spanish-speaking nation that freed its slaves and an English slave society it bordered. Belize's enslaved population, acutely aware of events transpiring across the uncharted territory that separated England's Central American foothold from the newly independent Spanish republic, saw an opportunity. "One hundred slaves, belonging to the English settlers at Belize," according to the English sources, immediately fled to Guatemala (then part of the Federal Republic of Central America) in pursuit of freedom. While the English press framed this as a new development, the fugitives from slavery joined their counterparts in a Black community on the shores of Lake Petén populated by previous escapees and their descendants, San Benito. Unsurprisingly, the English slaveholders based in Belize protested and petitioned for the return of their enslaved charges. *The African Observer* reported that, after perfunctory debate, Guatemalan authorities denied their request. In a concession to the English, they agreed to pay an indemnity to the slaveholders.

The English-language press only provided an approving and incomplete version of the events of 1825. In the perspective of the editor of *the African Observer*, the Central American assembly, with rhetorical flourishes that likely originate more in the author's imagination than from the Central American politicians, quickly sided with those who opposed the "restitution" of the escapees. This account downplayed the dissension in the ranks among Guatemalans, who appeared unanimous in their determination to abolish slavery, guarantee freedom to escaped slaves, and grant citizenship to the newly arrived.[6] English accounts omitted deep local opposition to resettlement of escaped slaves and the contentious nature of the debate over their fate that nearly led to their expulsion and forcible return to enslavement in Belize. Spanish-language records of the deliberations and the experiences of previous escapees show that Black refugees in Petén occupied a precarious place in Guatemalan society. Both English and Spanish accounts ignore the voice of the escapees.

Reading against the grain shows that escapees of 1824 and 1825 consciously sought to become legal, free residents in a land that hosted several escapees in a community of their own, San Benito, the Black Belizean community founded on the shores of Lake Petén. The Belizean refugees from slavery who crossed the blurry border between Belize and Guatemala had a clear destination in mind. Though it proved elusive and uncertain, these formerly enslaved migrants sought citizenship under Guatemalan rule, one of many options available to them. Numbering in the hundreds between 1795 and 1825, they made deliberate choices in setting their sights on San Benito. Informed by news of freedom, closed opportunities elsewhere, and the promise of subjecthood and citizenship drew them to the shores of Lake Petén.

The hundred or so Belizeans who fled to San Benito, Petén, in 1825, joined a town on the outskirts of the provincial capital of Petén founded by fugitive Belizean Blacks in 1795. Like many other enslaved inhabitants in British territory that bordered Spain's expansive holdings, the pueblo's first settlers secured their permission to stay on the Spanish side by requesting conversion to Catholicism. From 1693 until 1790, Spain's sanctuary policy granted refuge to enslaved peoples fleeing Protestant-ruled lands for Spanish territories if they sought baptism.[7] Yet the policy ended in Florida definitively in 1790. By 1800, neighboring Yucatan no longer consistently recognized the claims of Belizeans seeking freedom in pursuit of conversion, a policy revoked elsewhere throughout Latin America.[8] In contrast, hundreds of slaves from Belize continued to cross the imperial borderlands until 1825, bolstering San Benito's numbers. Their persistence in the face of an uncertain future ensured that the practice of accepting fugitives from Belize remained in effect through the early independence period, long after Spain had revoked the guarantee of refuge elsewhere. This chapter examines the pursuit of legality that characterized these former slaves and how their determination led to the persistence of a practice at a local level after its demise as an imperial policy. In doing so, they exploited the uncertainty and variability of law on the ground and entrenched practices that prevailed in border regions.

Spain's offer of sanctuary during the seventeenth and eighteenth centuries granted freedom to escapees from slavery from Protestant lands who professed a desire to become Catholic. Fugitives from slavery who took advantage of this offer of liberty came from English, Dutch, Anglo-American, and even Danish territories, mainland and island, to Spanish lands.[9] After an initial focus on flight from Georgia and the Carolinas to Florida, recent works have expanded the scope to include more regions within the Greater Caribbean and the Gulf Coast littoral, including flight from Saba, Curaçao, Essequibo, Belize, Saint Croix, Saint Eulalia to Yucatan, Honduras, Venezuela (*Tierra Firme*), Puerto Rico, Florida, and Cuba.[10] This chapter focuses on Black Belizean settlers of the town of San Benito in Petén, Guatemala, a region in which the end of sanctuary policy elsewhere did not stop the flow of new arrivals from Belize.[11] As a region with only minimal slavery and a small, sparsely populated Caribbean coast, fears of slave uprisings did not factor prominently into local administrators' considerations.[12] As a result, Guatemala provides a distinctive case study where the practice of offering sanctuary continued into the nineteenth century. The formation of a community of refugees raised questions about the citizenship of recent arrivals from the Anglophone world at independence. San Benito, the town they founded, stands out as the only community established as a result of this sanctuary policy still in existence today.

The 1790s marked the end of refuge in most Spanish colonies for enslaved people seeking sanctuary from Protestant lands (usually geopolitical rivals).[13] Guatemala continued to permit Belizean Black fugitives passage and resettlement, though with reservations and concerns.[14] Elsewhere, reciprocal agreements increasingly unfavorable to fugitives from slavery, limited the options in the second half of the eighteenth century, especially in the years leading up to the 1790s. Fears regarding slave revolts inspired by the example of Haiti no doubt played a role. In 1766 and 1783, individual governors of Spanish territories and Danish islands of St. Thomas, St. John, and St. Croix signed reciprocal return agreements.[15] In 1774, governors of Portuguese Brazil and Banda Oriental under Spanish rule agreed to return slaves and deserters.[16] Under pressure from the newly independent United States, Spanish Florida rescinded its offer of freedom to fugitives from its rising neighbor to the north.[17] By contrast, the largest population site of Belizean Blacks was founded by thirty-two escapees in 1795, and more arrivals pushed the community's numbers above one hundred in just five years.[18]

The Setting: The Atlantic World in the 1790s

The balance of power between Belize and Guatemala differed significantly. The reciprocal agreements involved undisputed overseas territories by rival powers that Spain did not challenge. Belize, then known as British Honduras, had never received recognition from Spain. In 1783, Spain conceded *only* logging rights to a section of modern-day Belize lying between the Rio Hondo to the north and the New River to the south and extended to the Belize River in further negotiations.[19] However, the agreement only allowed English settlement and logging and never represented a territorial concession. Upon achieving independence, Guatemala put the settlers on notice that it continued to view Belize as its territory.[20] Compared to colonial slaveholders elsewhere, the settlers of British Honduras had limited bargaining power. Enslaved Belizeans saw this legal opening and acted on it as hundreds of them fled to Petén.

The 1790s also witnessed an upsurge in fears regarding the spread of slave insurrections instigated by recently arrived slaves who had experienced or participated in uprisings in the Greater Caribbean. Guatemalan authorities had less to fear than the colonial authorities in slave societies elsewhere. Compared to the other regions discussed above, Guatemala—especially the interior region of Petén—had little connection to the Gulf Coast littoral or the Caribbean coastline. In part due to its landlocked status and distance from the rebellions that rocked the region, fears of slave revolts resonated less in Guatemala. Guatemala also had a much smaller enslaved population than many of the circum-Caribbean nations, just five hundred according to one contemporary estimate.[21] One of the key concerns local and regional authorities had regarding the arrival of slaves from rival colonial holdings was their propensity to inspire uprisings among the locally born and settled slave population of any given territory.[22] Guatemala was a society with slaves, and only a few of them, rather than a slave society. The Maya majority provided most coerced labor.

Instead of a sizeable enslaved population, Petén had a majority Maya population, consisting of some of the last indigenous groups conquered in Mesoamerica. The last centralized state, the Itzá kingdom based in Tayza, was only conquered nominally in 1697. While we do not know how the average Maya inhabitant felt regarding the newcomers, their leadership was diametrically opposed to any coexistence with the Black Belizeans, whose numbers grew in the 1790s. In league with the local clergy and the presidio commander, the Maya head of the community of San Andrés, don Raimundo Chatá, staunchly opposed the integration of fugitive Belizeans into the Maya pueblos surrounding Lake Petén. Within a year of the arrival of the thirty-two original Belizean fugitives, the founders of the town, Chatá petitioned for the forcible relocation of the recent arrivals to a new town on the other side of Lake Petén from San Andrés.[23] This new site, initially named San José de los Negros, was renamed San Benito, the name it retains today as a suburb of Flores, Guatemala.

Chatá's response provides an example of the reactions of Mayas living under Spanish rule, but many Mayas continued to defy the impositions of the Catholic church and the Spanish crown. Beyond the effective administration of Spanish officials, many Mayas lived independently. In uncolonized spaces, occasional evidence of sporadic cooperation between Black and Maya runaways surfaced in encounters.[24] However, when Mayas associated Black fugitives with Spaniards, they did not fare as well. In 1754, two Spanish soldiers escaped Belizean captivity with a Black Belizean prisoner. After he was injured during the crossing, the two Spaniards went to hunt food and returned to find their companion in the escape dying of arrow wounds.[25] In an earlier and more dramatic example, a "mulatto" from Campeche known as Juan Thomas escaped his confinement in the presidio of Petén in 1700 and fled to unconquered communities in Petén's interior. He sought to incite the Mayas who had not yet succumbed to Spanish rule against their colonizers, proposing that he serve as their captain. The Mayas rejected his overtures and killed him in a spectacular sacrifice.[26]

Though the fears of slave insurrections were minimal, Spanish authorities did have misgivings regarding fugitive Belizeans as potential instigators of resistance among the Maya. A small number of fugitive Belizean Blacks may have joined Maya communities beyond colonial control, but for the most part authorities had no serious fears that escapees from slavery would surmount cultural and linguistic divides to inspire rebellion on the part of the Maya. Even after 1790, Guatemala continued to accept Belizean refugees, but it did so with some ambivalence. The refugees were provided their own town, subject to close surveillance in civil and criminal matters and receiving much less attention spiritually than their indigenous neighbors.

Sanctuary and its Origins

Spain's century-long policy of sanctuary created the conditions necessary for the establishment of San Benito. This royally sanctioned offer of asylum to escapees enslaved in Protestant territories justified by a professed desire to convert nominally remained in force in Spanish colonies from 1687 until 1790. Yet it was only gradually implemented, unevenly enforced, and inconsistent in chronology. San Benito, Guatemala, continued to offer refuge even after 1790.

Sanctuary policy arrived late in Guatemala and persisted there longer than elsewhere. The florescence of scholarship on sanctuary policy and its implementation has taken the historical understanding of the process from a rough sketch to granular detail. Jane Landers's examination of eight escapees from slavery from the Anglo-American colony of South Carolina to Spanish Florida in 1687 was often seen as the starting point of sanctuary policy.[27] This incident did serve as a precedent for Charles IV's *real cédula* passed in 1693 extending the policy to all slaves in Protestant territories who sought freedom and baptism in Spanish territories.[28] Linda Rupert's recent research found an earlier date for locally observed sanctuary policy, applicable to escapees from slavery in 1680 bound for Trinidad. The royal decree marking a refusal to return escapees from slavery to their slaveholders ordered "that all blacks who came directly seeking baptism from whichever of the foreign nations that occupy the lands of the King, be declared free."[29] A professed desire to convert served as the rationale for offering freedom to formerly enslaved fugitives. Pushing the timeline for the practice of sanctuary back even further, a recent dissertation by Fernanda Bretones Lane uncovered an earlier escape from slavery in nominal pursuit of baptism, in 1664.[30] Fugitives from slavery in Belize, only settled in the early eighteenth century, attempted to gain freedom in Petén at least as early as 1727. This first cohort of six slaves met with failure. Authorities in Petén re-enslaved the escapees.[31]

Later, Petén's authorities were more receptive to the pleas of fugitives to receive freedom and baptism. In 1757, twenty-six Black and two Indian slaves arrived in Petén.[32] After they expressed a desire to convert to Catholicism, Petén's governor, don Francisco Joseph García de Monzabal, acquiesced, allowing them to remain and freeing them from slavery.[33] Indigenous slavery, banned throughout Spanish colonies, meant that the two indigenous slaves were guaranteed their freedom. The concession of freedom and the right to remain in Guatemala for the enslaved Black escapees marked a more significant legal precedent. Guatemalan authorities in Petén extended the royally mandated offer of sanctuary regularly from 1757 onward, though with occasional lapses in its consistency.

Despite the success of this 1757 cohort of escapees in receiving freedom and protection from being returned, enslaved Belizeans apparently fled in greater numbers to neighboring Yucatan until 1790. Geographical factors no doubt played a significant role, as escapees had less uncharted jungle terrain to cross before reaching Bacalar compared with the presidio of El Petén. Between 1750 and 1771, when a *real cédula* reaffirmed the order that "the king cannot deny the hospitality and protection to a foreigner of any condition who, professing another religion, seeks asylum from his place of origin with the desire to embrace the Catholic religion," this offer of asylum opened the way for fugitives from slavery to enter any nearby territory.[34] Yucatan was the closest. Repeatedly cited to deny the claims of English slaveholders, the law applied to slaves, permitting exceptions only in cases of lèse-majesté or other grave crimes. The law also meant that no English slaveholder would receive indemnification of any kind.

Different colonial administrators took distinct and inconsistent approaches to upholding sanctuary policy in practice. As research by Octavio García and Matthew Restall shows, not all fugitives from slavery in Belize were granted their freedom. Authorities often re-enslaved or resold slaves to Guatemalan, Honduran, or Yucatecan slaveholders, while others faced a return to English masters. Others became slaves of the king and were sent to work on royal projects such as the mines in Peru or fortifications in Cuba.[35] Sanctuary policy was not interpreted broadly, either. If enslaved people did not express a desire to convert or if Spaniards captured them during an invasion rather than arriving in Spanish territory as a result of their own efforts, a return to slavery was likely. In the aftermath of invasions aimed at expelling the English, slaves captured from the English were resold into slavery in Yucatan. Often their numbers were quite large; up to two hundred Black captives from Belize were sold into slavery under the Spanish in 1733.[36] Corsairs operating with royal approval regularly captured enslaved Belizeans and sold them into slavery in Yucatan with official sanction during the 1750s and 1760s.[37] A joint expedition by forces from Petén and Yucatan with naval support from Cuba led to the capture of twenty-three enslaved Black Belizeans who were treated as spoils of war. One died of a bullet wound.[38] Black Belizeans captured in war could be resold, but those seeking conversion were offered sanctuary. During the 1750s and 1760s in Yucatan and Petén, fugitives who proclaimed a desire to convert were indeed allowed to remain as free subjects. Yucatecan officials cited a cedula of 1750 that reaffirmed the application of the offer of religiously justified sanctuary in their denial of restitution to Belizean petitioners.[39]

Yucatan appears to have been the preferred destination for escapees from slavery in Belize from the mid-eighteenth century until the final decade of the eighteenth century.[40] By the 1790s, more fugitives made the arduous journey to Petén instead. Though royal reaffirmations of sanctuary policy that extended its scope to all of Spain's holdings nominally were to be applied consistently throughout the Americas, Guatemala's situation disposed it to be more generous. First, the source of escapees, Belize, was never recognized as English territory by Guatemalans during the eighteenth and nineteenth centuries. Unlike Jamaica or South Carolina, for example, Spain conceded logging rights but never officially acknowledged the de facto colonial state of Belize. Guatemalan and Yucatecan authorities vehemently opposed English administration and territorial claims unless compelled to do so by treaties.[41] In his correspondence regarding the 1757 decision to grant freedom and permission to remain in the presidio of Petén to the twenty-six enslaved Blacks and two Indians, don Francisco José García de Monzalba referred to the slaveholders as English and asserted that the territory was "of the jurisdiction of Yucatan."[42] Repeated attempts to dislodge the English met only with short term success and eventually failed. Within a year or two of an expedition to remove the English, newcomers from Jamaica took their place. However, authorities in Yucatan and Guatemala did manage to undermine the loggers' (Baymen) precarious economic standing by welcoming their forced laborers with open arms. The English, for their part, accused the Spanish of encouraging the escapees from slavery, a well-founded suspicion.[43]

After 1790, Petén became the most sought-after destination for fugitives from enslavement in Belize. Yucatan's authorities no longer offered asylum to all comers. Petén continued to allow former slaves to arrive in significant numbers. Yucatan's reluctance may have also resulted from pressure on Bacalar and its vulnerability to threats from neighboring Belize, whose population and arms continued to expand.[44] Both Petén and Yucatan sporadically attacked Belize, but incursions were launched from Yucatan more regularly. In one of the most thorough punitive expeditions in 1754, forces from Yucatan and Petén, with naval support from Cuba, launched a major effort to oust the English. Melchor de Mencos, whose name was given to the easternmost town in Petén on the border with Belize, led the Guatemalan contingent. Leaders of the attack believed they had effectively expelled the English permanently from the territory, burning the camps, food stores, and even the logwood, and scouring the land for any survivors. Two years later, however, an intelligence report alarmingly observed that 350 English and a great number of slaves had resettled there, this time with heavy artillery to defend their position.[45] English and Miskito allies raided Yucatan, but apparently never attacked the presidio of Petén itself.

It seems, in fact, that the British were only vaguely aware of the location of the presidio of Petén due to the impenetrable forest between the Belizean shore and the lake town. They suspected, however, that their former slaves knew it well. As Edward Bode, the superintendent of Belize in the 1820s wrote: "Indeed the distance is supposed to be short, and it is believed to be well known to many of the Negroes." He proposed that a road be built to connect the two: "It appears to me necessary that a road should be opened to this Town and a Tacit communication made to its Governor for the restitution of runaway Slaves who are harboured there."[46] (To this day, that road has yet to be completed; though roads reach the boundary from each country, crossing the border must be done on foot.)

The turmoil of independence struggles, English encroachment on Spanish boundaries elsewhere, and alternating alliances of convenience between Spain and England against a common foe, revolutionary France, led many local authorities to enact reciprocal agreements regarding the return of fugitives from slavery in the 1790s and early nineteenth century. Petén remained, in the words of the Superintendent Bode, "the refuge of the deserters."[47] The contrast between Petén and other territories became more consistent. In 1800, the year in which San Benito was founded as a site specifically for Belizean fugitives, now numbering more than one hundred, Yucatecan authorities re-enslaved six escapees from Belize to Yucatan.[48] At a time when the threat of revolutionary France inspired unprecedented cooperation between the longtime rivals Spain and England, the governor of Belize, Thomas Barrow, complied, noting the precedent set by Yucatan. He noted that "all those [slaves] claimed by us last year from the Province of Yucatan were delivered up."[49] He noted that the local administrators enjoyed significant latitude in enforcing or ignoring mandates, but agreements in 1794 and 1802 stipulated the mutual return of deserters from the military as well as slaves. Notice of these changes no doubt reached Belize's enslaved population. Verbal news networks spread useful information.[50] The preference for Petén as a destination undoubtedly stemmed from an awareness that other destinations were less likely to accept them. In Petén, however, escapees from slavery continued to profess a desire to convert upon arrival as late as 1825.[51] Even then, though most were allowed to remain, eleven fugitives were returned, a detail omitted from the reports celebrating Guatemala's offer of refuge to the rest.[52]

Belizeans' Best Option: San Benito

Fleeing slavery posed risks for an enslaved person anywhere in the Americas, but the dangers faced by enslaved Belizeans were lower and they had more options. Enslaved Belizeans likely had far more opportunities for flight than slaves elsewhere; Yucatan to the north, Petén to the east, and Honduras to the south all provided potential sites of freedom.[53] Petén was only one of many options. Growing numbers of refugees from slavery saw Petén as the preferred location after 1790.

Yucatan increasingly returned fugitives from Belize to their slaveholders and Honduras likewise became a destination with diminishing prospects for freedom. Both Yucatan and Honduras carried out more regular, though fraught, communications with British settlers. The proximity of Omoa to southern Belize and Bacalar's adjacency to Belize's northern border facilitated lines of communication while the seeming impenetrability of the forest between Belize's coastal and riverine settlements and Lake Petén Itzá deterred all but the most intrepid travelers. Honduras also had a larger enslaved population and on occasion sought the return of slaves who fled to British territory.[54] For example, don Antonio Gónzalez Hernández, commander of the fort of Omoa, requested the capture and return of three deserters and three slaves in 1803. Petén, on the other hand, had no significant slave population and thus no concern with turning slaves over in a reciprocal agreement. Authorities in Petén, using their own discretion, ignored such agreements. Petén alone remained a reliable safe haven.

Though it is difficult to determine the exact date for the foundations of maroon communities, marronage presented another option for enslaved Belizeans. As the eighteenth century progressed, accounts of fugitives in Belize's interior reached Spanish authorities. In 1768, after a brief skirmish between English settlers and Spanish corsairs, the English reported that they had captured Spanish interlopers to prevent them from reporting that three hundred armed Englishmen had gone into the interior (la montaña) to capture twenty-one escapees from slavery.[55] At some point, the numbers of maroons reached levels sufficient to sustain permanent communities. According to O. Nigel Bolland's research, reports from 1816 discuss slave towns and maroon communities near the Sibun River and the Blue Mountains.[56] Flight to maroon communities offered a less secure but geographically closer destination. Sporadic punitive expeditions against the maroons meant that their situation was more precarious than those who made the longer journey to Petén.[57]

Small uprisings also punctuate the accounts by the Belizean authorities. Minutes from the 1820 Meeting of Magistrates in Belize note that the "runaway negroes in the River Belize were becoming very numerous and turbulent."[58] More specific reports describe escapees from slavery threatening their slaveholders with guns and knives as well as attacking their cattle and pillaging settlements. On April 22, 1820, Alexander Anderson, a slaveholder, reported that two runaways, identified as Jem and William, threatened him on separate occasions, one with a gun and the other with a knife.[59] Three days later, William Markel and George Hyde reported that other runaways fired guns at them and skinned a bull in a cattle pen.[60] During the same month, Edward Meighan reported that a band of forty escapees—"all armed with guns"—broke into his provisions store and gratuitously shot his cattle, far more than they could possibly eat. Believing that they intended to ambush and shoot him, Meighan fled from his camp along the river.[61] Though no widespread slave uprising was ever threatened, small-scale rebellion was another form of resistance recorded in the English accounts of the slave society of Belize.

Scholars, as well, have long studied flight and marronage, forms of slave resistance practiced by enslaved Black Belizeans. Enslaved Belizeans, operating with relative autonomy and only limited supervision due to the nature of their work as loggers, also occasionally took part in a less common strategy, somewhat akin to *petit marronage*, but with a twist. Rather than fleeing slavery altogether, some hired themselves out to other slaveholders or as freemen across the border. Joseph Raboteau, a white resident of Belize who worked occasionally in Omoa, faced accusations that he had lured away "negro-men slaves named Simon, Robert, Fortune and Sampson" in 1825.[62] Surprisingly, Raboteau faced a more serious investigation than the enslaved escapees. In the end, however, his argument prevailed: "I am accused of having employed runaway slaves. This cannot be. This I most solemnly deny. Those men I am accused of employing by the laws of Guatemala ceased to be slaves from the moment they put their feet on their territory." He was declared not guilty by a jury of his peers.[63]

Despite the array of alternative approaches to resisting slavery, many fugitives sought to make their way to Petén for the three advantages it offered. First, during the final decades of colonial rule and the early years of Guatemala's independence, Petén's officials were the likeliest to grant freedom. Second, unlike other areas, Petén was the site of a town composed largely of Belizean runaways, which gave its inhabitants a small amount of self-government as well as proximity to others from similar backgrounds. San Benito offered permanence and freedom among fellow fugitives. Finally, it was close.

As Raboteau's defense demonstrates, setting foot in Guatemala made one free by some interpretations. Fleeing slavery, of course, was illegal in the slaveholding territory that the escapees sought to leave behind. But Petén's consistent offer of refuge, its provision of a minimally self-governed, autonomous town, and its tenuous concession of citizenship meant that it was the most legal option. The de facto continuation of the sanctuary policy received national approval codified in more forceful language in 1824 as the new nation abolished slavery and slave trading. Raboteau cited the exact law in his defense: "Section 2nd, Article 13. Every man is free in this Republic, he who is under the Protection of its laws cannot be a slave, nor can he who deals in slaves be a Citizen."[64] Slaves knew this when they chose to flee to Petén.

Despite couching the language of sanctuary policy in high-minded terms, practical aims almost certainly informed Guatemala's openness to formerly enslaved Belizeans. Guatemalan authorities, threatened by the encroaching settlement of Belize, knew that Belize—unique among the future Central American nations—was a slave society, not a society with slaves. Striking a blow at slavery severely weakened economic activity. Belize was an unwelcome neighbor. The Central American Federation claimed Belize as its territory. Undermining an economy based on slave labor no doubt would weaken the position of the English settlers. In 1825, George Westby, the Keeper of Records, noted in the minutes of the Meeting of the Magistrates that "it was now perfectly clear that this Law had evidently been made with a view of affecting this Settlement."[65]

"Welcomed and Protected"?

To the English, it seemed that the runaways were "enticed, welcomed and protected" by the Guatemalans. In their view, outside interference could entice the enslaved Belizeans to desert. According to an 1803 report by Superintendent of British Honduras Colonel Thomas Barrow, "There is not any part of the World where Negroes are better fed."[66] Thus, without Spanish efforts to lure away enslaved Belizeans, those enslaved runaways would have been perfectly content according to this line of reasoning. Despite this purported excellent treatment, escapees from slavery steadfastly resisted their forcible return. Reports stated that they were armed and mustered as troops.[67] In reality, the reception the runaways received was not so warm. Despite extending the offer of sanctuary long after its cessation elsewhere, Maya and ladino *petenero* officials, both military and ecclesiastical authorities, did not accept and embrace the Belizeans fully. At the behest of both Maya and ladino officials, the new arrivals were forcibly resettled at a distance from both the presidio and the Maya pueblos surrounding the lake.[68] Segregation ruled in the town, originally identified as San José de los Negros and later renamed after its patron saint, San Benito. Compared to a site of resettled Black Auxiliaries from Saint Domingue in Yucatan, San Fernando Aké, much less intermarriage took place. Both were sites of resettled former slaves from foreign rivals' territory, but integration with the Maya population took place much more rapidly in San Fernando Aké. By 1840 Mayas constituted 40 percent of the population in San Fernando Aké. By contrast Father

Domingo Fajardo, the vicar of Petén, noted in 1800 that San Benito's population consisted of "only blacks and their children."[69] In fact, the caciques of San Andrés and San José stridently objected to intermarriage with a vehemence not equaled in many instances where indigenous inhabitants encountered Black newcomers.[70]

Attention from ecclesiastical authorities was limited, while civil authorities closely monitored the new town. Compared to their concern over the state of the Maya pueblos and the "*caribes*," Mayas who continued to evade colonial impositions, the ecclesiastical hierarchy had less interest in ministering to the "nuevo pueblo de los negros," despite the fact that they had ostensibly crossed into Spanish territory to be converted.[71] Authorities cast doubt on the desire for baptism on the part of the new arrivals from Belize, asserting that they came more in pursuit of "liberty than in search of the true religion."[72] San Benito remained without a resident priest at least for the first five years of its existence.[73]

Civil authorities dedicated much more attention to surveillance and law enforcement of the townsfolk of San Benito, who remained at a remove from the ladino and Maya social networks. In 1803, two of San Benito's residents were charged with *lenocinio*, or procuring prostitutes. The opening description described the two suspects, Juan Pablo Berges and José María Guerra, as "Negros de Walix," or Blacks from Belize, rather than as townspeople of their Petén community.[74] In a rare intersection of interests, Maya leaders along with Spanish civil and ecclesiastical authorities coincided in creating an image of "libertinage" on the part of the recent arrivals as a justification for their enforced segregation.[75] The indigenous leadership of the pueblos of San Andrés and San José argued for their removal due to their harmful influence, specifically their "vices and disorders."[76]

Even descriptions of the new settlement's location vis-à-vis the presidio and nearby pueblos hint at the vigilance and mistrust on the part of the authorities. After the forcible relocation of the original thirty-two inhabitants of the town, the commander of the Guatemalan presidio of Petén, José de Gálvez, described the town as a "rifle shot" away from the presidio.[77] In another communique, the top priest, Fajardo, described the new town as "under the cannon" of the fortress.[78] And, contrary to the belief on the part of the English that "the deserters were enrolled as Troops" when large numbers fled to Petén in 1824 and 1825, the new arrivals were not even permitted to keep the firearms they arrived with.[79]

Conclusion

Escapees from slavery made calculated decisions regarding the risks of their flight. Unlike enslaved peoples elsewhere, Belize's enslaved population had many potential ways to resist slavery. Belize had an uncharted interior that permitted the foundation of maroon communities, completely independent but threatened by armed bands sent out to re-enslave them. Outright rebellion was another option. For runaways,

Yucatan to the north, Petén to the east, and Omoa, Honduras, to the south offered the possibility (but not the guarantee) of freedom. In a distinct form of *petit marronage* some slaves sought not to abandon the settlement but to find work under new overseers.

Fleeing to Petén offered the highest likelihood of legal freedom. Once they crossed the poorly demarcated and undefended border between British Honduras and Guatemala, fugitives from slavery entered a legal gray zone. Guatemala, part of the Federal Republic of Central America, was among the first nations to abolish slavery, in 1824. It guaranteed the right of any enslaved person who entered its territory to immediately attain free status, a measure directed at undermining the neighboring settlement of British Honduras, a territory whose existence antagonized the Spanish-speaking republics. Refugees from slavery exploited the rivalry, since crossing the border meant leaving slavery behind. Leaving slavery did not always entail immediate acceptance as citizens of Guatemala. However, no matter how marginalized they were, most Belizean fugitives had a legal right to remain, free from fear of a return to Belize and slavery.

Notes

1. "Art. IX–1. Correspondence with the British Commissioners relating to the Slave-Trade. 1825, 1826," 585.

2. Barnwell, "Anti-Slavery Press," 89.

3. "Report of Proceedings Relative to the Slave Trade in Guatimala," 30.

4. "Report of Proceedings," 30.

5. Other chapters by Christina Villareal, Cameron Jones, and Alex Borucki in this volume also address the transimperial nature of opportunities for flight from slavery.

6. In fact, Guatemalan authorities did return eleven escapees. Belize Archives & Record Service (BARS), "Dispatches and letters Outwards," Records 4C (3rd of 4) (1823–1825), Government House Belize, June 6, 1825, No. 39, f. 5.

7. Other chapters in this volume that add geographical depth to the scholarship on sanctuary include Christina Villareal's essay on the Spanish Gulf Coast borderlands, Alex Borucki's discussion of the Rio de la Plata as a zone for fugitivity, and Cameron Jones's chapter on Spanish California's free-Black settlements.

8. The National Archives (TNA), Colonial Office (CO) 123/15, "Letter from the Governor of Walis to the President of Guatemala," March 26, 1803, f. 57v.

9. See TePaske, "The Fugitive Slave," 1–12; Landers, "Spanish Sanctuary," 296–313; Landers, "Gracia Real de Santa Teresa de Mose," 9–30; Landers, *Black Society in Spanish Florida*, for a fuller treatment of Black settlers in Spanish Florida.

10. Recent works on slave flight enabled by sanctuary policy include Hall, "Maritime

Maroons," 476–98; Rupert, "Marronage, Manumission and Maritime Trade in the Early Modern Caribbean," 361–82; Tompson, "Between Slavery and Freedom on the Atlantic Coast of Honduras," 403–16; Stark, "Rescued from Their Invisibility," 551–86; Restall, "Crossing to Safety? Frontier Flight in Eighteenth-Century Belize and Yucatan," 381–419; and Lane, "Spain, the Caribbean, and the Making of Religious Sanctuary."

11. Rupert, "Marronage, Manumission and Maritime," 366–67.

12. "Report of Proceedings," 30. Guatemala's entire enslaved population consisted of fewer than five hundred enslaved individuals at the time of its independence, according to *the African Observer*.

13. The other town established as a direct result of the sanctuary policy was Gracia Real de Santa Teresa de Mose. It was abandoned in 1763. See Landers, "Gracia Real de Santa Teresa de Mose."

14. The Audiencia of Guatemala included Honduras, whose port of Omoa was also a destination for escapees into the 1790s. English settlers in Belize petitioned for the return of the fugitives in 1795. Unfortunately, the correspondence does not indicate exact numbers, only a "numerous party" (*en partida numerosa*). Madrid's reply, made by the Secretary don Antonio Ventura de Taranco, stands out for its restatement of the policy of sanctuary with its emphasis on conversion and baptism *after* 1790. Estado 49, No. 74, Cuad. 1, "Da cuenta scon testimonio sobre si debe ser restituidos los Negros que pasan de Walis a aquellos Reynos." 1795, ff. 1–5v. The English attempted to have slaves remitted from Omoa as early as 1765 with little success. TNA, CO, 123/1, "Copy of a Letter to Don Francisco Aybar, Commandant of ST. Fernando de Omoa," September 2, 1765.

15. Grinberg, "Illegal Enslavement," 37–38.

16. Grinberg, "Illegal Enslavement," 36, n16.

17. Landers, "Spanish Sanctuary," 311.

18. AGI, Estado 49, No. 74, Cuad. No. 2, "Testimonio del expediente sobre trasladar 32 Negros que se pasaron al Petén del Walix al Paraje Nombrado Sn. Jossef," f. 4v; and AGI, Estado 49, No. 74, Cuad. No. 3, "Testimonio del Expediente del común del Peten," (1800).

19. Chalmers, *A Collection of Treaties Between Great Britain and Other Powers*, 233–35.

20. BARS, "Meeting of Magistrates," 1825–1826; "At a Council held at the government House Belize Honduras," February 15, 1825, f.189.

21. "Report of Proceedings," 30.

22. See, for example, Rupert, "Marronage, Manumission and Maritime," 366–67.

23. AGI, Estado 49, No. 74, Cuad. No. 3, "Testimonio del Expediente del común del Peten," 1800.

24. Lentz, "Black Belizeans and Fugitive Mayas," 670–71.

25. Lentz, "Black Belizeans," 671.

26. Arias Ortiz, "El caso del mulato Juan Thomas y la Conquista de El Petén (1695–1704)," 173–98.

27. Landers, "'Giving Liberty to All,'" 125–26.

28. Ibid., 126.

29. Rupert, "'Seeking the Water of Baptism,'" 201.

30. Bretones Lane, "Spain, the Caribbean, and the Making of Religious Sanctuary."

31. García, "African Slavery and the Impact of the Haitian Revolution in Bourbon New Spain: Empire-Building in the Atlantic Age of Revolution, 1750–1808."

32. AGI, México 3099, "Expediente sobre el permiso del corte del palo de tinte," June 15, 1757, f. 954.

33. AGI, México 3099, "Expediente sobre el permiso del corte del palo de tinte," June 15, 1757, ff. 953–56.

34. AGI, México 3099, "No. 23—Copias del nuevo oficio repetido por el Capitan del Navio de Grra Yngles," 1771, f. 1396v.

35. García, "African Slavery," 217–26, recounts instances of re-enslavement in Guatemala and Restall, "Crossing to Safety?," 381–84, discusses re-enslavement of escapees who availed themselves of the sanctuary law in Yucatan.

36. AGI, México 3099, "Noticia que se han recibido sobre la ocupación de la Costa de Mosquitos," (1737), f. 800.

37. AGI, México 3050, Consejo 4, "Expediente originado de una representación . . . sobre haver apresado el corsario Dn. Juan Francisco de Sosa . . . dos negros y dos negras . . ." (1760–1762), ff. 94–188.

38. AGI, México 3099, "Expedición de orden de S.M. en la Provincia de Yucatán para la despoblación de los Yngleses intrusos. . . ." 1754, f. 635.

39. AGI, México 3099, "Expediente sobre el permiso del corte del palo de tinte," June 1, 1765, f. 1233.

40. Restall, "Crossing to Safety?," 386.

41. Guatemala's president complained of Robert Hodgson, acting governor of the English settlements of the Mosquito Coast, behaving as if the Central American coast "were incontestably the dominion of Great Britain." AGI, México 3099, "Minuta de Extracto de lo ocurrido en el expediente sobre desalojar a Yngles," 1758, f. 30.

42. AGI, México 3099, "Expediente sobre el permiso del corte del palo de tinte," June 15, 1757, f. 954.

43. AGI, México 3099, "Copia de Carta escrita por el Almirante de la cuadra Ynglesa con destino a Jamayca al Gobernador de Yucatán," April 2, 1765, f. 1291.

44. See AGI, México 3099, "No. 23—Copias del nuevo oficio repetido por el Capitan del Navio de Grra Yngles," 1771, f. 1396v.; and AGI, México 3099, "Expediente sobre el permiso del corte del palo de tinte," 1770, 1366–69.

45. AGI, México 3099, "Expediente sobre el permiso del corte del palo de tinte," 1754, ff. 507–13; AGI, México 3099, "Copia de Melchor de Navarrete en asumptos de establecimiento de Yngleses en el Rio de Valix," 1756, ff. 739–42v.

46. BARS, "Dispatches and letters Outwards," Records 4C (3rd of 4) (1823–1825), Government House Belize, "Precís," ff. 57–58.

47. Ibid., f. 63.

48. Restall, "Crossing to Safety?," 380–84; and AGCA, A1.56, Leg. 186, Exp. 3809, "Sobre la traslación de los Negros nuevamente poblados al otro lado de aquella Laguna," 1800, f. 4v.

49. TNA, CO 123/15, "Letter from the Governor of Walis to the President of Guatemala," March 26, 1803, f. 57v.

50. For example, John Christophers, representing the British settlers of the Mosquito Coast, blamed "the persuasions of some Mulattos, subjects to His Catholick Majesty," for instigating the flight. Honduras's governor harbored the fugitives, justifying his decision based on the fact that the escapees from slavery "came to seek Christianity among them." TNA, CO 123/1, "Copy of a Letter to Don Francisco Aybar, Commandant of St. Fernando de Omoa," September 2, 1765, f. 105v; and TNA, CO 123/1, "A Report containing an Account of my Transactions on His Majesty's Service in consequence of my having been ordered from Black River," f. 101v.

51. AGCA, B7.11, Leg. 135, Exp. 03149, 1825, "La comisión de puntos constitucionales en la nota del gobierno," 1v.

52. BARS, "Dispatches and letters Outwards," Records 4C (3rd of 4) (1823–1825), Government House Belize, June 6, 1825, No. 39, f. 5.

53. Flight to Honduras lacks careful study. See Restall, "Crossing to Safety?" for Belizean flight to Yucatan, and Lentz, "Black Belizeans and Fugitive Mayas," for a brief overview of Belizean flight to Petén.

54. TNA, CO 123/15, "Letter from the President of Guatemala to the Governor of Walis," February 5, 1803, f. 55. For a brief description of slave life in late eighteenth-century Omoa and Trujillo, see Tompson, "Between Slavery," 403–16.

55. AGI, México 3099, "Expediente sobre el permiso del corte del palo de tinte," (1768), ff. 1337–38.

56. Bolland, *Colonialism and Resistance in Belize*, 72–73.

57. BARS, "Meeting of Magistrates," 1820–1821, No. 107 and 111, and April 27, 1820, and No. 111 "Memorandum," May 3, 1820.

58. BARS, "Meeting of Magistrates," 1820–1821, No. 105, April 22, 1820.

59. BARS, "Meeting of Magistrates," 1820–1821, No. 106, April 24, 1820.

60. BARS, "Meeting of Magistrates," 1820–1821, No. 107, April 27, 1820.

61. BARS, "Meeting of Magistrates," 1820–1821, No. 108, April 22, 1820.

62. BARS, "Grand Court," 1825–1826, Box 3, Vol. 19, No. 41, "The King on complaints of M. W. Bowen on behalf of himself & on behalf of the Estate of Mary Hickey dec.d," March 1825, f. 251.

63. Ibid., ff. 253–63.

64. Ibid., f. 254.

65. BARS, "Meeting of Magistrates," 1825–1826, "At a Council held at the government House Belize Honduras," February 15, 1825, f.189.

66. TNA, CO 123/15, "A Sketch of the Present State of Honduras," Colonel Thomas Barrow, March 31, 1803, f. 20.

67. BARS, "Meeting of Magistrates," 1825–1826, "At a Council held at the government House Belize Honduras," February 15, 1825, f.189.

68. AGCA, A1.56, Leg. 186, Exp. 3809, "Sobre la traslación de los Negros nuevamente poblados al otro lado de aquella Laguna," 1800.

69. Ibid., f. 4v.

70. AGI, Estado 49, No. 74, Cuad. No. 2, "Testimonio del expediente sobre trasladar 32 Negros que se pasaron al Petén del Walix al Paraje Nombrado Sn. Jossef," f. 4v. The original text reads that "los Casiques y Justicias repugnan estos casamientos."

71. AHAY, Mandatos, 1809, Exp. 18, "Expediente instruido sobe la ilegalidad de los derechos cobrados en la revisión de la cuenta de cofradías del Peten," no. 10.

72. AGI, Estado 49, No. 74, Cuad. No. 2, "Testimonio del expediente sobre trasladar 32 Negros que se pasaron al Petén del Walix al Paraje Nombrado Sn. Jossef," ff. 4v–5.

73. AGCA, A1.11.7, Leg. 186, Exp. 3813, "El Padre Cura de aquel Presido sobre que de cuenta de la Real Hazienda se expense un sacerdote mas," 1800, f. 38.

74. AGCA, A1. Legajo 46918, No. 3, "Contra Juan Pablo Berges y José María Guerra Negros de Waliz por el delito de Lenosinio," 1803, ff. 1–3.

75. AGI, Estado 49, No. 74, Cuad. No. 2, "Testimonio del expediente sobre trasladar 32 Negros que se pasaron al Petén del Walix al Paraje Nombrado Sn. Jossef," f. 1.

76. AGCA, A1.1, Leg. 217, Exp. 5110, "El común de el Peten sobre que no se repartan Yndios para las labores de Mulatos. Que estos vivan fuera de la reducción," 1795, f. 1.

77. AGI, Estado 49, No. 74, Cuad. No. 2, "Testimonio del expediente sobre trasladar 32 Negros que se pasaron al Petén del Walix al Paraje Nombrado Sn. Jossef," f. 3v.

78. AGCA, A1.56, Leg. 186, Exp. 3809, "Sobre la traslación de los Negros nuevamente poblados al otro lado de aquella Laguna," 1800, f. 4v.

79. AGCA, B7.11, Leg. 135, Exp. 03149, 1825, "La comisión de puntos constitucionales en la nota del gobierno," 1v.

CHAPTER SIX

"LORDS OF THE LAND"

Maroon Challenges to Spanish Sovereignty in Panama and Hispaniola, 1520–1610

Robert C. Schwaller

DURING 1555-1556, Pedro de Ursúa led Spanish forces against Africans who had resisted slavery by running away and forming their own settlements on the Isthmus of Panama. These African *cimarrones*, as the Spanish called them, were led by a man named Bayano. Frequently called a king by Spaniards, Bayano led hundreds of Africans living in hidden communities spread across the eastern half of the isthmus. In his retelling of the campaign, Fray Pedro de Aguado, a Franciscan friar, narrated an extended speech by Ursúa as he motivated his men for battle. Ursúa denigrated Bayano and his people for their presumption to become "lords of the land."[1] In raising up Bayano to be their king, the *cimarrones* went "against all laws and rights, human or divine." For Ursúa, the Africans' presumptuousness justified a deceitful plan that involved drugging Bayano and his men during peace negotiations. While Ursúa's treachery succeeded, many of Bayano's subjects escaped the ruse and would remember Spanish duplicity for decades.

Over a half century later, Baltasar López de Castro, the *escribano de cámara* (clerk of the high court) in the Audiencia of Santo Domingo, wrote to the king proposing a plan to mitigate the dual threats to Spanish control over Hispaniola, that of contraband trade and African *cimarrones*. López de Castro opined that the Africans wished "to make themselves lords" of Spanish settlements and would have "become lords of the island" had the residents of Santo Domingo not taken up arms against them.[2] To mitigate these threats, López de Castro proposed forcibly relocating Spanish settlements on the northern and western coasts to the interior, a plan that would be enacted beginning in 1603. Although the plan radically redefined Spanish settlement on the island, it did not end the threat of *cimarrones* or foreign interlopers. These two episodes reveal the magnitude of the threat posed by African *cimarrones*, hereafter maroons, to Spanish control of these regions in the early colonial period.

While phrases like "lords of the land" served a rhetorical purpose for the Spanish authors who deployed it, the phrase was not mere hyperbole. Spanish law recognized *señores naturales* (natural lords), a category that applied to traditional elites within a society. In the Americas, this concept justified the extension of special rights and privileges to indigenous elites. In describing Africans as aspiring to be "lords of the land," these Spanish authors implied that the maroons had, or were attempting, to establish dominion over these lands, effectively conquering lands that Spain had only recently acquired through its own conquests. Ursúa's speech tacitly recognized that Bayano's dominion over people and land had established a *señorío* (seigniory) that imbued him with a right to rule. Although Ursúa attempted to dismiss the validity of such a claim, the extreme ends taken to defeat Bayano highlight the urgency felt by the Spanish to vanquish the maroon leader's dominion.

During the sixteenth century, maroons acquired, settled, and defended significant territories in the Caribbean and adjacent mainland. On Hispaniola and in the Isthmus of Panama, maroons threatened stability in two of Spain's oldest and most important American holdings. Despite being overshadowed by the mineral wealth and human capital found in Mexico and Peru, Hispaniola remained a key gateway to the Americas. It defended the Caribbean from foreign intrusion, provided a safe haven for fleets arriving from Spain and produced valuable commodities, including sugar and ginger. Panama, known as *Tierra Firme* or *Castilla de Oro*, served as the gateway to the Pacific and to the wealth of Peru. Almost all goods destined for Peru had to be transshipped across the isthmus from Nombre de Dios to Panama City. Silver and gold from the Andes made the return journey, eventually enriching the royal treasury and private coffers.

Despite the importance of both regions, the Spanish did not undertake expansive settlement in either region. In 1510, Hispaniola boasted fifteen Spanish settlements, but by the 1540s the number of Spanish towns had dwindled as many residents left the island to seek more lucrative alternatives on the mainland. By 1574, the island had ten settlements.[3] Yet none except Santo Domingo boasted more than one hundred Spanish *vecinos* (residents). The two mining communities of Santiago and la Vega had more than fifty. The remaining settlements, largely scattered along the coast, had between ten and forty *vecinos*. In the 1520s, Panama held only four Spanish settlements. By the late 1530s, the two oldest settlements, Santa María de la Antigua del Darién and Acla, had ceased to exist. Instead Spanish Panama existed entirely as the two port cities of Nombre de Dios and Panama City. Between these two ports lay two transshipment routes: an overland track that looped its way over the mountains and a mixed riverine and overland path, loosely following the course of what would later become the Panama Canal.

On Hispaniola, indigenous Taínos led by the cacique Enrique fled Spanish estates to become the first maroons in 1519. Two years later, a widespread revolt by enslaved Africans added to Enrique's numbers.[4] A peace treaty negotiated in 1533 pardoned Enrique and his indigenous subjects allowing them to resettle as an autonomous community. The agreement left out the Africans who had joined Enrique in the remote mountains of the Bahoruco. For the remainder of the century, Africans continued to flee sugar estates, ranches, mining camps, and urban homes.[5] While the Bahoruco remained the most prominent refugee, maroons inhabited almost every part of the island.

In Panama, marronage began almost immediately as enslaved Africans fled Spanish settlements. By the 1540s and 1550s, African maroons had established several settlements in the interior river valleys of the isthmus. While Ursúa's campaign scattered these maroons, their numbers continued to grow. By the 1570s, enslaved Africans represented the majority of the region's inhabitants and served in countless occupations associated with trade, subsistence, service, and construction. As on Hispaniola, those Africans who fled enslavement joined maroons occupying vast stretches of land.

Various scholars have explored marronage in both regions, although most work has been published in Spanish by scholars in Latin America and Spain. Carlos Deive's examination of slavery on Hispaniola offers an excellent overview of marronage on the island.[6] In 2018, I argued that during the sixteenth century African marronage represented a unique form of conquest that reversed earlier Spanish conquests and laid bare the tenuous Spanish control on the island.[7] In the 1970s, Armando Fortune drew increased scholarly attention to Panama's maroons.[8] More recently, Ruth Pike introduced the most comprehensive English study of the Spanish-maroon conflict.[9] In 2009, Jean Pierre Tardieu published the first monograph to tackle the social and political development of Panama's maroons.[10] Significantly, no scholar has directly compared the patterns of Spanish-maroon conflict on Hispaniola to that in Panama.[11] However, in 2007, Ida Altman astutely noted that the peace offered to Enrique prefigured later negotiations undertaken with maroons.[12]

This chapter builds upon Altman's observation in order to better understand why Spanish authorities in Panama chose to entreat with maroons while those on Hispaniola did not. This comparison first highlights similarities in maroon tactics and practices before turning to an analysis of Spanish efforts to subdue maroons. Although Spaniards pursued similar strategies, the Spanish choice to negotiate an end to maroon conflict in Panama reflected a pragmatic solution that offered greater security to a vital economic corridor. In contrast, the geopolitical, economic, and racial dynamics of Hispaniola led its leaders to follow a divergent, arguably more radical path. Ultimately, both solutions exacerbated the underlying problem that Spaniards claimed sovereignty over lands they could not effectively control.

It is important to know that this chapter highlights the unique contexts and landscapes navigated by African maroons during the sixteenth century. Unlike the fugitives that appear in the chapters by Christina Marie Villareal, Mark Lentz, and Alex Borucki, the maroons examined here could not exploit territorial interstices found between European empires, although they certainly exploited imperial rivalries when possible. Instead, like the *mulatos* of Esmeraldas discussed by Charles Beatty-Medina, the maroons of Hispaniola and Panama exploited landscapes depopulated and transformed by Spanish conquests of Native Americans. While the maroons of Hispaniola and Panama certainly inhabited a borderlands that extended beyond areas of Spanish control, in a very real sense the territories they occupied were not liminal spaces on the periphery. Maroon-Spanish conflicts were direct contestations over sovereignty.

The Maroon Threat

The growth of maroon communities on Hispaniola and in Panama proceeded steadily during the sixteenth century. Most of the Africans who fled enslavement to join these communities did so individually or in small numbers. Spanish accounts rarely mention instances of mass revolt and flight.[13] Some of these individuals may not have necessarily intended to flee permanently.[14] Yet, by chance or intent, these scattered individuals found others, joining existing communities or forming nascent ones beyond Spanish settlement and control in the *monte* (a term loosely equivalent to the English "the bush").[15] This steady stream of individuals eventually formed larger subsistence communities sometimes numbering in the hundreds, but many likely numbered a dozen to a score of individuals. Spanish accounts attest to the subsistence base of these communities.[16] Nevertheless, their remote location offered scant resources for the production of tools, weapons, and clothing familiar to their African residents. Consequently, maroons regularly raided Spanish settlements and pack trains to acquire items they could not produce themselves. Frequently these raids also allowed maroons to capture other enslaved Africans. In many cases, enslaved persons taken by maroons joined their communities, although in some cases captives fled maroons to return to the Spaniards that owned them.[17]

Spanish complaints of such raids appear with great regularity in both regions. For example, in 1536 the king responded to a complaint from Panama City that noted that the maroons "go about robbing *estancias* (rural estates) and committing other very grave insults and countless crimes."[18] In 1545, Spaniards in Hispaniola's mining towns of Santiago, Puerto Plata, and la Vega reportedly slept with lances in their hands in fear of nighttime raids. Regular raids on roadways led residents of Hispaniola to travel in groups of fifteen to twenty.[19] Testifying on behalf of the cabildo of Nombre de Dios, Pero García Marqués recounted several raids targeting muleteers and travelers venturing across the isthmus.[20] Figures 1 and 2 show the approximate extent of maroon activity in each region during the first half of the sixteenth century.

In 1569, Pedro González de Meceta offered one of the most detailed

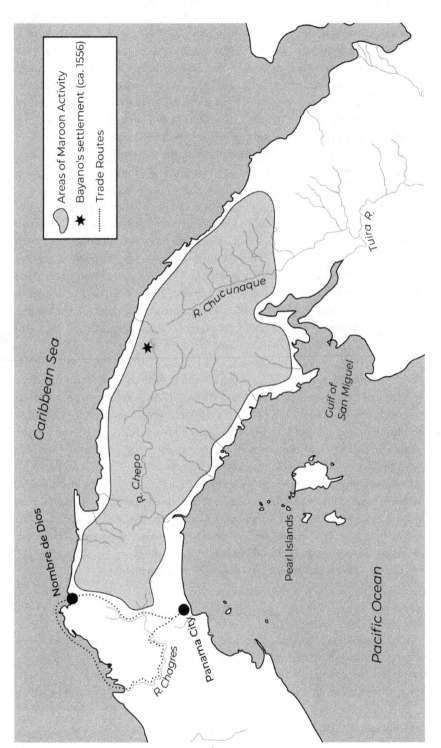

FIGURE 1. Maroon Activity in Panama, ca. 1556. Map by author.

accounts of a maroon raid.[21] González de Meceta lived outside of Nombre de Dios near the Cerro de Nicuesa, a large hill that overlooked the bay's anchorage. One night the previous September, as he and his household sat eating dinner, a "large quantity" of maroons assailed his home. They killed or wounded several dependents and carried off an enslaved woman whom he had purchased for three hundred pesos.[22] The maroons also stole "clothing, furniture, [and] weapons" before burning the home. González de Meceta and his wife escaped by fleeing into the bay and making their way to the port city. He believed that the maroons attacked his estate because it was situated along the route they used to raid Nombre de Dios. By destroying his homestead, the maroons would be able to enter the port unseen.

Although raids by maroons frequently appeared in Spanish official reports, maroons developed subtler ways to acquire items and information from Spanish cities. As early as 1542, the archdeacon of Hispaniola reported that enslaved women in Santo Domingo served as fences selling goods stolen by maroons. By 1560, authorities suspected that free-colored residents of Santo Domingo also offered aid and comfort to the island's maroons.[23] As Christina Marie Villareal has shown in chapter 2 on fugitives in the Spanish gulf coast, networks connecting fugitives to free and enslaved urban dwellers proved vital for maroon survival regardless of time and place. Such ties frequently frustrated colonial authorities.

In 1570, the cabildo of Panama City drafted new ordinances designed to police the enslaved and free African population.[24] Authorities felt that the city's free residents of color hid enslaved persons fleeing Spanish owners and covered up crimes committed by maroons and enslaved Africans. When authorities in Panama decided to propose a pardon and peace to maroons, they announced it within the cities knowing that some of the enslaved and free residents of color would pass the decree to the maroons.[25] In 1573, maroon intelligence allowed Francis Drake to attack a bullion shipment as it wound its way from Panama City to Nombre de Dios.[26] In 1579, when maroons finally chose to entreat with the Audiencia of Panama, they did so by having a *negro ladino* (Hispanicized Black) give Alonso Criado de Castilla (the senior judge) an arrow as a token of peace.[27] Although Spaniards always had an advantage in arms and supplies, clandestine networks of trade and intelligence offered maroons significant advanced warning of Spanish actions.

Spanish Responses

In both Hispaniola and Panama, Spaniards relied on a shared set of strategies for responding to maroon attacks and preventing marronage. Initially, ad hoc mobilization of private Spaniards represented the most frequent response to enslaved revolt or maroon raids. In 1521, when enslaved Africans revolted on Diego Colon's Hispaniola estate, Colon frantically rallied other Spaniards to put down the uprising.[28] In 1549, after an African man named Felipillo fled Panama's Pearl Islands with other

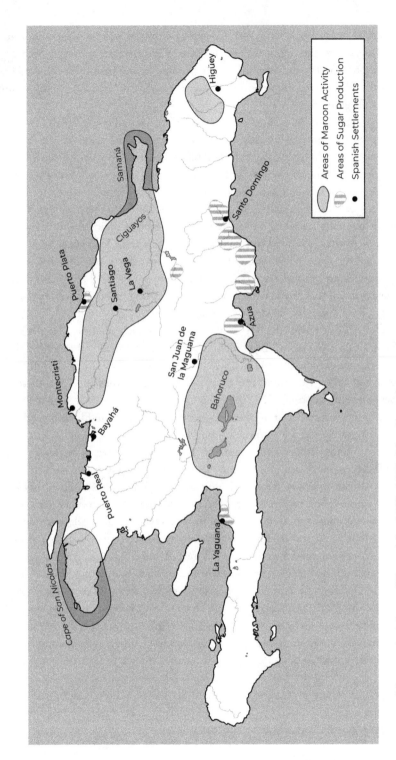

FIGURE 2. Maroon Activity on Hispaniola, 1520–1550. Map by author.

enslaved pearl divers, Francisco Carreño organized a private expedition to search and recapture the fugitives.[29] In the face of large-scale uprisings, Spanish efforts sought to stem the spread of insurrection. Smaller scale efforts like that of Francisco Carreño's occurred infrequently enough to make little headway against steady flight by enslaved persons.

Such ad-hoc efforts reflected a lack of formal mechanisms for recapturing enslaved persons and an unwillingness on the part of slave owners to undertake such ventures. In these early decades, magistrates such as *alcaldes ordinarios* (municipal magistrates) or *alcaldes mayores* and *corregidores* (rural magistrates) had authority to pursue maroons; however, few chose to do so given the immediacy of routine matters of justice. Since the salaries of such officers came from the penalties they assessed on delinquents, spending days or months in search of fugitives with no guarantee of success further mitigated their participation. Similarly, Spanish slave owners rarely felt that the time, effort, and risk of recapturing slaves warranted personal participation. Spanish slave owners frequently complained of the growing numbers of maroons, but they neither refrained from importing more enslaved persons nor did they take a direct role in stemming marronage.

The earliest efforts to overcome these obstacles came during the mid-1520s. Spanish slave owners of Panama City collectively contributed to a fund that would pay salaries to individuals tasked with pursuing and recapturing a group of maroons that had taken to raiding the city's outlying agricultural estates and roadways.[30] Several years later, in 1534, the lieutenant governor raised a similar force. These efforts represented an important ad hoc solution that could be repeated as needed but, ultimately, did not result in institutional changes.[31]

Early institutionalization of antimaroon strategies began in the 1530s. Authorities on Hispaniola attempted to limit raids and movement of indigenous and African maroons by establishing three "flying squads" that would patrol the roads around Spanish settlements.[32] A decade later during another period of intense maroon raiding, the Audiencia commissioned two flying squads as a rapid response force that could hem in maroon movements. Initially, these patrols represented an ad-hoc solution paid for out of royal funds. By the 1560s, the government had institutionalized the units levying new taxes to pay for their continuation.[33] The city of Santo Domingo also created the position of *alcaldes visitadores de negros* (slave estate inspectors).[34] These magistrates were charged with visiting estates to ensure that enslaved persons received adequate treatment and to prevent excessive cruelty. None of these measures stopped enslaved Africans from engaging in marronage, although they did appear to mitigate periods of particularly intense maroon raiding.[35]

During the sixteenth century, Panama did not see the same degree of institutionalization in responding to maroon threats, although authorities established similar types of measures. In 1534, Governor Barrionuevo established a tax on imported wine and wheat to support a fund dedicated to road maintenance and antimaroon patrols. Ten years later the crown authorized the continuation of the tax and, in 1549, expanded the tax to include a duty assessed on every enslaved African imported to the region.[36] In the 1560s, both port cities established additional taxes to maintain funds for antimaroon activities. During the 1570s, the most active period of conflict, the crown bolstered these locally raised funds with an authorization to use up to 10,000 *ducados* (ducats) from the royal treasury. Unlike on Hispaniola, Panama's authorities did not create flying patrols. Instead, the funds appear to have supported guards to protect trans-isthmus pack trains and outfitting of periodic campaigns against maroon settlements.

Entradas (military campaigns or sorties) against known or suspected maroon communities could be used to recapture or kill maroons. In the 1540s, the flying patrols of Hispaniola appear to have engaged in some campaigning against suspected maroon communities.[37] Most patrols on the island, however, only entered the bush while in pursuit of maroon raiders.[38] The exception to this pattern came in the 1590s when at least four campaigns targeted the Bahoruco.[39] The overall impact on maroon life in the Bahoruco appears to have been minimal. Within a decade of these campaigns, the drastic reconfiguration of the island's Spanish communities would place the Bahoruco well beyond the border of Spanish territorial control.

Officials in Panama adopted this approach with greater frequency than those on Hispaniola. Periodic *entradas* became a staple of Spanish Panama's anti-maroon strategy. Nevertheless, their timing, scope, and duration varied. Although it is likely that some *entradas* occurred in the 1530s and 1540s, there are few specific accounts before the 1550s. Writing in 1551, the cabildo of Nombre de Dios noted that previously, magistrates had "sent captains with men against the rebellious negros."[40] These campaigns did little to stem the growth of maroon communities, which appeared to house more than six hundred persons.

In 1553, Governor Alvaro de Sosa initiated regular patrols of the *monte* in which the maroons had established themselves.[41] Prior campaigns had gone out yearly and cost more than four thousand pesos. Sosa proposed smaller but more frequent campaigns. Over the next two years, Sosa commissioned four expeditions, two of which were led by Francisco Carreño presumably due to his success capturing Felipillo.[42]

In 1555, Peru's newly appointed viceroy, the Marques de Cañete, arrived in Panama on his way to take up his post. The viceroy took control of the matter and commissioned Pedro de Ursúa to take a large force that included both recruits and press-ganged convicts.[43] Spaniards considered Ursúa's campaign a success because his treachery resulted in Bayano's capture. Nevertheless, a close reading of Aguado's hagiographic account suggests that Spaniards had few clear victories except the slaughter they initiated after drugging Bayano and his military leaders.[44] Not surprisingly, within a few years, authorities once again began to commission campaigns. In 1562, the governor requested more tax levies in order to make "constant war" on the maroons for at least one year.[45] Escalating raids, like the one against González de Meceta, led the Audiencia to appoint Esteban de Trejo *capitán general* of a new campaign in 1569. After several months, the 140-man *entrada* returned with only a handful of captured maroons.[46]

The course of campaigning in Panama changed drastically in the 1570s. French and English corsairs began to raid ships traveling to Panama and even undertook assaults on Nombre de Dios. During late 1572, Francis Drake raided Nombre de Dios. After being rebuffed, Drake allied with maroons and spent several months recovering and planning with them. In early 1573, maroons assisted Drake in raiding a bullion shipment as it crossed the isthmus. Shortly afterward, the maroons and English allied with French corsairs to attempt a second raid just outside Nombre de Dios. The audacity of these attacks spurred Spanish officials to bolster the defenses around Nombre de Dios and undertake two campaigns, neither of which made headway against the maroons.[47]

In 1576, John Oxenham, a member of Drake's crew, led a return journey to the region. He renewed alliances with the maroons. In early 1577, a maroon-English expedition raided the Pearl Islands off the Pacific coast and captured a merchant vessel traveling to Panama from Guayaquil. These attacks spurred more forceful action by Spanish authorities and initiated a four-year period of war against the English and the maroons that aided them.

During this period, the Spanish commissioned three major expeditions. In early March 1577, the Audiencia commissioned Pedro de Ortega Valencia to quickly respond to the attacks on the Pearl Islands.[48] He led more than 250 men on a forty-day campaign. Although Ortega Valencia destroyed a maroon settlement and recaptured stolen goods, many of the Englishmen and maroons escaped.[49] Claiming victory, Ortega Valencia returned to Spain in the hopes of securing royal reward. Simultaneously, the viceroy of Peru commissioned a separate expedition under the leadership of Diego de Frías Trejo.[50] After seven months of campaigning, Frías Trejo succeeded in capturing most of the English, including Oxenham, and dispersing maroons from their settlements.[51] As with earlier campaigns, the recorded number of captured or killed maroons paled in comparison to their presumed numbers. Figure 3 illustrates the areas in which Spanish-maroon conflict took place during the late 1570s.

Ortega Valencia returned to Panama in early 1579 with a royal commission to undertake further campaigns against the maroons. Shortly after his return, overtures by maroons raised hopes of a negotiated peace.[52] Although some maroons surrendered and received pardons in mid-1579, fears of Spanish duplicity and news of Francis Drake's attacks on Spanish ports in the Pacific led to vacillation among the region's maroon leaders.[53] From late 1579 through 1581, Ortega Valencia sent out smaller squads to pursue maroons, burning their fields and homes and capturing those they could. In late 1581, both sides, wary of conflict, renewed negotiation and secured the rendition and pardon of the region's remaining maroons.[54]

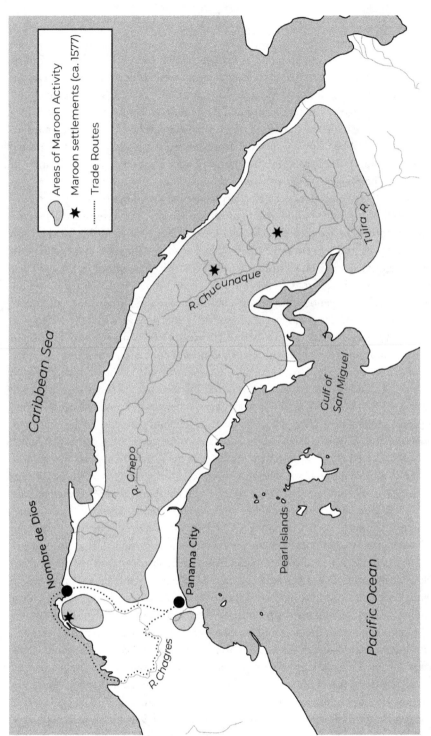

FIGURE 3. Maroon Activity in Panama, ca. 1577. Map by author.

Despite rhetoric that cast maroons as bringing about the perdition of the Indies, officials and Spanish citizens alike sought permission to negotiate with maroons rather than prolong military conflicts. In 1544 and 1545, the king gave the newly appointed *oidor* (judge of the high court) and *juez visitador* (visiting judge) Alonso López de Cerrato a free hand to "enact that which you believe is best" against the maroons of Hispaniola.[55] The following year, officials exercised this latitude. Cerrato reported that his captains had approached the maroon leader Diego de Ocampo with terms for peace. The Spanish proposed freeing the maroon leaders, while returning other maroons to their Spanish owners. Not surprisingly, the maroons declined the offer.[56] As the Spanish patrols continued to pressure the maroons, eventually Diego de Ocampo approached authorities offering to surrender in return for his freedom and that of his wife and two cousins.[57] Soon after Diego de Guzmán, another maroon leader, negotiated a personal pardon in return for assisting authorities against other maroons, an obligation that had been part of the 1533 peace with the cacique Enrique and his indigenous maroons.[58] The efforts of these former maroons appear to have helped stem the frequency and severity of maroon raids into the 1550s.

Roughly a decade later, in Panama Francisco Carreño approached the maroon leader Bayano during a campaign ordered by Governor Sosa. Accounts of this expedition do not specify who authorized negotiation. Carreño claimed credit for entreating with Bayano.[59] According to his account, he coaxed Bayano and other maroon captains to negotiate in Nombre de Dios. In return for peace and pardon, Bayano pledged to bring his people to Nombre de Dios. Yet, after leaving the Spanish port, Bayano did not return. Sosa ordered a new military expedition, but maroon ambushes decimated its numbers.[60] Soon after, Carreño once again sought out Bayano. In an effort to appease the Spanish, Bayano reportedly turned over several Africans who had recently fled Spanish owners and arrived in his communities. These overtures did not spark further negotiation.

A year later, Pedro de Ursúa's expedition reached Bayano's main settlement, in the upper reaches of the Rio Chepo or Rio Chucunaque. Outnumbered and facing an elevated, fortified settlement, Ursúa approached Bayano under a flag of truce. Bayano allowed the Spanish to establish a camp at the foot of the hilltop community. The two leaders agreed that Bayano and his community would surrender, receive pardons, and be relocated to a site on the Rio Francisca, near Nombre de Dios. The maroons promised to seek out any enslaved person who fled and to supply goods to the port and overland travelers. Yet, Ursúa had no interest in honoring the plan. Instead, he pursued his plan to drug and capture Bayano. Ursúa spared Bayano's life, and the maroon leader supposedly lived out his days in Spain.[61]

In the wake of the assaults committed by the maroon-English alliance in 1573, the king authorized a military campaign and the Audiencia held an open session to determine the best course of action.[62] Most residents of Panama strongly supported a military reprisal.[63] The high court authorized a fifty-man expedition led by Luis de Torres Guerrero. Yet the court simultaneously sent out a Dominican friar to attempt to negotiate with the maroons. At the time Pedro de Ortega Valencia, then serving as royal treasurer, lambasted the decision for sending mixed messages to the maroons, which resulted in the death of the friar and several African porters sent to accompany him. The court's indecision over a policy of peace or war only served to exacerbate the conflict.

In 1574, the king explicitly authorized the Audiencia to negotiate a peace with the maroons.[64] When the order reached Panama, the Audiencia held a new public session. Popular sentiment had shifted toward peace. The court agreed and proclaimed an offer of pardon and freedom for maroons that surrendered within four months.[65] Given the duplicity of 1573 and the memory of Ursúa's treachery, only three maroons presented themselves in the first two months of the amnesty.[66] Although the Spanish genuinely wished to negotiate a peace in 1575, the maroons did not appear to trust them. Oxenham's expedition and the subsequent campaigns by Ortega Valencia and Trejo sidelined any future peace during 1577 and 1578. Yet the Spanish had not fully abandoned the peaceful option.

In late 1578, the Audiencia sent messages to maroons through "faithful" Africans, informing them that if they came in peace the Audiencia would receive them, presumably under similar terms to those of 1575.[67] When Ortega Valencia arrived in January 1579, two maroon captains from the region formerly inhabited by Bayano entered Nombre de Dios to initiate peace talks.[68] In March, a maroon from a separate group of maroons near Portobelo approached the Audiencia to sue for peace.[69] One month later, a small group of maroons from the hinterland of Panama City likewise sought peace.[70] By early summer, Spanish authorities believed that the maroon problem would soon be resolved.

Although negotiations with the maroons of Portobelo and those from near Panama City proceeded well, by June the negotiations with the maroons from Bayano had faltered. Ortega Valencia presided over negotiations from a camp on the Gulf of San Miguel. The Spanish considered a maroon leader named Domingo Congo to be "king" of the maroons, a successor of sorts to Bayano. Yet the political organization of the maroons likely resembled more of a confederation than a kingdom. After Ortega Valencia and Domingo agreed to terms, the maroon captains in attendance were to collect their people and return to the Spanish camp.

The maroons did not return. The Spanish suspected them of duplicity. Several factors appear to have contributed to the breakdown.[71] Domingo Congo had requested that the Spanish transport the maroons from the Gulf of San Miguel to a new site near Panama in boats but without military escort. Ortega Valencia appears to have balked at that suggestion, likely raising fears that Spanish soldiers might re-enslave his people. As the negotiations transpired, word of Francis Drake's arrival in the Pacific reached Panama.[72] While the maroons offered to help the Spanish defeat Drake, even proposing to lure Drake to the Spanish, the English presence destabilized the negotiation. When maroon leaders returned to their communities, internal disagreement stymied the terms negotiated by Domingo Congo. Later accounts suggest that he died "of anger" because other leaders would not comply.[73] At least one maroon leader, Antón Marchena, vociferously rejected the peace.

By October 1579, the Spanish had secured a peace with maroons living near the bay of Portobelo even as they returned to a state of war with those from the Bayano. Yet the peace with the Portobelo maroons changed the dynamic of war. After establishing the *villa* of Santiago del Príncipe, near Nombre de Dios, the maroons of Portobelo began to assist Ortega Valencia in raids through the Bayano. During 1580 and 1581, these raids forced maroons to scatter into small bands, burn their larger settlements, and establish small *rancherías* (camps) in remote areas.[74] Some maroons found themselves pushed far to the southeast towards *indios de guerra* (unconquered indigenous groups).

The cost of war weighed heavily on both sides. In late December 1581, one of the major leaders of the Bayano maroons approached Spanish forces offering to surrender in return for pardon and freedom. The Spanish quickly accepted and by mid-February had relocated hundreds of maroons to a new community, named Santa Cruz la Real (see figure 4). For the remainder of 1582, newly freed maroons helped the Spanish locate scattered holdouts hiding throughout the isthmus.

Even after the successful reduction of Panama's maroons into the new free-Black towns of Santiago del Príncipe and Santa Cruz la Real, authorities in Hispaniola remained resistant to negotiation. Despite an escalation of antimaroon expeditions during the last two decades of the century, only one instance of Spanish-maroon negotiation occurred. In 1592, Antonio de Ovalle led an *entrada* into the Bahoruco. He succeeded in negotiating terms with a small community of maroons. Authorities allowed Ovalle to resettle the maroons and named him *corregidor* of their community.[75] Authorities would not entertain further negotiations with maroons on Hispaniola until the late eighteenth century.[76]

Divergent Responses

Given the parallels in Spanish-maroon conflicts between these two regions, the radically divergent outcomes bear consideration. Explanations lie in the broader context of Spanish-maroon conflict and how peace with maroons could bring solutions to other problems facing the Spanish crown. In particular, the issues of foreign interlopers, contraband, and rebellious or disobedient Spanish residents appear to have shaped the context of Spanish responses.

While both regions faced the increasing presence of foreign ships during the second half of the seventeenth century, these ships and their crews interacted with each region in vastly different ways. In Panama, foreign ships preyed on the trade to and from Nombre de Dios. In some cases, daring captains attempted to bypass the port and capture goods traveling between Nombre de Dios and Panama by

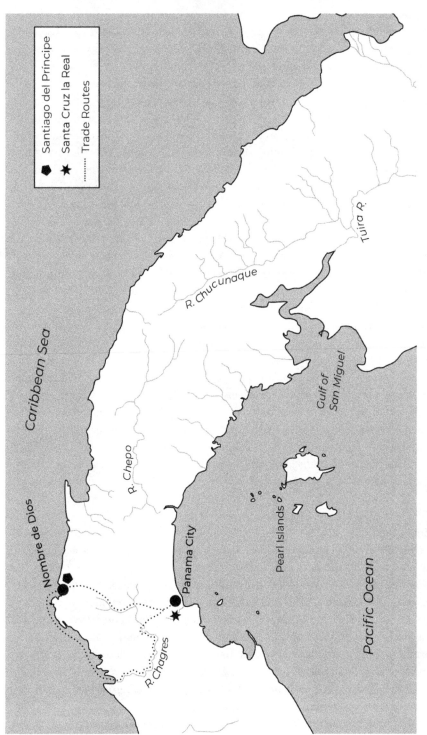

FIGURE 4. Free-Black Towns of Panama, ca. 1582. Map by author.

either ascending the Chagres River or ambushing the overland path. On Hispaniola, foreign ships did prey on shipping, but unlike in Panama the majority of ships sought to partake in illicit contraband trade with the island's residents.

From the 1570s onward, Hispaniola became increasingly isolated within the Spanish economic system. Only a handful of merchants financed voyages between Seville and Santo Domingo, resulting in exorbitant prices for imported goods and limited options for export.[77] Moreover, residents of smaller coastal communities had to first ship goods to Santo Domingo before they could be sent back to Europe. Given these obstacles, foreign ships filled a vital niche that allowed residents of Hispaniola access to otherwise barred commercial networks. Some maroons even joined into this trade killing feral livestock and selling tanned leather to foreign traders.[78]

Such contraband trade did not develop in Panama, in large part because the only two Spanish settlements were the very ports through which authorized trade passed. Unlike neighboring regions of the circum-Caribbean, Panama simply did not have secondary coastal settlements that would welcome contraband trade. Unlike maroons on Hispaniola, those in Panama had little to offer foreign ships other than information and assistance.

Given the heated religious landscape of the period, fears that foreigners might spread Protestant heresy compounded the economic threat posed by foreign contraband traders. On Hispaniola, the dual threat posed by contraband and fears of spreading heterodoxy fueled repeated campaigns of prosecution. Although most residents simply saw foreign traders as a means to greater economic prosperity, for authorities contraband trade threatened religious and political impropriety that needed correction.[79] While Panama did experience some internal strife from disgruntled Spaniards the problem never became compounded by fears of heresy.[80] These differing contexts help explain why Spanish-maroon conflict in these regions resulted in such different outcomes. Royal officials sought solutions that could remedy multiple problems facing the region.

In the case of Panama, defending against foreign interlopers and maroon raids had resulted in a prolonged and excessively costly period of warfare. Negotiation with maroons provided a solution that could alter the status quo on both fronts. By making peace with existing maroons and relocating them to sites closer to Spanish interests, Spanish authorities enhanced their strategic position in several ways. First, authorities improved their ability to defend against foreign attacks by enlisting former maroons into the colony's defenses. Second, in addition to defending against external attack, former maroons pledged to seek and return fugitives. Third, the communities settled by maroons would provide much needed foodstuffs and local goods to the two Spanish ports. These policies bore fruit. In the decades that followed, maroons played crucial roles in repulsing Drake's 1596 raid, assisting with the relocation of Nombre de Dios to Portobelo, patrolling for maroons, and defending against attacks from indigenous groups migrating into the eastern isthmus.

On Hispaniola, marronage represented a less pressing concern; yet one that

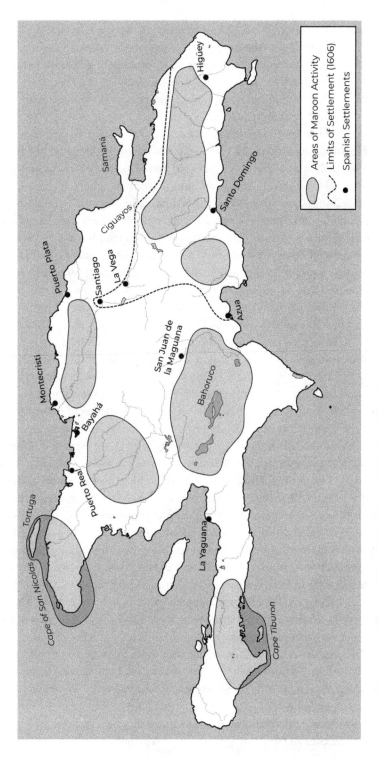

FIGURE 5. Maroon Activity on Hispaniola, 1570–1610. Map by author.

Areas of Maroon Activity
Limits of Settlement (1606)
Spanish Settlements

Higüey

Samaná

Ciguayos

Santo Domingo

Puerto Plata

Santiago
La Vega

Azua

Montecristi

San Juan de
la Maguana

Bayahá

Bahoruco

Puerto Real

Tortuga

Cape of San Nicolas

La Yaguana

Cape Tiburon

could not be divorced from the problems of contraband. In fact, the 1598 proposal that would precipitate the forced relocations of the *banda del norte* (north coastline) explicitly used marronage as a rationale for consolidating Spanish settlements closer to Santo Domingo. In adopting the proposal, authorities hoped that the relocations would inhibit contraband trade, make it easier to prevent marronage, and consolidate Spaniards into more defensible positions.

While the process in Panama achieved most of its desired ends, the outcome in Hispaniola generated less conclusive results. In the long run, the abandonment of the north and western coasts allowed French *boucanes* (buccaneers) to establish a presence that would eventually result in the French colony of Saint-Domingue. In consolidating enslaved persons and Spaniards into a smaller area, the relocations likely made preventing marronage slightly easier. Indeed, reports of grand marronage diminished greatly during the early seventeenth century. Nevertheless, the relocations effectively ceded large swaths of the island to the maroons who occupied them (see figure 5). Some areas, such as the Bahoruco, remained under maroon control well into the eighteenth century.

Although the scope and impact of grand marronage appear to have diminished in each region, the policies adopted significantly weakened Spanish territorial control. French occupation of Hispaniola steadily increased during the seventeenth century leading to the formal cession of the western half of the island in the Treaty of Ryswick (1697). In Panama, the Spanish ability to control the eastern isthmus slowly diminished. During the first decades of the seventeenth century, migrating indigenous groups, likely the predecessors of the Kuna people, began to occupy the region. By the late seventeenth century, renewed raids by foreign privateers, including Charles Dampier and Bartholomew Sharp, once again laid bare the lack of Spanish control. In 1698, the audacious Darien Scheme resulted in a short-lived Scottish colony.

The territorial fragility that followed the sixteenth-century Spanish-maroon conflict cannot be wholly attributed to maroons or the Spanish policies that sought to ameliorate their threat. Rather, successful grand marronage during the sixteenth century revealed the divergence between Spanish claims to sovereignty and their ability to effectively govern those regions. Maroons sought out, settled, and defended regions that the Spanish could not, or would not, occupy or secure. The responses to sixteenth-century marronage did not alter this underlying weakness.

Quite the opposite, the solutions exacerbated the problem. On Hispaniola, authorities relocated Spanish settlements, the key loci of Spanish dominion, consolidating control over a much smaller region while effectively ceding over half of the island. In Panama, the choice to relocate maroons away from the eastern isthmus produced similar results. Spanish and free-Black settlements became consolidated in a narrow band between Nombre de Dios-Portobelo and Panama City. The inability of Spaniards to project authority over territory they claimed put the lie to their presumption of sovereignty. More important, these episodes reveal the effectiveness of maroons in carving out sanctuaries and tenaciously defending them from Spanish reprisals.

Notes

1. Aguado, *Historia de Venezuela*, 2:218–19.

2. "Second memorial," November 20, 1598, in Rodríguez Demorizi, ed., *Relaciones historicas de Santo Domingo*, 2:186–87.

3. López de Velasco, *Geografía y descripción universal*, 100–105.

4. Altman, "Revolt of Enriquillo," 587–614.

5. Stone, "America's First Slave Revolt," 195–217.

6. Deive, *La esclavitud del negro*, vol. 1; Deive, *Los cimarrones*; Deive, *Los guerrilleros negros*.

7. Schwaller, "Contested Conquests," 609–38.

8. Fortune, "Los primeros negros," 56–84; Fortune, "El esclavo negro," 1–16; Fortune, "Bayano," 1–15.

9. Pike, "Black Rebels," 243–66.

10. Tardieu, *Cimarrones de Panamá*.

11. Other notable works examining maroons and Africans in these regions include: Arrom and García Arévalo, *Cimarrón*; Batlle, *La rebelión del Bahoruco*; Diez Castillo, *Los cimarrones y los negros*; Franco, *La diaspora africana en el nuevo mundo*; de la Guardia, *Los negros del Istmo de Panamá*; Guillot, *Negros rebeldes y negros cimarrones*; Jopling, ed., *Indios y negros en Panamá*; Landers, "*Cimarrón* and Citizen"; Mena García, *La Sociedad de Panamá*; Thompson, *Flight to Freedom*. See also Schwaller, *African Maroons*.

12. Altman, "the Revolt of Enriquillo," 613–14.

13. Scholars have often distinguished between *petit marronage*, short-term flight by individuals or small groups, and grand marronage, long-term or permanent flight by large groups. These categories date from later French Caribbean slavery. In sixteenth-century Spanish America, such distinctions are harder to identify. Schwaller, "Contested Conquests," 610.

14. See Diouf, *Slavery's Exiles*, 73–76.

15. The term *monte* generally applied to areas in which vegetation or topography made travel difficult or impossible. These features could exist in various ecological zones from tall shrub-lands to tropical forest.

16. Aguado, *Historia de Venezuela*, 2:227; AGI-Patronato 234, R. 6, 656–58; AGI-Santo Domingo 53, R. 1, N. 24, "Gonzalo Mejía de Villalobos a su Mag," (1609), bloque 2; AGI-Santo Domingo 54, R. 2, N. 42, "Gómez de Sandoval a su Mag," (1611).

17. AGI-Panama 29, R. 5, N. 11 (1551), 13; AGI-Patronato 234, R. 6, 376v–380.

18. AGI-Panama 235, L. 6, "Perjuicios que causan los negros cimarrones" (1536), 24v–25.

19. Archivo de la Real Academia de la Historia, Colección de Juan Bautista Muñoz, 09–04846, Tomo 66, N. 1231, fol. 142v.

20. AGI-Panama 29, R. 5, N. 11 (1551), 12v–14.

21. AGI-Patronato 151, N. 5, R. 1. "Probanza de Pedro González de Meceta" (1569). Transcripción available in Jopling, *Indios y negros en Panamá*, 338–39.

22. Three hundred pesos was a significant sum. González de Meceta estimated the damage caused by the maroons, the theft and destruction of his entire estate, exceeded three thousand pesos.

23. Utrera, *Historia militar*, 2:398.

24. AGI-Panama 30, N. 15. Abridged transcription in Jopling, *Indios y negros en Panamá*, 353–55. Translation in Schwaller, *African Maroons*, 90–102.

25. AGI-Patronato 234, R. 6, fs. 337–341v.

26. Nichols, "Sir Francis Drake Revived," 173–87.

27. AGI-Panama 13, R. 18, N. 91, "Alonso Criado de Castilla a su Mag," (1579).

28. Stone, "America's First Slave Revolt," 195–217.

29. AGI-Patronato 150, N. 14, R. 2, "Probanza de Francisco Carreño" (1562), 753–805.

30. Mena García, *Sociedad de Panamá*, 402.

31. Ibid., 406.

32. Utrera, *Historia militar*, 1:206.

33. Utrera, *Historia militar*, 2:178–79, 399.

34. AGI-Santo Domingo 899, L. 1, 389–90.

35. Schwaller, "Contested Conquests," 623–24, 628–29.

36. Mena García, *Sociedad de Panamá*, 411.

37. AGI-Santo Domingo 49, R. 18, N. 112, "Licenciado Grajeda a su Mag," (1548), 3.

38. Schwaller, "Contested Conquests," 624.

39. AGI-Santo Domingo 51, R. 8, N. 156, "Presidente Lope de Vega Portocarrera a su Mag," (1596), 2; Utrera, *Historia militar*, 3:342.

40. AGI-Panama 29, R. 5, N. 11.

41. AGI-Panama 39, N. 29, 162. Also, AGI-Patronato 192, N.1, R.56.

42. Tardieu, *Cimarrones de Panamá*, 72–75.

43. Ibid., 77.

44. Aguado, *Historia de Venezuela*, 2:183–229.

45. AGI-Panama 29, R. 9, N. 37, "Luis de Guzmán a su Mag," (1562), 2–2v.

46. AGI-Panama 13, R. 10, N. 35, "Licenciado Diego de Vera a su Mag," (1570), 2v–3.

47. AGI-Patronato, R. 7, N. 1, "Probanza de Luis de Torres Guerreo" (1587); AGI-Panama, 11, "Cabildo de Panama a su Mag," (1574), 23–26.

48. AGI-Panama 33, N. 104, "Oficiales reales a su Mag," (1577).

49. AGI-Panama 13, R. 16, N. 68, "Dr. Loarte a su Mag," (1577).

50. AGI-Panama 41, N. 23, "Diego de Frías Trejo a su Mag," (1577).

51. AGI-Panama 41, N. 49, "Diego de Frías Trejo a su Mag," (1578).

52. AGI-Panama 13, R. 18, N. 89 "Audiencia de Panama a su Mag," (1597).

53. Pike, "Black Rebels," 262–63.

54. AGI-Panama 13, R. 20, N. 132, bloque 3, "Pedro González de Meceta a Dr. Criado de Castilla," (1581).

55. AGI-Santo Domingo 868, L. 2, fs. 204, 246.

56. AGI-Santo Domingo 49, R. 16, N. 98, "López de Cerrato a su Mag," (1546).

57. AGI-Santo Domingo 49, R. 16, N. 101, "Los licenciados Cerrato y Grajeda a su Mag," (1546), 1v.

58. AGI-Santo Domingo 49, R. 16, N. 102, "Licenciado Cerrato a su Mag," (1546), 1v.

59. AGI-Patronato 150, N. 14, R. 2, "Probanza de Francisco Carreño," (1562), 753–805.

60. AGI-Panama 29, R. 6, N. 25, "Alvaro de Sosa a su Mag," (1555), 4–4v.

61. AGI-Panama 13, R. 21, n. 137, "Alonso Criado de Castilla a su Mag," (1582), 2; Vega, *Historia General del Peru*, 277.

62. AGI-Panama 229, L. 1, 8v–9.

63. AGI-Panama 11, "Pedro de Ortega Valencia a su Mag," (1573), 119–24.

64. AGI-Panama 42, N. 21, 622–23.

65. AGI-Patronato 234, R. 6, 337–341v.

66. AGI-Panama 11, "Audiencia de Panamá a su Mag," (1575), 8–12.

67. AGI-Panama 13, R. 18, N. 89, "Audiencia de Panamá a su Mag," (1579).

68. AGI-Patronato 234, R. 5, "Pedro de Ortega Valencia a su Mag," (1579), 83–92.

69. AGI-Panama 42, N. 35, "Memorial de Antonio de Salcedo," (1580), 1102.

70. AGI-Panama 42, N. 35, "Memorial de Antonio de Salcedo," (1580), fs. 1100v–1101.

71. AGI-Panama 234, R. 5, 95–109.

72. AGI-Panama 42, N. 6, "Pedro de Ortega Valencia a su Mag," (1579).

73. AGI-Panama 13, R. 20, N. 123, "Presidente Cepeda a su Mag," (1581).

74. Ibid.

75. Rodríguez Demorizi, *Relaciones historicas de Santo Domingo*, 2:349–52.

76. Deive, *Los cimarrones*.

77. Ponce-Vázquez, *Islanders and Empire*, 59–60.

78. AGI-Santo Domingo 54, R. 2, N. 49, "Gómez de Sandoval a su Mag," (1611), 2.

79. Ponce-Vázquez, *Islanders and Empire*, 100.

80. Mena García, *Sociedad de Panamá*, 303–9.

CHAPTER SEVEN

MINE OWNERS, MONEYLENDERS, ENSLAVERS, AND LITIGANTS

Free-Black Miners and Black Mining Dynasties in the Colombian Chocó, 1744–1784

Juliet Wiersema

Introduction

SPANISH COLONIAL archives preserve countless tales of African oppression and abuse. Stories of African autonomy and entrepreneurship are more difficult to find, but they do exist. One unlikely source is a manuscript map of the Atrato River and its accompanying *descripción* (see figure 6).[1] The Atrato River in the Chocó represented a major fluvial artery and an important gold mining area in a remote frontier within the viceroyalty of New Granada (see figure 7). The map *Curso de el río de Atrato. Plano de la provincia del Zitará* (figure 6) identifies every tributary and calls attention to numerous mining sites (rendered as simple huts). What is not immediately apparent is that many of these mines were owned by free Africans (*negros libres*) and their descendants.[2] Sites of mining in the Spanish Americas were most often spaces of enslaved African labor and hardship; however, various factors in the Chocó opened a door to African autonomy. My aim in this essay is to shine a light on a few remarkable instances of Black opportunism, entrepreneurship, and freedom along the Atrato in the mid- to late-eighteenth century.

Africans were brought to Colombia's Pacific Lowlands (the Greater Chocó) in the late seventeenth century. Here they were forced to mine for gold along remote rivers and streambeds in *cuadrillas* (teams of enslaved workers), overseen by Spanish mine owners and administrators. The gold mined in the Chocó fed the regional and global economy but at the same time brought opportunities for enslaved Africans. In this chapter, I examine a handful of cases of Africans and their descendants living in the Chocó who, by the mid-eighteenth century, had acquired their freedom, owned mines and enslaved workers of their own, and operated in niche markets which addressed local demands including money lending and canoe transport. These same individuals successfully navigated the complex Spanish legal system, safeguarding their livelihoods. They gained *vecindad* and created strong multi-generational communities with other free-Black mining families.

To get at these underrepresented narratives, I draw from a handful of accessible primary sources.[3] Through these, we are introduced to members of free-Black mining dynasties—the Velascos, Caycedos (Caicedos), and Thovars (Tovars)—who, having broken the bonds of enslavement, went on to build successful mining enterprises in family-based communities with other *negros libres*. As we will see, neither gender nor former enslavement were impediments to entrepreneurial success for Africans and their descendants in this part of the Chocó.

New Granada, The Chocó, and the Extraction of Gold

New Granada, one of four Spanish viceroyalties, encompassed today's Colombia, Panama, Venezuela, and Ecuador.[4] Similar to New Spain and Peru, New Granada was discovered and colonized by Spaniards in the early sixteenth century. Motivated by declining revenues and threats of foreign encroachment, New Granada was first established as a viceroyalty in 1717.[5] In 1723, the Spanish crown concluded that the cost of maintaining New Granada as a viceroyalty outweighed any benefits, stripping it of its viceregal status. Another fifteen years would pass before it was reinstated, in 1738, with Spanish officials claiming that New Granada's rich natural resources and its great economic potential were sufficient reason to bring it back into the fold.[6] Gold provided the rationale for establishing New Granada as a viceroyalty in 1717 and the best argument for reinstating it twenty years later.[7]

New Granada's economy was built around the extraction of gold. From the beginning of the Spanish colonial period until 1780, gold represented nearly 100 percent of New Granada's exports.[8] Gold financed external commerce and fostered the development of other internal economic sectors such as agriculture, ranching, and manufacturing.[9] These regional industries—including cloth produced in Quito, Pasto, Tunja, and Socorro, and livestock and crops from Pasto and the Cauca Valley—fed the mining industry. By the eighteenth century, much of the gold mined in New Granada came from the Pacific Lowlands, of which the Chocó formed part.[10] All New Granada's economies (agricultural, textile, mining) were powered by enslaved laborers.[11]

In many parts of the Americas, it was difficult for an enslaved person to break the bonds of slavery. However, a confluence of circumstances in the Chocó—its mineral wealth, the area's isolation from Spanish colonial centers, the relative absence of Spaniards in the region, the critical mass of Africans as well as their access to gold and to mines, and the fact that Black labor was always in demand—provided Africans and their descendants more avenues to freedom and more opportunities for self-realization than were possible in other areas of New Granada.[12] As we will see, freedom appears to have been more obtainable in New Granada's goldfields than

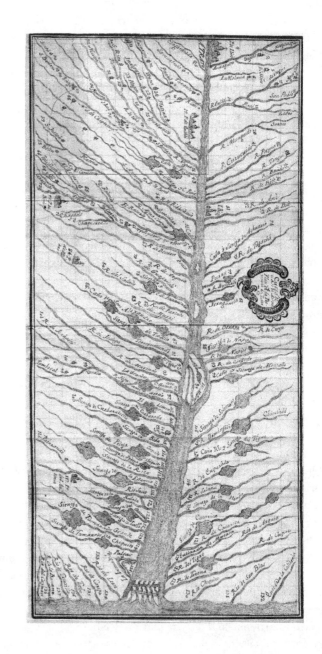

FIGURE 6. Curso de el río de Atrato. Plano de la Provincia del Zitará, included in the manuscript "Descripción de la Provincia del Zitará y el curso del río Atrato," ca. 1780, oriented with west at top. The Atrato River flows horizontally across the page, from Lloró at left to the Gulf of Urabá at far right. The section at bottom left was inhabited by free-Black mining families. Map courtesy of The Poetry Collection of the University Libraries, University at Buffalo, The State University of New York.

in other slave-dominant zones, such as the sugarcane fields of greater Cali or the upper Cauca River basin. (For additional cases of African autonomy resulting from tenuous or failed Spanish colonization, see Schwaller's chapter on sixteenth-century Panama and Hispaniola and Beatty-Medina's chapter on sixteenth- and seventeenth-century Esmeraldas. For the role of geography in creating spaces of refuge, see Lentz's chapter on San Benito.)

The Chocó, one of fourteen provinces in New Granada, was famed for two things: its unhospitable climate—characterized by scorching heat, inescapable humidity, and diluvial rainfall—and its rich placer mines.[13] As early as 1688, a Spaniard portrayed the area as an abyss; a horror of mountains, rivers, and marshes.[14] Another report described the Chocó as hot and humid, a set of climatic conditions which led to illness.[15] An eighteenth-century *descripción* of Nóvita characterized the Chocó as an area of abundant mosquitos and copious snakes, centipedes, frogs, bats, and cockroaches.[16] Despite its many disadvantages, the Chocó was of central economic importance to the Spanish crown from the early Spanish colonial period until the very end.[17]

The Chocó, a frontier zone in Colombia's Pacific Lowlands, is bordered by Panama and the Caribbean Sea to the north, the Pacific Ocean to the west, the Cauca

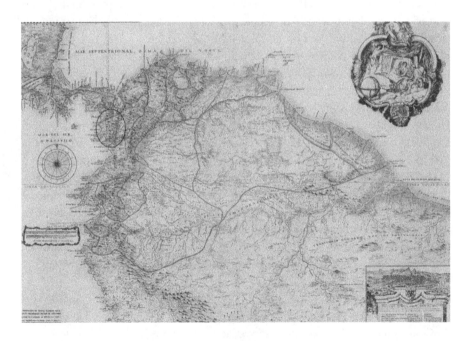

FIGURE 7. Plano geográfico del virreinato de Santa Fé de Bogotá, Nuevo Reyno de Granada (1772), Francisco Antonio Moreno y Escandón. Archivo General de La Nación-Colombia. Sección Mapas y Planos 2 Ref. 1248. The Chocó, near Panama, is circled in black.

River Valley to the south, and the Cordillera Occidental to the east (see figure 7). Nearly every stream that flows from the Cordillera Occidental and empties into the Atrato or San Juan rivers is gold bearing.[18] Antonio Manso, President of the Audiencia of Santa Fé de Bogotá (1724–1731), noted in 1729 that gold in the Chocó was not extracted by *arrobas* (a measure equating to approximately 11.5 kilograms) but instead by *cargas*, or loads.[19] In the 1720s, this was not mere hyperbole, but such bonanza could not last.

Differing from vein mining in Zacatecas or Potosí, which occurred in wealthy, heavily populated, and geographically connected urban centers, mining in the Chocó was alluvial (or placer), and occurred along rivers and streambeds in small, scattered, and isolated mining camps. At these camps, cuadrillas of enslaved laborers extracted gold using simple technology and subsisted largely on maize and plantains.[20] Gold mining of this sort had been going on elsewhere in New Granada since the middle of the sixteenth century, with early mining centered in Cartago and Santa Fé de Bogotá. Antioquia was a prominent gold mining center from the early to mid-seventeenth century. In the late seventeenth century, gold mining was concentrated in Popayán.[21] The Chocó, along with Popayán and Amazonia, represented the last frontier.

Africans and their descendants comprised the largest portion of the Chocó's inhabitants.[22] According to the 1778 census, enslaved Africans represented 39 percent of the population while free people of all colors (*libres de todos colores*), many of African ancestry, comprised an additional 22 percent.[23] By 1808, free people, or *libres*, comprised 75 percent of the population.[24] Their critical mass contributed to their ability to assert their rights and carve out opportunities in this remote frontier.

Africans had come to New Granada from West and West Central Africa through the Transatlantic Slave Trade as well as through traffic with the British and Dutch Caribbean.[25] The transatlantic trade brought Africans to New Granada from the Gold Coast and the Bight of Benin (corresponding to today's Ghana, Togo, Benin, and western Nigeria), as well as from West Central Africa (Congo and Angola).[26] Enslaved Africans were destined for the remote mining areas on the Pacific coast, including the Chocó, where they replaced the decimated indigenous labor force.[27] Mining censuses and inventories offer clues to the origins of Africans in the Chocó. In these documents, Africans are often listed by first name and ethnonym.[28] Ethnonyms, or approximate geographic designations—Mina, Araras, Popo, Chamba, Carabali, Ibo, Congo, etc.—often became an enslaved individual's last name in this region.[29]

From *Negros Esclavos* to *Negros Libres*

As Orían Jiménez Meneses has observed, to be Black in the Chocó was to be enslaved.[30] Nevertheless, notarial records from the eighteenth century reveal increasing numbers of *negros esclavos* (enslaved Africans) who became *negros libres*. Freedom in the Chocó was obtained most often through self-liberation or self-emancipation, where an enslaved person was able to purchase their freedom with money they had made or gold dust they had collected on off days.[31] Some enslaved people were manumitted, or granted their liberty, by those who had enslaved them, but this was rare.[32] In addition to self-purchase, enslaved and free people in the Chocó purchased the freedom of their children or other junior relatives.[33] A more fraught freedom could be obtained by fleeing, perhaps to a *palenque* (community or encampment with elements of permanency) where terms of liberty for the palenque's members were negotiated with Spanish officials but often came with strings attached.[34] (For fugitive communities in the Pacific Andes, see O'Toole's chapter.) There was also the possibility, even before the first law of emancipation in 1821, of being born with free status. Any person born to a mother who was free was understood to be free by birth.[35]

Negros Libres as Mazamorreros and Dueños de Minas y Esclavos

Evidence for Africans as free prospectors (*mazamorreros*) and mine owners in the Chocó can be gleaned from mining censuses, court cases, and official reports. We also learn about the commercial activities of negros libres from a close reading of historical maps. Each of these sources enables us to construct a preliminary picture of a pioneering group of Africans and their descendants living along tributaries in the Chocó in the second half of the eighteenth century.

A mining census from 1759 documents dozens of negros libres who worked as free prospectors along the San Juan River. This census recorded all enslaved people associated with alluvial mines in the province of Nóvita. A page from this census preserves for posterity the names of forty-eight negros libres who mined at the *partido* (district) of San Agustín (see figure 8).[36] Included in this list were details about each free person's marital or family status which, in turn, offers a rough sketch of a community of negros libres living and mining along a tributary of the San Juan River near Nóvita (see figure 9).[37]

Among the forty-eight free-Black miners at San Agustín were mothers, fathers, and children who formed nuclear families. There were also single women (Magdalena), single men (Gerónimo, Mathias, and Thomas Moreno; Ventura and Manuel Caycedo; Matteo, Juan, and Nicolas Vivero; and Juan Velasco), and single mothers (Cathalina Moreno), as well as widows (María Vivero) and widowers (Lázaro Diaz). One family unit was comprised of Juan Antonio and his two sisters. There were also at least five extended families, where several individuals shared the same last name—Thovar, Velasco, Caycedo, Moreno, Vivero—suggesting familial mining dynasties within this enclave.[38] One negra libre, Cathalina, was married to Martín, an enslaved person, indicating that family ties at San Agustín extended to nearby *cuadrillas*.[39] (For Black strategies of emancipation as well as connections between free and enslaved communities along the late-eighteenth century Spanish Gulf Coast, see Villareal's chapter.) From this rather straightforward register (figure 8), we gather rich information about the social structure of free-Black, family-based communities in Colombia's Pacific Lowlands.

FIGURE 8. List of forty-eight negros libres who mined at the *partido* (district) of San Agustín, Archivo General de la Nación-Colombia, Negros y Esclavos 43 4 D 38 (1759), fol. 570r.

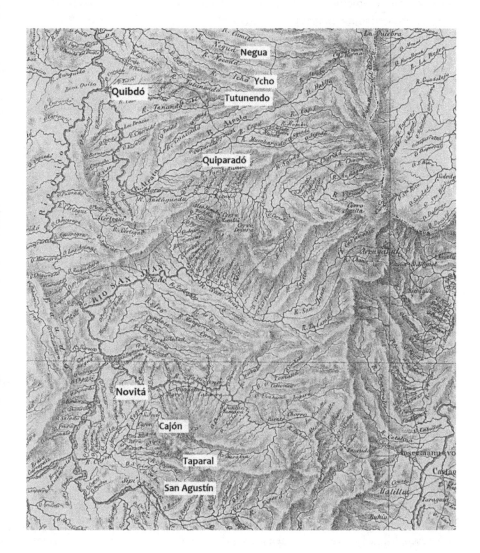

Map labels: Negua, Ycho, Quibdó, Tutunendo, Quiparadó, Novitá, Cajón, Taparal, San Agustín

FIGURE 9. Detail of *Carta corográfica del estado del Cauca construida con los datos de la Comisión Corográfica i del orden del gobierno general por Manuel Ponce de León, Ingeniero, i Manuel María Paz, Bogotá, 1864*, showing areas of free-Black mining operations near Novitá and the San Juan River at Cajón, Taparal, and San Agustín. Further north, near Quibdó and the Atrato River, are sites of free-Black mines at Negua, Ycho, Tutunendo, and Quiparadó, Archivo General de la Nación-Colombia, Sección Mapas y Planos 6, Ref. 5.

A roughly coeval report (*descripción*) provides information about other ne-gros libres who mined in the Chocó. The *Descripción del gobierno del Chocó* (undated but possibly written sometime around 1755–1759) mentions the mines of Jesús, María, and José, located in the *partido*, or district, of el Cajón in Nóvita (see figure 9). These mines were owned by Diego de Thovar, a negro libre, and were worked by his three enslaved men and an enslaved woman.[40] This same descripción mentions Miguel de Velasco (Miguel Belasco), another negro libre, and his mines at San Antonio, which were worked by his four enslaved men and two enslaved women.[41]

In another report (likely later in date)—the anonymous and undated "Descripción superficial de la provincia del Zitará"—Miguel de Velasco appears again. This time he is recorded as mining near the Negua River with a cuadrilla of between fourteen and sixteen people (see figure 9).[42] This change in location alludes to the mobile nature of alluvial mining, where new profitable placers were con-stantly sought to replace depleted ones.[43] This descripción also suggests that Miguel de Velasco's mining enterprise had tripled in size. Meanwhile, this same report doc-uments a family of free Blacks, the Caycedos, who lived and mined nearby with their respective cuadrillas. In addition to Narciso (possibly the father or an older brother), there was Agustín and his sister, Susana, a free-Black woman who also owned mines and cuadrillas of her own.[44]

Evidence for African prospectors and mine owners can also be teased from a roughly coeval map, the *Curso de el río de Atrato. Plano de la provincia del Zitará*, undated but likely created around 1780 (figure 6).[45] Oriented with west at the top, the map depicts the Atrato River as it flows from the Spanish town of Lloró (at far left) to the Gulf of Urabá and the Caribbean Sea (at right). Glossed on the map are over a hun-dred tributaries and a handful of Spanish towns. Meanwhile, numbers 1 through 138 identify the whereabouts of additional places of interest, including more than forty mines, marked with an emblem of a small hut (see figure 6).[46] Many places located on this map and discussed in the associated descripción preserve valuable information about negros libres in the Chocó.[47]

Of particular interest are the mines owned by negros libres (see figure 10). In the "Descripción de la provincia del Zitará y el curso del río de Atrato," Miguel de Velasco is again mentioned, but, by this date—c. 1780—it is his descendants who own houses, mines, and cuadrillas of enslaved people (no. 33; see figure 10).[48] Gerónima de Velasco, Miguel de Velasco's sister, is recorded as owning a large mine, the Real de Santa Rita (no. 30; see figure 10), which was worked by a cuadrilla of ten enslaved peo-ple.[49] These descripcións and archival documents provide evidence of generations of free-Black mining families, or dynasties, living and mining in the Chocó. Both mines and assets were passed on to their heirs. These same documents reveal that free-Black women were important actors in the later eighteenth-century Chocó mining economy.

In this same descripción, the Caycedo family, another multi-generational dynasty of negros libres who owned mines and cuadrillas, is referenced. The house

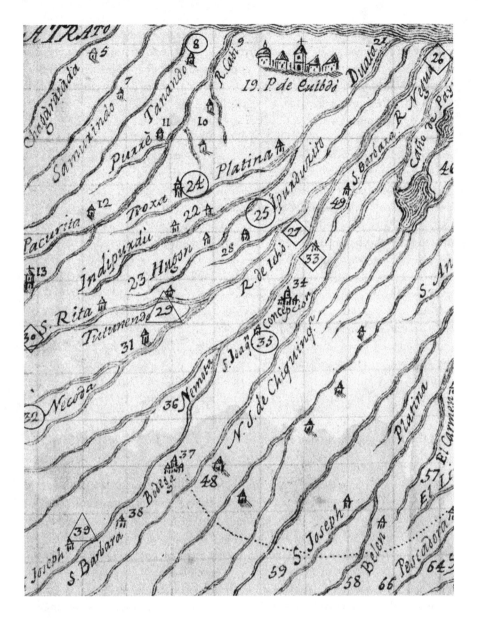

FIGURE 10. Detail of map included in the manuscript "Descripción de la Provincia del Zitará y el curso del río Atrato," ca. 1780, with the locations of mines owned by free Blacks. Areas mined by the Velascos are indicated by a diamond [26, 27, 30, 33], those of the Caycedos are indicated by a triangle [29, 39], and those of unnamed free-Black miners are indicated by a circle [24, 25, 32, 35]. The Thovar holdings are located further south at Taparal and Cajón, beyond the scope of this map (see figure 9).

and mine of Susana Caycedo and her cuadrilla of eight enslaved workers were located near Tutunendo (no. 29; see figure 10).[50] Nearby was another large mine, the Real de San José (no. 39; see figure 10), and a house belonging to the descendants of Narciso Caycedo.[51] If we look to *Curso de el río de Atrato. Plano de la provincia del Zitará*, we see that the mines belonging to negros libres and their families were clustered in a fairly concentrated area, just east of the Atrato River not far from the Spanish colonial administrative town of Quibdó (figure 6). In this same corner of the Chocó, several unnamed negros libres lived and mined as *mazamorreros* along the Atrato's tributaries (nos. 1, 2, 5, 24, 25, 32, 35, 40; see figure 10).

From this cursory examination of a handful of historical documents—a mining census, three roughly coeval official reports, and a map—we have evidence that extended families of negros libres owned and operated successful mining enterprises in the Chocó during the second half of the eighteenth century. In a handful of cases, these free-Black miners' full names were recorded, enabling us to unearth additional details in archival records about their lives, their commercial activities, and their communities. Through individuals like Diego de Thovar, Miguel de Velasco, Gerónima de Velasco, and Susana Caycedo, we are given concrete examples of what Marta Garrido has described as "self-made" men and women who successfully reinvented themselves amidst and despite their difficult life histories. For the Thovars, the Velascos, and the Caycedos, their place in Chocó society was constructed from scratch.[52] (For the regional unity of Black experience, see Clark's chapter on late seventeenth-century borderlands in the Caribbean and North America.)

Miguel de Velasco y Solimán and Gerónima de Velasco, negros libres y dueños de minas y esclavos

Much of what we know about Miguel de Velasco (y Solimán), a *negro libre* and *dueño de minas y esclavos* (owner of mines and enslaved workers), concerns his mining activity, which spanned from 1744 to 1771. In addition to registering rights to several mines along the Atrato's tributaries near Quibdó and acquiring up to twenty enslaved laborers, Velasco spawned a small mining empire together with his sister, Gerónima.

Some of the earliest information we have for Miguel de Velasco stems from 1744, when he was given the *quebrada* (ravine) of San Isidro by two *vecinos* (residents, citizens) of the province of Zitará, both owners (*dueños*) and discoverers of said mine.[53] As part of this transfer of ownership, Velasco formally changed the name of the mine from San Isidro to San Antonio and agreed to develop it as well as pay the *quintos* (crown mining tax) on all gold that he extracted there. Eleven years later, in 1755, Velasco continued to mine the quebrada at San Antonio with a team of six enslaved workers, comprised of four men and two women,[54] indicating that the mine given to him in 1744 by the two vecinos of Zitará had become—in Velasco's hands—profitable.[55]

Four years later, Velasco was included in the large 1759 mining census of

Nóvita, where he was documented at río Ycho (no. 27), with twenty enslaved workers in his employ.[56] Seven years later, in 1766, Velasco registered what was likely a contiguous mine. This quebrada, which flowed into río Ycho, he named Nuestra Señora de los Dolores de Quiparadó, referencing the indigenous place name—Quiparadó—of the nearby tributary.[57] That same year, Velasco registered mines near Tutunendo, which he named San Francisco. These, we learn, were contiguous to the quebradas mined by his sister, Gerónima de Velasco.[58]

Gerónima de Velasco, *dueña de minas y esclavos* (female owner of mines and enslaved workers), oversaw operations at the large mine of Santa Rita (no. 30; see figure 10), worked by a cuadrilla of ten.[59] A few years later, in 1784, Gerónima was documented at the mines of San Isidoro de Tutenendo where Pablo Escobar, one of her enslaved laborers, stated under oath that Gerónima gave workers Saturdays to tend to their crops or mine for their own benefit. According to Escobar's testimony, Gerónima ensured that her enslaved laborers were taught Christian doctrine.[60]

These documents, which span four decades (1744–1784), introduce us to a mining dynasty in the Chocó built by two free-Black siblings. Miguel de Velasco began with a small, sufficiently productive mine and a small cuadrilla. He went on to obtain rights to contiguous quebradas, successfully mining them and growing his enterprise in the process. His sister, Gerónima, did the same, identifying promising areas nearby. A few of their mines are identified in *Curso de el río de Atrato* (figure 6), revealing that the Velascos chose to exploit alluvial mines which were geographically proximal to one another. The quebradas mined by the Velasco family fell within a circumscribed area, lying within a day of Quibdó (figure 6).[61] The sites chosen by Miguel and Gerónima de Velasco also had local sources of salt (*ojos de sal*) and were fertile areas for the cultivation of plantains, sugar cane, and cacao.[62] Río Ycho, in particular, seems to have offered a rare kind of abundance for the region, with groves of cacao, sugarcane, star apple (*caimito*), and avocado.[63] These areas, pertaining to free-Black miners, were likely coveted locations, especially in the Chocó where supplies and staples had to be brought in from elsewhere at irregular intervals and at exorbitant prices.[64]

While the Velascos—a prosperous mining and agricultural family of negros libres—might strike us as unusual, archival documents reveal that they were not an anomaly. In this same part of the Chocó, in close geographical proximity to Miguel and Gerónima de Velasco's quebradas, lay the mines of other extended families of negros libres. For example, the mines at Tutunendo (no. 29; see figure 10), owned by Susana Caycedo and worked by a cuadrilla of eight, were located just upriver from Gerónima de Velasco's mines at Santa Rita (no. 30; see figure 10). A few tributaries to the north, along río Nemota, were the *reales de minas* de San José (no. 39; see figure 10) pertaining to the descendants of Narciso Caycedo. These were famed locally for their rich mineral and infinite number of tributaries.[65] Mines owned and operated by the Caycedo family were not far from Negua (no. 26; see figure 10) and Ycho (no. 27; see figure 10), where the mines of Miguel de Velasco, alias "Solimán," were located.[66]

Negras libres, dueñas de minas y esclavos

Our introduction to the Velascos, Caycedos, and their mining activity in the south-western Chocó, sheds light on free men—and free women—in late Spanish colonial New Granada who owned both mines and cuadrillas. Yesenia Barragan has observed that female enslavers have largely been omitted from extant studies of women, slavery, and everyday life in Colombia. Barragan's work investigates important cases of female enslavers in the nineteenth-century Pacific Lowlands, revealing that European women (*blancas*) as well as free-Black women (*negras libres*) owned mines and enslaved laborers.[67] Karen Graubart has identified free-Black women enslavers in seventeenth-century Lima, including Beatrice de Padilla who died owning several enslaved people and 2,500 pesos.[68] David Wheat has brought to light free women of color in the Spanish Caribbean including Francisca de Miranda, who owned slaves and appears, additionally, to have been involved in the trade.[69] Meanwhile, María Elena Díaz has noted that while free miners at El Cobre in eastern Cuba owned enslaved people, it was not uncommon for the royal slaves working the copper mines to have their own enslaved laborers.[70]

Little, if anything, has been written on free-Black women mine owners and enslavers in the eighteenth-century Pacific Lowlands. The women identified in this chapter—Gerónima de Velasco and Susana Caycedo—demonstrate that free-Black women did, in fact, own mines and cuadrillas, and managed successful, long-term mining operations in the frontier zones of New Granada. As documents and maps indicate, these negras libres—along with their family members—chose to situate themselves near resources and sources of sustenance and within larger communities of negros libres. In the next section, we look to Diego de Thovar, another negro libre with mines and enslaved laborers, who ran a canoe transport business and moonlighted in money lending.

Diego de Thovar, negro bozal libre, dueño de minas y esclavos, usurero

Little would be known about Diego de Thovar had he not been accused of usury. One of the earliest mentions of Thovar comes from a 1755 mining census for the province of Nóvita, where he was listed as a free Black working at Taparal with four enslaved people, three men and one woman.[71] This entry would be unremarkable had Thovar been a Spaniard, but as a negro libre with his own mines and enslaved laborers, it stands out. The following year, in 1756, Thovar found himself in the throes of a legal battle (ultimately decided in his favor) which brought to light many interesting details about this man, a native African, living in the Chocó a half century before Colombia's Independence.[72]

One of the first things we learn about Thovar is that he was allegedly ninety years old and, in his words, "very near death" when charges were filed against him.

In the documents, Thovar is repeatedly referred to as a *negro bozal*, indicating he had been born in Africa, a victim of the Transatlantic Slave Trade.[73] The term "bozal" also suggests that Thovar had a minimal command of Spanish and was considered by Spaniards as "unacculturated" or "un-Hispanicized."[74] At some point in his life, Thovar married Isabel Alexandra, a *negra criolla*, or Afro-criolla, a designation which suggests that, while of African descent, she had been born in the Americas.[75] Thovar had at least two sons, Santiago, who lived with Thovar and his wife, and Raymundo who, at the time of the legal dispute, lived elsewhere.

Thovar possessed rights to the productive mines of Taparal (see figure 9) and, by 1756, owned nine enslaved people, two of whom were children. The names of some of these individuals appear in the case file.[76] Thovar owned a house where his cuadrilla lived. He owned the mining tools they used including *barras, almocafres*, axes, and a *barreton*. He also owned the house (with a kitchen) where he and his family resided, and a corn field that, at the time of the court case, was ready for harvest. His other possessions included a silver knife (*mojarra*) and two desks for papers and letters (*papelera*), one of which had a new lock. All these things—Thovar's worldly goods—were impounded by colonial authorities.[77]

The accusations against Diego de Thovar had been filed by Agustín de Arboleda, a recently freed slave, who was noted as a *criollo libre*. Thovar had loaned Arboleda 50 pesos, an amount which enabled Arboleda to pay the final installment on his *carta de libertad*, or freedom papers. Arboleda complained that the loan terms, as stipulated by Thovar and originally agreed upon by both parties, had been excessively harsh. The 50-peso loan was to be repaid at 100 percent interest, where the original 50-peso debt would be paid in cash and the 50 pesos of interest would be given in the form of in-kind labor. While Arboleda had initially agreed to these terms, he complained that the labor Thovar required of him—as a free man—was more grueling than any work he had undertaken as an enslaved person.[78] In particular, Arboleda noted that, under Thovar, he had not been given time off to procure food and clothing for himself and his family.[79] The local presiding official, Lucas de Estaio y Fortún, lieutenant governor of Quibdó, decided in favor of Arboleda. In doing so, Estaio y Fortún waived the original 50-peso debt that Arboleda owed Thovar. Estaio y Fortún additionally fined Thovar 100 pesos for engaging in usury (loaning money at high rates of interest), leaving Thovar 150 pesos in the red.[80] But this case, as we will see, was far from over.

Finding this ruling unfair, Thovar chose to appeal, sending the case to the Audiencia in Santa Fé de Bogotá for review and adjudication. In Santa Fé, the case was decided in Thovar's favor. In the end, both negros libres (Thovar and Arboleda) were vindicated. Thovar's belongings were returned to him along with the 100 pesos he had been fined by Estaio y Fortún. Additionally, Thovar was reimbursed the 50 pesos he had loaned to Arboleda and was compensated for days of lost labor. In the end, it was the Spanish colonial official, Estaio y Fortún, who was found to be at fault.

Estaio y Fortún was accused of surreptitiously extracting mineral from Thovar's mines while Thovar's goods were impounded. The more significant transgression seems to have been that Estaio y Fortún did not document the gold taken from Thovar's mine, meaning that no percentage (royal fifth) was paid to the crown. In the end, Estaio y Fortún was forced to pay 420 pesos in damages, an amount which included all legal fees, expenses incurred by Thovar and his son while traveling to and remaining in Santa Fé for the hearing, and the 35 pesos in gold illicitly taken from Thovar's mine.[81]

Apart from shedding light on savvy negros libres suing for sizeable sums, elevating court cases on appeal, and outing corrupt Spanish officials, there are other fascinating details that emerge from this case. For one, we learn that both Thovar and Arboleda were aware of their legal rights and knew how to exercise them to their advantage. Both Thovar and Arboleda understood that they had a legal right to protest and that such protest was worthwhile. Arboleda chose to petition against his unfair treatment and exploitation at the hands of Thovar; Thovar, meanwhile, fought against excessive penalties assessed by a Spanish colonial official. As this case makes clear, even in a frontier zone, negros libres possessed the knowledge and the acuity to assert their legal rights and stand up to colonial officials who abused their power.

In the Spanish colonial Americas, there are many examples of enslaved and free Blacks who exercised their legal rights. The royal slaves of El Cobre (in today's Cuba) litigated, protested, and filed complaints with the aim of receiving better treatment, claiming land, outing abusers, and seeking avenues of freedom for their community. As María Elena Díaz has shown, royal slaves traveled to regional as well as high courts in Santo Domingo and Madrid.[82] In viceregal centers like Mexico City, Lima, and Trujillo, slaves who filed suits in royal courts exercised their legal rights, but additionally, as Bianca Premo has argued, helped shape Spanish law on slavery.[83] Michelle McKinley has examined the ways that enslaved women in seventeenth-century Lima successfully leveraged the Spanish legal system to secure their freedom, keep their families intact, negotiate lower self-purchase prices, and arrange transfers of ownership.[84] Differing from McKinley's cases—where enslaved litigants resided in cosmopolitan centers in the households of viceregal and ecclesiastical administrators, curates, judges, and magistrates—free Blacks in the Chocó lived in isolated hamlets in a peripheral area of a fringe viceroyalty.[85]

Thovar's case is also important because it sheds light on the economic prospects for negros libres in the Chocó during the second half of the eighteenth century. Through court testimony, we learn that Thovar actively participated in several local economies.[86] In addition to his mines at Taparal, Thovar also had a canoe transport business.[87] While he charged for the trip itself (from departure point to destination), he also imposed an extra fee for each additional passenger. Arboleda, in his testimony, noted that a trip charge should have been sufficient, but because people in the area had limited means of mobility, Thovar found that he could bring in extra money by charging for extra travelers. According to Arboleda, Thovar's canoe business had enabled Thovar to acquire everything that he owned.[88]

In addition to his mines and his canoe business, Thovar also profited from lending money. In the case file we learn that Thovar had lent fifty pesos to Arboleda, a negro moving from enslaved to free status. These same documents reveal that Thovar loaned money to others, as well. One of his clients was Miguel Asprilla, a miner. Asprilla, because he is never described as a negro or a negro libre, was most likely a *blanco*, perhaps a Spaniard.[89] Besides profiting from high rates of interest, Thovar also leveraged his debtors' collateral. As part of his loan to Asprilla, Thovar took as collateral one of Asprilla's enslaved laborers.[90] In the case of Arboleda—who had no possessions when he borrowed from Thovar—it was Arboleda himself who became collateral. The vivid details of this case reveal that Diego de Thovar was economically enterprising as well as legally astute.

Other aspects of this case shed light on the complexities of linguistic and cultural assimilation for native Africans living in a remote periphery of the Spanish empire in the second half of the eighteenth century. In the documents, Thovar is frequently referred to as a *negro bozal*. In addition to signifying a person who had been born in Africa, captured, sold into slavery, and brought to the Americas, the term *bozal* also implied an individual who retained aspects of his or her native culture, including language. If we can lend any credence to the ethnic notation of "Ibo" recorded next to Thovar's name in the 1755 mining census, it may be that Thovar had come from the Bight of Biafra (today, Bight of Bonny), and spoke a Niger-Congo language.[91]

Documents in the case file from 1756–1757 reveal that Thovar had successfully charted his way through Spanish colonial society. Apart from acquiring his freedom, he had identified profitable quebradas at Taparal and registered his rights to mine them.[92] Before that, he had made enough money to purchase enslaved laborers of his own. In addition to gold mining, Thovar had identified other niche markets including canoe transport and money lending which brought in additional revenue. He also successfully navigated the complex Spanish legal system. All these triumphs are noteworthy for a native African but become all the more striking when we learn that Thovar had a minimal command of the Spanish language, both spoken and written.

Francisco Martínez, the then governor of Chocó, had expressed concern that Thovar, when presented with the final court ruling (which sided in Thovar's favor), might not comprehend it.[93] As it happened, Santiago del Castillo, who presented the court's decision to Thovar, confirmed Martínez's concerns. Castillo noted that, despite the great lengths Castillo had gone to—reading and re-reading the court documents to Thovar—Thovar was unable to understand any part of the decree (*decreto*). Castillo did not attribute this lack of understanding to Thovar's advanced age, nor to failing faculties such as sight or hearing, but to Castillo's belief that Thovar was "*demasiadamente bozal*," or too African, implying he had not learned

Spanish or assimilated to Spanish culture. Castillo added that, while Thovar had had a hard time understanding Castillo, Castillo had had an equally hard time understanding Thovar.[94] Later, when Castillo again presented the ruling to Thovar, Thovar's son, Raymundo, was with him. Raymundo read the written notice aloud to the older Thovar, enabling him to understand its contents.[95]

This seemingly small detail has several interesting implications. While it is possible that Thovar did not want to deal with the authorities and so pretended not to understand, the decree favored Thovar. This narrative suggests that a person of African origin could—at least in the more remote Pacific Lowlands—pursue a path to freedom, establish multiple businesses, and effectively operate in Spanish colonial society *without* speaking Spanish. This, in turn, indicates that much of Thovar's day-to-day verbal communication transpired in his native tongue. If so, this implies that Thovar engaged with others who did the same, participating in daily transactions communicated in a language other than Spanish. Thovar's son, Raymundo (who was likely born in the Americas), appears to have had a much stronger command of Spanish, as indicated by a letter he wrote which is preserved in the case file. Raymundo's letter and signature, while of a rustic calligraphic style and orthography, demonstrates that he was literate.[96]

From this example, we have evidence that some Africans and their descendants living in the Chocó during the second half of the eighteenth century acquired their freedom and established themselves in the local mining economy. They identified market needs and created businesses that met market demands. They exercised their legal rights, securing strong representation, challenging damaging accusations, and safeguarding their livelihoods. Furthermore, some of these Africans, like Diego de Thovar, appear to have navigated their way through Spanish colonial society without having or needing proficiency in the *lingua franca* of the Spanish empire.[97]

Negros Libres as Vecinos

In addition to establishing that negros libres in the Chocó participated in Spanish colonial society as owners of mines and cuadrillas, archival documents indicate that negros libres residing in New Granada's frontier zones could also become vecinos. Miguel de Velasco—a free Black discussed earlier in this chapter—acquired this status. In 1744, when registering the mines of San Isidro, Miguel de Velasco was noted as a negro libre and a vecino.[98] In 1766, documents which discuss his mines at Quiparadó also note Velasco as a negro libre and a vecino.[99]

The term vecino denoted a person who was a long-term resident, the head of a household, or a property-owning, permanent resident.[100] Becoming a vecino, or obtaining *vecindad* (subjecthood, citizenship) additionally indicated local belonging. As Tamar Herzog has argued, "vecino" denoted the rights—the privileges as well as the duties—of citizens. To be a vecino was to be identified as a member of the community but, specifically, a "civilized" member.[101] Hugues Sánchez Mejía has written that, for New Granada, becoming a vecino meant accepting Catholicism. Vecindad also granted a person access to communal lands.[102] In sum, becoming a vecino—especially for someone of African ancestry—was a hard-earned privilege that came with economic, moral, and political expectations and dimensions.[103]

Scholarship undertaken in the past few decades has demonstrated that free Blacks throughout the Spanish colonial Americas earned this distinguished place in society. Alejandro de la Fuente has shown that some of the free Blacks in late sixteenth century Havana, working in the service, commercial, agricultural, and maritime industries, were described as vecinos.[104] Karen Graubart has identified free-Black female vecinas in late sixteenth to mid-seventeenth century Lima who owned property and enslaved people.[105] Meanwhile, Chloe Ireton has found evidence for first generation African and free-Black vecinos in Veracruz, Santo Domingo, Portobelo, and Veraguas. In exceptional cases, free Blacks came to be vecinos in not just one but several places.[106] These cited cases stem from large urban ports and coastal cities. That free Blacks living in a tropical, riparian, mining frontier could also become vecinos adds to our body of knowledge about Africans and autonomy in the Spanish Americas.[107]

Conclusions

It seems fitting to end where we began, with the forty-eight negros libres at San Agustín documented in the 1759 mining census (figure 8). Within this group, we find Diego de Thovar and his wife, their son Raymundo and his spouse, and another son, Santiago, and his wife. There are seven additional Thovar family members documented at San Agustín at this time.[108] In total, the Thovars comprised over one-fourth of this sizeable mining enclave. Meanwhile, one man and his wife had the surname Caycedo and three members shared the last name Velasco.[109] It is not clear if these Caycedos were related to Susana, Agustín, and Narciso or if these Velascos were relations of Miguel and Gerónima. If they were, it suggests that familial dynasties of negros libres lived and worked in each other's orbit, probably for generations. Given the proximity of mines along the Atrato established by families of negros libres, it seems likely that Miguel and Gerónima would have known Susana Caycedo. They may have heard about the seemingly infamous Diego de Thovar. The extended familial groups who engaged in mining at San Agustín do not end here, however. Seven people at San Agustín had the last name Moreno and six people had the last name Vivero, indicating other extended family groups of negros libres working at this site.

From these cases, we learn that negros and negras libres living in the Chocó in the second half of the eighteenth century followed in the footsteps of Spanish enslavers, becoming dueños de minas y esclavos (owners of mines and enslaved), entrepreneurs, and even vecinos (residents or citizens). As important actors in the local economy, they identified niche markets and diversified their assets. They also navigated the complex Spanish legal system, exercising their rights and protecting their livelihoods. With other negros libres, they created communities that functioned within, yet remained somewhat apart from, Spanish colonial society.

Notes

I am grateful to Kris Lane, Max Deardorff, and Spencer Abruzzese for their careful reading of this chapter and for their valuable suggestions for edits and connections to other scholarship. Yurany Perdomo Forero guided me through stickier parts of the Diego de Thovar case file and Alex Borucki kindly advised me on aspects of the slave trade. Mauricio Tovar at the Archivo General de la Nación in Bogotá provided me with copies of important maps and documents and Alison Fraser, Jessica Hollister, and Jim Maynard at SUNY Buffalo's Poetry Collection graciously facilitated a visit to see the map and manuscript vital to this essay. I thank Diógenes Patiño for our rich conversations about Africans in Spanish colonial Popayán and Jay Harrison and Cameron Jones for providing the opportunity to explore new material for this volume. A National Endowment for the Humanities Fellowship (2020–2021) funded the research and writing of this chapter.

1. The undated and anonymous map and descripción are housed today in the Gran Colombia collection at SUNY Buffalo's Poetry Collection.

2. The term *negros libres* refers to people who had been formerly enslaved and had acquired their freedom as well as to those born with free status.

3. These include archived mining censuses, court cases, official reports, and historical maps, many of which have been digitized. See consulta.archivogeneral.co.gov/Consultaweb.

4. Principle regions in New Granada included the Caribbean (Cartagena, Mompox), the Eastern Cordillera (Bogotá, Tunja), and the Southern provinces (Popayan, Caloto, Cali, Buga, Anserma, Pasto, and parts of the Pacific Lowlands). By 1740, Chocó was an independent mining province. McFarlane, *Colombia before Independence*, 61.

5. McFarlane, *Colombia before Independence*, 28.

6. Fears that New Granada's riches would end up in the hands of foreigners fueled the decision to reinstate New Granada as a viceroyalty. See McFarlane, *Colombia before Independence*, 192, 194–95.

7. West, *Colonial Placer Mining*, 112.

8. Jaramillo Uribe, "La economía del virreinato," 49; Barona, "Problemas de la historia económica," 65; and Kris Lane, "In the Shadow of Silver." For extractive economies in the Pacific Lowlands, see Leal, *Landscapes of Freedom*, 11 and chap. 2; and Tubb, *Shifting Livelihoods*.

9. Williams, *Between Resistance and Adaptation*, 17; see also West, *Colonial Placer Mining*, 1. Key agricultural products included tobacco, sugar, wheat, and cacao. See McFarlane, *Colombia before Independence*, chap. 2. For more on these economies in Medellín, see Twinam, *Miners, Merchants, and Farmers*.

10. Jaramillo Uribe, "La economía del virreinato," 49, 51.

11. Many of the Chocó's white mine owners lived outside the Chocó, in Cali, Buga, Popayán, or even Santa Fé; see Boyd-Bowman and Sharp, *Description of the Province of Zitará*, 17.

12. Autonomy and opportunity were possible within the context of place but were not necessarily transferrable to larger centers with more dominant white populations, greater oversight, or more restrictions. And despite greater freedom in parts of the Pacific Lowlands, numerous cases attest to the deplorable treatment of enslaved Africans. The Barbacoas mines of Casimiro Cortés drove enslaved laborers to infanticide to escape the horrors of slavery. See Romero, "Sociedades negras"; and Herrera Ángel, "En un rincón de ese imperio." See also Echeverri, "Enraged to the Limit." The tragic case of the foiled palenque of Cartago provides another example; see Pablo Rodríguez, "La efímera utopía." In addition to physical abuse, enslaved Africans endured malnourishment, disease, snake bites, drowning, depression, and separation from family members.

13. See Herrera Ángel, "Las divisiones político-administrativas," 80, table 1. Barona et al., *Geografía física y política*, 55, 105. See also Cantor, *Ni aniquilados ni vencidos*; Sharp, *Slavery on the Spanish Frontier*; West, *Colonial Placer Mining*; and Williams, *Between Resistance and Adaptation*.

14. See Sharp, *Slavery on the Spanish Frontier*, 13ff., 9.

15. Barona et al., *Geografía física y política*, 55.

16. Anonymous, "Compendiosa noticia," 452.

17. See Sharp, "The Profitability of Slavery," 469–70.

18. Sharp, *Slavery on the Spanish Frontier*, 13.

19. *"el Chocó . . . de donde se saca [el oro] no por arrobas sino a cargas."* Colmenares, *Relaciones e informes de los gobernantes*, 1:28.

20. Sharp, *Slavery on the Spanish Frontier*, 46–49, 133.

21. See chart in Jaramillo Uribe, "La economía del virreinato," 51.

22. Today, Afro-Colombians make up 82 percent of the Chocó's population. DANE, *Colombia. Una nación multicultural*, 38.

23. Indigenous, meanwhile, represented 37 percent and Spaniards and Europeans only 2 percent. Tovar Pinzón et al., *Convocatoria*, 353–57; and McFarlane, *Colombia before Independence*, appendix A, table 8, 362.

24. Sharp, *Slavery on the Spanish Frontier*, 142.

25. See Borucki et al., *"Atlantic History and the Slave Trade";* and Lovejoy, "The Impact of the Atlantic Slave Trade."

26. For the earlier trade (1570–1640), see Wheat, "First Great Waves," 12; del Castillo Mathieu, *Esclavos negros en Cartagena*,160–61; and Colmenares, *Historia económica y social*, chap. 2.

27. McFarlane, *Colombia before Independence*, 74–77; Sharp, *Slavery on the Spanish Frontier*, 111; and West, *Colonial Placer Mining*, 78.

28. Ethnonyms in archival records from New Granada were assigned by Europeans and reflect

only a vague notion of an African's ethnicity or place of origin. See Colmenares, *Historia económica y social*, 21–22; see also DeCorse, "Oceans Apart: Africanist Perspectives," 135–36; Lovejoy, "The Impact of the Atlantic Slave Trade," 378; and Lohse, "Slave-Trade Nomenclature," 74.

29. See Colmenares, *Historia económica y social*, 21–30, chart 25. Colmenares refers to caste designation, or ethnonym, as a hypothetical ethnic origin, 21.

30. Jiménez Meneses, *El Chocó. Un paraíso del demonio*, 30–31.

31. Sharp, *Slavery on the Spanish Frontier*, 142; and Lane and Romero, "Miners and Maroons," 35. Colombia's Pacific Lowlands stands out for being one of few places in the Americas where self-purchase accounted for the largest percentage of manumissions. See Leal, *Landscapes of Freedom*, 45; as well as manumission records in the Archivo Central de Cauca, Cali.

32. Jiménez Meneses, *El Chocó. Un paraíso del demonio*, 35.

33. See Lane and Romero, "Miners and Maroons," 35; and Meiklejohn, "The Observance of Negro Slave Legislation," 197–207.

34. For palenques, see Navarrete, "Palenques: Maroons and Castas," 269–96; and *San Basilio de Palenque*. See also Lane and Romero, "Miners and Maroons," 32–37.

35. Sharp, "El negro en Colombia," 91; see also Barragan, "Free Black Women," 61.

36. AGN Negros y Esclavos , 43 4 D 38 (1759), fol. 570r. The larger document is broken down by mine, fols. 558r–590r.

37. For African autonomy and community formation in the Dagua River region, see Lane and Romero, "Miners and Maroons," 32–37; and Wiersema, "Importing Ethnicity, Creating Culture," 267–90; and "The Manuscript Map of the Dagua River."

38. Moreno and Caycedo were surnames of wealthy and influential Spanish families. Sharp, *Slavery on the Spanish Frontier*, 115.

39. Two mulato men, Manuel de Zuniga and Joseph Antonio, were noted as *casado con negra*, or married to Black women. These women were not, however, counted in the census, indicating that they lived outside of San Agustín. AGN Negros y Esclavos Cauca, 43 4 D 38 (1759), fol. 570r.

40. Muñoz de Aronja, "Descripción del gobierno del Chocó," 467. Aronja's "Descripción" includes mines at San Agustín but does not mention the forty-eight libres at San Agustín, possibly because his report predates their appearance there.

41. Muñoz de Aronja, "Descripción del gobierno del Chocó," 469.

42. Anonymous, "Descripción superficial," 432.

43. Williams, *Between Resistance and Adaptation*, 17.

44. Anonymous, "Descripción superficial," 432.

45. See discussion in Boyd-Bowman and Sharp, *Description of the Province of Zitará*, 10–16.

46. All 138 sites presented on the map are annotated in an associated report, the "Descripción de la provincia del Zitará y el curso del río de Atrato" held at SUNY Buffalo's Poetry Collections.

47. This map, first published in José Manuel Arrubla, "Descripción de la provincia del Zitará," is also held in SUNY Buffalo's Poetry Collections. A copy of the map published by Arrubla has been digitized by the AGN, MP 5, Ref. 316B. http://consulta.archivogeneral.gov.co/ConsultaWeb/imagenes.jsp?id=3255866&idNodoImagen=3255867&total=1&ini=1&fin=1.

48. Boyd-Bowman and Sharp, *Description of the Province of Zitará*, 48. A slightly different version of the same descripción was transcribed and published by Antonio B. Cuervo; see Anonymous, "Descripcion de la provincia de Zitará," 306–24.

49. Boyd-Bowman and Sharp, *Description of the Province of Zitará*, 48. Miguel and Gerónima are established as brother and sister in AGN Minas Cauca 38 5 D 2 (1766), fol. 108r. A *real de minas*, or large mine, was any mine with ten or more enslaved laborers.

50. Boyd-Bowman and Sharp, *Description of the Province of Zitará*, 47.

51. Boyd-Bowman and Sharp, *Description of the Province of Zitará*, 49-50.

52. Garrido, "'Free Men of all Colors,'" 168–69.

53. AGN Minas Cauca 38 5 D 13 (1744), fol. 740r. Miguel de Velasco y Solimán is noted in archival records as Miguel Solimán, AGN Negros y Esclavos Cauca, 43 4 D 38 (1759), fol. 585r; Miguel de Velasco y Solimán and Miguel Velalcázar y Solimán, AGN Minas Cauca 38 5 D 13 (1744), fols. 740r–740v; Miguel de Velasco, alias "Solimán." Anonymous, "Descripción superficial," 432; and Miguel Velasco in Boyd-Bowman and Sharp, *Description of the Province of Zitará*, 48.

54. AGN Negros y Esclavos Cauca, 43 2 D 20 (1755), fol. 963r. See also Muñoz de Aronja, "Descripción del gobierno del Chocó," 469.

55. That the quebrada was given to Miguel because it was unproductive is my assumption.

56. AGN Negros y Esclavos Cauca, 43 4 D 38 (1759), fol. 585r. See also Anonymous, "Descripción superficial," 432, where Miguel de Velasco, alias "Solimán," is noted as mining near Negua and Ycho with fourteen to sixteen slaves.

57. AGN Minas Cauca 38 5 D 2 (12 April 1766), fol. 109r.

58. AGN Minas Cauca 38 5 D 2 (12 April 1766), fols. 109r–109v.

59. Boyd-Bowman and Sharp, *Description of the Province of Zitará*, 48.

60. AGN Visitas Cauca 62 5 D 3 (1784), fols. 371r–371v. "*Pablo Escobar, esclavo de Gerónima Velasco.*" During this same *visita*, at the mines of San Joséf de Memerado (?), two of Susana Caycedo's enslaved workers, Pedro Palomeque and Juan Joséf, testified that they received Saturdays to work for themselves, were taught Christian doctrine, and were not rigorously punished. AGN Visitas Cauca 62 5 D 3 (1784), fols. 369v–371r.

61. See Anonymous, "Descripción superficial," 432.

62. Salt was an invaluable commodity for curing meats in this tropical climate.

63. Boyd-Bowman and Sharp, *Description of the Province of Zitará*. Some of this information appears to be pulled from *visitas* and other official documents but some of it seems to reflect actual reconnaissance; see also Cantor, "Extracción de oro," 67–96.

64. Both the Atrato and San Juan Rivers were closed to traffic and commerce for much of the eighteenth century. Sharp, *Slavery on the Spanish Frontier*, 9–10.

65. Boyd-Bowman and Sharp, *Description of the Province of Zitará*, 49.

66. Anonymous, "Descripción superficial," 432. Not far from the free-Black Caycedo family mines were the mines of Doña Maria Clemencia Caycedo (no. 40). While I have not found evidence to suggest that negros libres with the Caycedo surname were former slaves of Maria Clemencia, it was not uncommon for enslaved people, once freed, to take the surname of their former enslaver. Sharp, *Slavery on the Spanish Frontier*, 115.

67. See Barragan, "Gendering Mastery," 1–26. Archival documents from the eighteenth-century record names female enslavers with mining operations in the Chocó; see for example, AGN Negros y Esclavos Cauca 43 4 D 38 (1759), fols. 567r–567v and 584v–585r.

68. Graubart, "Lazos que unen," 637.

69. Wheat, *Atlantic Africa*, 156.

70. Díaz, *The Virgin, the King*, 179.

71. AGN Negros y Esclavos Cauca, 43 2 D 20 (1755), fol. 963r. *"Diego Ibo de Thovar, negro libre en rico minas del Taparal, tres negros, y una negra."* If "Ibo" is an ethnonym referring to Igbo, Ebo, Eboe, or Heboe, it suggests that Thovar had ties to this ethnic group, which, in the Spanish colonial period, corresponded to the Bight of Biafra. For the complexities of Igbo and the Transatlantic Slave Trade, see Chambers, "'My Own Nation': Igbo Exiles in the Diaspora," 72–97; and Northrup, "Igbo and Myth Igbo." Diego de Thovar is briefly mentioned in Jiménez, *El Chocó*, 34–35.

72. For the case file, see AGN Minas Cauca 38 2 D 23 (1756–1758), fols. 467r–504v. Thovar is mentioned briefly, but not named, by Sharp who references this court case, *Slavery on the Spanish Frontier*, 150–51.

73. AGN Minas Cauca 38 2 D 23 (1756–1758), fols. 471r, 473r, 497r. *Bozales*, or native-born Africans, were brought to the Chocó in the late seventeenth and early eighteenth century and comprised large portions of slave inventories until the mid-eighteenth century. Sharp, *Slavery on the Spanish Frontier*, 111–19.

74. See Wheat, *Atlantic Africa*, 216.

75. The term *criollo* is also used to describe *negros* born in Spain, Portugal, and Cape Verde.

76. One is referred to as *"negro Antonio Carabali,"* another *"negro Pedro,"* and a third *"Joseph Mandinga."* AGN Minas Cauca 38 2 D 23 (20 September 1757), fols. 502r–502v. Carabali and Mandinga are ethnonyms, or approximate geographic designations.

77. For a list of items seized in Taparal, see AGN Minas Cauca 38 2 D 23 (16 July 1756), fols. 485v.

78. *"sujetarlo en mayor cautiverio y esclavitud que la que tenía antes de su rescate."* AGN Minas Cauca 38 2 D 23, fol. 489v.

79. AGN Minas Cauca 38 2 D 23, fol. 489v.

80. AGN Minas Cauca 38 2 D 23, fols. 473r–473v.

81. AGN Minas Cauca 38 2 D 23, fols. 487v; 502r–504r.

82. Díaz, *The Virgin, the King*, 15.

83. See Premo, *The Enlightenment on Trial*, 191.

84. McKinley, *Fractional Freedoms*.

85. While free Blacks in the Chocó had greater legal protections than enslaved Blacks, relatively few free people appear to have exercised these rights. Sharp, *Slavery on the Spanish Frontier*, 150. For legal and other strategies employed by enslaved in Barbacoas, see Echeverri, "Enraged to the Limit."

86. For free Blacks as central actors in Spanish American economies, see also Wheat, *Atlantic Africa*; Ireton, "They Are Blacks," 579–612; Graubart, "Lazos que unen," 625–40; and de la Fuente, *Havana and the Atlantic*.

87. Canoe navigation in New Granada was a highly valued skill. Evaluations in mining inventories reveal that the assessed value for a *boga* or *canoero* could be equal to or higher than that of a cuadrilla captain; see ACC Sig. 11347 (1764), fols. 4r–5v.

88. AGN Minas Cauca 38 2 D 23, fol. 490r.

89. AGN Minas Cauca 38 2 D 23, fol. 486r.

90. AGN Minas Cauca 38 2 D 23, fols. 486r–486v.

91. AGN Negros y Esclavos Cauca, 43 2 D 20 (1755), fol. 963r, "Diego Ibo de Thovar." Wheat has cautioned that Africans of the same ethnic background sometimes spoke different languages and, in some cases, could not readily comprehend one another; *Atlantic Africa*, 236.

92. It is not clear when or how Thovar acquired his freedom. Given his enterprising nature and business acumen, it seems likely that he purchased it rather than having it granted by an *amo*, or enslaver.

93. The reason Martínez gave was "*por su ninguna capacidad*," (inability to understand), referring to Thovar's limited understanding of Spanish. AGN Minas Cauca 38 2 D 23 (14 September 1757), fol. 503v.

94. AGN Minas Cauca 38 2 D 23 (September 1757), fol. 497v, "*aunque muchas veces le leí el dicho decreto, y trabajé mucho sobre dárselo al entender en mi inteligencia, no entendió el dicho negro Diego libre cosa alguna de las que por dicho decreto se manda por su incapacidad a causa de ser demasiadamente bozal que lo es tanto en tanta manera que si él a mí no me entendió tampoco no le entendí yo cosa alguna de la que me dijo.*"

95. AGN Minas Cauca 38 2 D 23 (September 1756), fol. 503v. Castillo saw Raymudo as having "*alguna más capacidad por ser criollo.*" I thank Yurany Perdomo Forero for identifying the importance of this passage.

96. AGN Minas Cauca 38 2 D 23 (22 May 1757), fols. 500r–500v.

97. For preservation of native African customs in the archaeological record, see Patiño Castaño and Hernández, "Arqueología e historia de africanus," 125–62.

98. AGN Minas Cauca 38 5 D 13 (1744), fol. 740v. "*Miguel de Velalcázar y Solimán, negro libre, vecino de esta provincia [Zitará], y dueño de esclavos en ella.*" For cases of negros and pardos libres

noted in wills and testaments as vecinos, see Jiménez Meneses and Pérez Morales, *Voces de esclavitud y libertad*. It is not clear if *vecino* in sixteenth-century Havana conveyed the same meaning that it did in seventeenth-century Lima nor is it known if the designation of vecino in a will or last testament held the same weight that it did in a land deed. Chloe Ireton has emphasized the need to interrogate the meaning of vecino as well as the contexts of its use; see "They are Blacks," 608–9.

99. AGN Minas Cauca 38 5 D 2 (1766), fol. 108r, *"negro libre, vecino, dueños de minas y esclavos en esta provincia* [de Zitará]."

100. Wheat, *Atlantic Africa*, 146.

101. Herzog, *Defining Nations*, 6–7.

102. See Sánchez Mejía, "De arrochelados a vecinos," 459; and "De esclavos a campesinos," 137.

103. Flórez Bolívar et al., "Liberalismo, ciudadanía y vecindad," 173.

104. de la Fuente, *Havana and the Atlantic*, 175.

105. Graubart, "Lazos que unen," 630–31.

106. Ireton, "They are Blacks," 592–93, 596, 601–3.

107. In many parts of the Spanish Americas, slave owning and vecindad seem to have gone hand in hand. In the Chocó, where mining was the principal industry and economy, vecinos—both blancos and negros—demonstrated their worth and social position through slave ownership; Sharp, *Slavery on the Spanish Frontier*, 115.

108. Blas, his wife, and child; Manuel and his wife; and Julio and his wife. AGN Negros y Esclavos Cauca, 43 4 D 38 (1759), fol. 570r.

109. Bentura and Manuel Caycedo are listed, as are Juan Velasco, Joseph Antonio Velasco, and his wife. AGN Negros y Esclavos Cauca, 43 4 D 38 (1759), fol. 570r.

CHAPTER EIGHT

AFRICAN MAROONS AND NATIVE PEOPLES ON THE "ATLANTIC" BORDERLANDS OF COLONIAL QUITO

Charles Beatty-Medina

"Few Americans realize that the continental seacoast most rarely viewed and least known in every geographic aspect lies not at the antipodes but, rather, close at hand, and just beyond the threshold of one of the world's concentrated trade routes."[1]

"Some five hundred miles from Panama, on the Pacific Coast of South America, lies a region which may be considered a veritable paradise from the point of view of the beauty of its landscapes, the astonishing fertility of its soil, and its rich minerals. There flourished, in remote epochs, very advanced civilizations intimately related to those of Yucatan and Central America. Nevertheless the province of Esmeraldas is very little known. Although it is so short a distance from the Canal which unites the two oceans; although its coast was the first point of the vast Inca Empire to be trodden by the conquistadores; and although from that moment attention was attracted by the wealth of the country and reports of the famous emeralds to which this province owes its name, it remains to the present time one of the least familiar sections of the Republic of Ecuador."[2]

DESPITE ITS proximity to the bustling isthmus that links the world's largest oceans, the Pacific coast of South America from Darien, through Colombia, into northern Ecuador forms one of the more isolated frontiers of the Ibero-Atlantic world. Four centuries before renowned geographer Robert Cushman Murphy journeyed down the "littoral of Pacific Colombia and Ecuador," Pizarro's chroniclers described many of the peoples and the environments of this region in plainly uninviting terms.[3] As they repeatedly sailed out and returned to Panama across this six-hundred-mile coastland, inching their way toward Peru, the conquistadors invented place names like the "port of hunger" and the "devil's playground."[4] And indeed, they experienced years of deprivation, death, and suffering as they endured repeated attacks from the coast's native peoples. It was not only the human elements but nature itself aimed to exclude them from the region.

The reset to Pizarro's journey took place when he reached the coast of Esmeraldas. That magical name, like El Dorado, referred to the precious stones and Spanish dreams of riches that propelled them to subjugate native peoples.[5] Esmeraldas became a place of possibilities and myths. Admired at first landing in 1526, in the decades to follow the region became a transitory space with a geography that challenged Spanish explorations. Its northern reaches near the Ancón de Sardinas continued the dense and impenetrable vegetation found along the coast of Pacific Colombia. But the Esmeraldas River and the bays of San Mateo and Atacames marked a shift to a dryer seasonal littoral better suited to large settlements with interspersed natural bays where ships could easily set anchor. Esmeraldas logically became the first beachhead in the conquistadors enterprise to find the empire of Peru. Though quickly eclipsed by the discovery of the Inca heartland, Esmeraldas continued to lure conquistadors and colonizers all through the colonial period. After establishing an audiencia to govern from the highland city of Quito in 1563, crown authorities and *encomenderos* (conquistadors granted indigenous labor drafts and tribute) also saw Esmeraldas as essential to their prosperity. Less interested in potential mineral wealth, they wanted to establish a seaport to reduce the cost of importing goods to the highland capital that was served by the port of Guayaquil and an overland route that was slow, costly, and susceptible to seasonal rains. For a variety of reasons, however, repeated expeditions and plans throughout the colonial period failed to achieve that goal.

Instead, uncolonized Amerindians and African maroons, who had escaped enslavement, dominated the province and regulated its interactions with outsiders. In the wake of Spanish incursions, Africans planted roots in the region and carved out roles for themselves as agents of commerce, diplomacy, and salvage. Their exchanges with outsiders on the shoreline and beachheads became the borderland of trade and encounter. Although the coast faced the "South Sea" or Pacific Ocean, their activities formed part of the Atlantic economy. As Alison Games points out, "Places and people on the Pacific coast of the Americas were engaged in processes originating from the Atlantic, regardless of their actual geographic location."[6] Coastal Esmeraldas, as such, came to form an "Atlantic borderland" where African and native peoples regulated the flow of goods and people in the area.

Like several essays in this volume, this chapter centers on the intersections where Spaniards, African maroons, and Amerindians came into contact, as also explored in Mark Lentz's study of late colonial Guatemala. Temporally, however, the world of Esmeraldas was closely associated with regions like sixteenth-century Panama described by Robert Schwaller. Additionally, Juliet Wiersema's chapter on eighteenth-century Chocó links geographically to northern Ecuador. Indeed, Colombia's Pacific coast mining camps have been cited as the source for eighteenth-century African arrivals to Esmeraldas. Finally, the local geographies of marronage plays a key role in these chapters. As demonstrated by Rachel O'Toole, fugitivity marked specific places on the colonial landscape.

Through an examination of the northern Ecuadorian coastland, within the context of Amerindian autonomy and African marronage, this chapter argues that Atlantic borderland history provides unique insights into the role of coastlines for autonomous groups and imperial motivations to utilize and pacify them. First, I examine how coastlines played a distinct role in the contest for territorial and maritime control. Then I explore how colonizers, pirates, Amerindians, and maroons utilized specific geographic and geopolitical knowledge to further their aims of dominance, survival, and continuity in the early Atlantic borderlands. For Europeans, coastal lands were essential transit points as well as places associated with colonial material desires. For semi-sedentary Amerindians and African maroons, the coastal borderland became a buffer zone for trade, communication, and diplomacy in their interactions with the outside world. While popular impressions often highlight the self-secluding features of maroons and often view them as relatively free of outside influence, this essay argues that the opposite is truer to the lived reality of life on the coastal Atlantic borderland. It reveals that these societies aimed to integrate to the broader Atlantic world on terms of their own making and underwent significant change over time. They adapted to the commercial and political surroundings of the day with the coast providing an essential space for communication and interaction. In utilizing these zones, the Atlantic borderlands people formed a unique interface between local and global cultures, peoples, and economies.

Constructing the Early Modern Atlantic Borderland

While the coastline may be considered the originating point of all Atlantic activities— the first place of departure, arrival, encounter, and exchange—it is often overlooked in the larger movement of people and goods that formed the Atlantic world. Additionally, as activities came to include regions linked to other oceanic realms, sensu stricto, regions of America's Pacific coast largely networked into Atlantic economies. Nonetheless, the activities that occupied coastlines, ports, and harbors typically capture historical attention only briefly, and mainly insofar as they facilitated the movement of goods and people from mining centers, trading camps, and plantations.[7] Aside from the penchant for raising flags, naming lands, and capturing local Amerindians, the shoreline is often a space foreshadowing the success or failure of subjugation and ignored as a key location of ongoing interactions.[8] Charters and landmarks set them up spatially, but their temporal isolation implies an evanescent moment of ceremony servicing the larger aim of territorial conquest. This chapter explores how the coastline acted as a location of repeated encounters with long-term implications, less an entryway or point of encounter and more a place of changing relations among people occupying the divide between land and sea.

To date, the concept of *Atlantic borderlands* has been applied mostly to locations where Europeans competed for dominance. Examples of American Atlantic borderland histories include Nathanial Millet's examination of the movement of peoples and competition in North America between British and Spanish colonies.[9] In conceptualizing Atlantic borderland history, Millet traces its origins to Eugene Bolton's work with a specific context in North American history and its later application to Africa, Asia, and the Middle East. He considers how the growth of Atlantic history, like borderlands, has accelerated since the 1960s and provided a space to integrate voices of people often marginalized in national histories geared toward Western expansionism. Millet goes on to define Atlantic borderlands as "real places in which powerful global forces intersected with exceptional local conditions to create societies that displayed distinct power dynamics, economies, and cultures."[10]

Similar influences appear in Nicholas Rogers's work on the eighteenth-century Miskito coast of Central America where the coastline was subject to British interventions and utilization of local native communities in their rivalry with Spanish authorities. Like several circum-Caribbean peoples, the Miskito maintained long-running relationships with buccaneers and sea rovers. They traded and supplied provisions while intermixing with runaway Africans. Furthermore, the Miskito engaged in raiding and tribute extraction from native groups along the Central American coast. More formal relationships with the English followed as Miskito were converted to "ethnic soldiers" and transported to Jamaica to track and capture maroons. This complex system of Atlantic integration subsided in the mid-nineteenth century, allowing for a reimagined Miskito vision as "gentle savages" of the littoral.[11]

The Miskito coast shares some aspects with Esmeraldas though it preceded them by a century. The Afro-indigenous communities of the region interacted with freebooters, smugglers, and commercial traders but also with Spanish administrators and soldiers, thus eschewing the open animosity claimed by the Miskito. However, Esmeraldas, like Nicaragua, constituted a borderland to the sea where maroon presence added a competitive dimension to the outcome of incursions and plans for permanent Spanish settlements. It is important that the oceanic spheres intermingled on South America's western coast as the Manilla Galleons and voyages of circum-navigation flowed east to west and back again. But the core of movement remained Atlantic centered. Though situated on the Pacific side of Spanish America, Atlantic trade patterns and processes of colonization played the most significant role in Esmeraldas's post-contact transformations. As with the Miskito, competition on the Esmeraldas coast was a dynamic involving international rivalries with a prominent focus on maroon-Amerindian relations and African-Spanish interactions alongside regional intercommunity conflicts.

In a hemispheric sense, these locations (Spanish Florida, Miskito Coast, and Esmeraldas) constituted the frontiers of imperial core regions.[12] The circum-Caribbean, especially the Mesoamerican parts of North and Central America and the Inca Empire, comprised the areas most explored and colonized by Europeans in the sixteenth and seventeenth centuries. Regions like Esmeraldas became "near-frontiers" that felt the wake force of intense colonizing efforts (often based on strategic concerns) but remained on the periphery of hubs that formed key administrative and judicial centers. Intensely "undercolonized," these areas were on the front line of developing imperial objectives and goals but remained the backwaters of colonial geography. Unlike the peripheral frontiers, Spaniards made repeated incursions into these zones but often failed to establish authority or populate their own settlements.[13] Many coastlands throughout the Americas fit this description. One key difference to inland borderlands was that the sea, the other side of the border, played a significant part in their development.

While territorial competition formed one half of Atlantic borderland conflicts, the other half, rivalry for the ocean, was no less impressive or antagonistic. As the Iberian empires expanded into Africa, the Americas, and Asia, control of the sea was deemed to be as essential as ruling over land and people.[14] However, while land territories could be occupied, there was no effective way to prohibit the use of the oceans to any country or person. Additionally, territorial claims had a strong basis in European law, but staking ownership of the open sea did not. Nonetheless, Iberian powers asserted their rights to the seas through acts of discovery, mapping, and papal authority. Though dissimilar to land masses that European Atlantic powers could claim possession over, treaties (based on papal bulls) such as Tordesillas (1494) and the Treaty of Zaragoza (1529) drew lines dissecting the globe along meridians that ran through the oceans (see figure 11). Scholars have argued over the meaning of these rights. Philip Steinburg stresses that such treaties were meant to indicate spheres of operation and stewardship rather than possession in the sense of *dominion*. Nonetheless certain provisions, like Portuguese claims to fishing rights off the coast of Africa, demonstrated a desire to retain their privileges over specific ocean resources and areas of open sea.[15] Passages abutting land, like the Straights of Magellan, were among the most contentious. In many cases these claims did spell out functional zones of operation for Portuguese and Spanish vessels. However, other European seaborn nations refused to recognize them. From the onset English, French, and Dutch vessels breached Iberian waters when and where possible in order to colonize, trade, and plunder American territories in the Caribbean Sea, Brazil, and on the Pacific coast.[16]

Although competition for land and attempts to wrest wealth away from Spanish ships occupied competing nations' vessels along the East and West Coasts of North and South America, far more activity occurred in the circum-Caribbean region. This was where the Spanish transported more wealth, and it was closer to the trunk lines connecting Europe, America, and Africa. Whether from having to sail around the horn of South America or swashbuckle across the Isthmian routes, the Pacific remained more remote and experienced far fewer outbreaks of international competition in colonial times.

Nonetheless, the forces of early modern maritime and territorial competition were linked in Esmeraldas. From the earliest Spanish engagements with native peoples to the transformative arrival of African maroons, the goings on along the coastline reverberated to the administrative centers locally and across the Atlantic. It brought together and encouraged the arrival of conquistadors, Africans, crown representatives, soldiers, sailors, missionaries, freebooters, smugglers, and traders.

FIGURE 11. Juan de la Cosas's map of 1500 showing the vertical line division of Tordesillas. Source: Wikicommons.

In 1524–1525, when Almagro and Pizarro's first expeditions reconnoitered the same coast traversed by Murphy in 1937, the region presented innumerable challenges and nearly halted Spanish advances into western South America. The Levant or eastern coast of the Pacific (from the perspective of Panama City) was viewed as nearly impenetrable for much of its distance. Described by Lockhart as "the treacherous coast," hundreds of miles of mangrove forest combined with very high rainfall and a plethora of wild life (including hordes of mosquitos) challenging Spanish presence in the area.[17] A few places, like Isla Gorgona (named after the Gorgon's hair to symbolize the many snakes that harried Pizarro and his men) and Isla de Gallo provided protection for extended, if torturous, stops along the way. While furnishing a haven from native attacks, the islands offered few resources and ultimately left the invaders bedraggled and infirm. The tropical vegetation and fauna proved physically and psychologically distressing and as many as 240 men died before these expeditions even reached the northern coast of modern-day Ecuador.[18]

The turning point in this drama of disaster came on Pizarro's second expedition in 1526 when pilot Bartolome Ruiz sailed further south to see if there were signs of larger settlements. Near the Cape of Pasao in Esmeraldas, Ruiz came upon a large raft, or *balsa*, laden with merchandise and he took six natives aboard his ship. The balsa, its contents, and Ruiz's captives (said to be from Tumbez) were critical to confirming Pizarro's hunch of larger populations and wealth further south.

Landing on the Esmeraldas coast, conquistador and early chronicler Francisco de Jerez described it as "buena tierra" even as the Spanish encountered thousands of warriors in large settlements near the shore. Regions north of the bay of San Mateo were said to be made up of *cienagas y anegadizos inhabitables* (uninhabitable swamps).[19] At San Mateo and points south the Spanish captured gold, silver, and clothing; spurring them on to the Andean peoples and immense treasures.[20] At the coastal town of Lacamez (Atacames), Jerez noted a population of 10,000 inhabitants. Recent archeology estimates a total precontact population between 13,000 and 19,000.[21] Additionally, the Esmeraldas coast provided the Spanish their first opportunity to land horses and rove the land. They immediately marched south, attacking native settlements at Coaque north of Manta and at the Island of Puná.

Following news of Pizarro's landing, Juan Ruiz de Arce left Nicaragua, arriving with fourteen horsemen at San Mateo Bay in 1532. At first, Ruiz followed the Esmeraldas River and invaded a hamlet with twenty houses. Inside he found baskets with bits of clothing, colored thread, and silver needles. Ruiz also stole some balled cotton that contained good-sized emeralds (*razonables*) and made off with enough corn to feed his horses and men. Returning to the coast, he described his elation at finding the hitching post erected by Pizarro's men to indicate the direction they were to follow. Ruiz continued south along the coast for four leagues (about fourteen miles) until they reached a swampland that contained many small fish and crocodiles so large that when they tried to kill some, their lances broke against their hides.[22] At their next stop, the village of Coaque (Quaqui) they rested for eight days. This location had gained notoriety as the first large settlement Pizarro pillaged where he claimed to have gained 18,000 castellanos in gold and "many emeralds."[23] Pedro de Alvarado would later land here in his quest to take part in the conquest and gain a share of Peruvian riches.

Once Pizarro reached Cajamarca, Spanish forces focused on subjugation of the Inca Empire, and Esmeraldas's role diminished as the conquistadors traversed the highlands searching out sources of population and ready wealth. For a few however, the mystique of hidden caches of gold and emeralds on Ecuador's coast continued to fire the imagination. The Italian traveler and chronicler Girolamo Benzoni, ever eager to criticize Spanish excesses, noted this and their repeated torture of the region's Amerindians: "The natives have many emeralds and they still hold the mines. However much the Spaniards have tormented them, and killed many, they still did not want to tell where they were."[24]

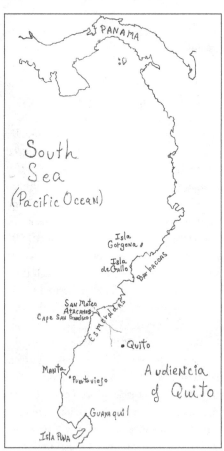

Benzoni also described a pattern that would come to typify the northern Ecuadorian coast. Jumping ship with twenty-three others near the Cape of San Francisco to search for food, Benzoni failed to encounter any native villages. Marching south to Cape Pasao, they "found that the Indians had burned their houses and had gone into the woods."[25] Thus, destruction and abandonment became a hallmark of the region throughout the sixteenth and seventeenth centuries, and it marked the coast as an uninhabited borderland: a neutralized territory still used for encounters but otherwise denuded of native populations.

The decades after 1540 witnessed numerous expeditions (*entradas*) to place settlements in Esmeraldas. But

FIGURE 12. Map of the Littoral from Panama to Guayaquil (map by the author).

attempts to populate the Bay of San Mateo and Atacames failed repeatedly. Many entradas looked only to pillage an easy windfall in gold and emeralds. *Capitanes* well-known to the area launched expeditions from the recently founded Spanish cities of Quito, Guayaquil, and Pasto. Some descended from the highlands, while others arrived by way of the coast. Several traversed a more northern route through the region of Barbacoas, others sailed up from Guayaquil, while another set of expeditions traveled from Quito attempting to arrive at San Mateo by way of the Esmeraldas River.[26]

Esmeraldas's weather and geography played a role in Spanish incapacity to inhabit the region. The contrast between interior and shoreland climates underpinned distinct settlement patterns. While the Bay of San Mateo typified a drier seasonal tropical zone also found at Atacames, rainfall levels and vegetation density increased as one moved to the interior of the littoral where pluvial forests created wetter year-round conditions. Equally, the depopulation of the coast described by Benzoni was more apparent further south along the dry tropical and evergreen lowland regions with moderate rainfall and better conditions for larger town life.

Although wetter interior regions were less adaptable to forming sizeable villages, they were well suited to the formation of smaller, elevated, dispersed hamlets that provided a sanctuary to Amerindians eager to steer clear of the Spanish invaders.[27] This proved to be ideal for defensive purposes as Amerindians and African maroons could conceal their villages and fields. In addition, the *monte* or hilly landscape mixed with thick vegetation, robust insect life, and wetter conditions discouraged Spanish soldiers from exploring and kept settlers away. Finally, knowledge of local topography was essential to navigate these densely forested lands. More than a few expeditionaries found themselves hopelessly lost as they crisscrossed the region, and many considered themselves lucky to have found an exit to the *selva* (jungle). Thus these regions were ideal for low density semisedentary native communities, and they accommodated new populations of African runaways after 1550.[28]

Arrival of African Maroons and Rekindling the Borderland Interface

From its inception the coastland played a meaningful role in promoting the escape of enslaved Africans. The same features that helped native communities evade Spanish subjugation aided Africans eager to cast off the yoke of servitude. By various accounts African maroons first landed in Esmeraldas after 1550 or so. Typically, they arrived because of shipwrecks and escaped their captors to the interior. The density of the local forests and mangroves enabled their escape when compared to regions further south that were flatter, drier, and more populated, making runaways more vulnerable to recapture.

Even so, perhaps no more than a few dozen Africans escaped enslavement and went on to intermix with the Amerindian population of Esmeraldas initially.

Though small in numbers, these intrepid individuals soon formed mixed-ethnic societies, and some gained notable positions of leadership. In addition, they became principal intermediaries with Spanish authorities. Reports of Spanish-maroon encounters date to the 1560s, but detailed accounts of their presence began to appear in the 1570s.

Salazar de Villasante, governor and judge for the Audiencia of Quito, described a shipwreck prior to 1570 near a point called Portete where "many blacks . . . escaped and could not be recaptured. They formed a village, took Indian women, and married them. And they multiplied and sometimes come to the coast where if they see Spaniards land to take water, they robbed and killed them. They also robbed the Indians."[29] These were not unusual descriptions of African maroons often portrayed as criminal, bloodthirsty, and a detriment to native communities. Other sources indicate a more complex set of interactions, admitting that the African maroons regularly rescued shipwrecked Spaniards and integrated themselves into preexisting Amerindian circuits of alliance and competition.

In 1577, Quito's royal authorities commissioned Miguel Cabello de Balboa, a priest and former soldier, to offer the maroons legitimacy and settle them in a mixed-race free township, to be named San Mateo, near the mouth of the Esmeraldas River. Cabello later sent a report of his expedition to the crown and followed it with a longer manuscript, the *Verdadera Descripción de la Provincia de Esmeraldas* (True Description of the Province of Esmeraldas). Both became key firsthand sources demonstrating the role of the coastland in Spanish-maroon interactions.

Cabello's mission, and the proposals he arrived with, indicate that just as the Africans were establishing themselves, Spanish administrators were moving to bring the region into closer contact with Quito. This period was marked by African cooperation and contestation as they intermingled and married into local native chieftaincies. They also became leading figures in warfare and raiding throughout the region. While the interior lands of Esmeraldas underwent political realignments and ethnic mixing, the coastline, still denuded of native populations, remained the site of Spanish incursions and periodic shipwrecks. Its borderland status developed as a result of regional geography and Amerindians' decision to move inland. Although Cabello's mission failed to permanently occupy San Mateo or Atacames, these locations and the Cape of San Francisco remained attractive stopping points to replenish stores and discharge passengers on the sometimes difficult journeys out of Panama.[30]

Examining interactions from 1577 and after provides a better understanding of how the coastal borderland could both serve and thwart the interests of maroons, Amerindians, Spanish traders, and local authorities. Significantly, the sources only allow us glimpses at specific times and places. Many interactions were never recorded in detail. But they hint at the types of exchanges that regularly occurred. To delve into these episodes is to piece together events based on partial or momentary views, filling in brushstrokes to better understand what may have been the habits of coastal relations and encounters.

Miguel Cabello Balboa, as the first diplomatic envoy to the region, provided insights to the maroon-Spanish dealings at the shoreline. A priest with a desire to subjugate the region, Cabello's skills identified him with both the cross and the sword. His expedition and subsequent writings provided a detailed record of the coastal borderland.

Commissioned by the Audiencia and the Bishop of Quito, Pedro de la Peña, Cabello was to offer the maroons and their followers a peace treaty and settle them at the Bay of San Mateo. Cabello left Quito with a small company at the end of July 1577 taking the quickest, but not the shortest, route. While Esmeraldas was closer, as the crow flies, to Quito, the only reliable way for Spaniards to make the journey was a long trudge to the city of Guayaquil and then sail up the coast, stopping at smaller settlement like Puerto Viejo, the northernmost town before embarking to Atacames, a known meeting place for the maroons. They landed six weeks after initial departure, on September 16. Abandoned and deserted, the silent seashore bore witness to the decimation of the once populated coast.

For the first twelve days of Cabello's stay they hardly saw a person. Toward the tenth day they caught sight of some natives "spying," although they soon disappeared. On the twelfth day, the maroon's leader, Alonso de Illescas, finally arrived. Like a scene from a novel, Cabello saw a canoe approach at a distance, driven by native oarsmen. As they advanced, he warned his companions to stay calm and go about their business. The long boat drew closer and Illescas exchanged words with one of its party, a man named Juan de Reyna. Once Illescas knew their purpose, he came ashore to embrace Cabello and the others. They read the orders of the Audiencia to the maroon leader, and he knelt below the papers, kissed them, and swore fealty to the crown. In just a matter of a few hours, the beach had been transformed into a diplomatic, religious, and performative space, where Spaniards and the maroons enacted their reconciliation.[31] After a ritual of prayer in a small set-up chapel and more conversation, the maroons and their allies left with a promise to return.

The Spanish waited uneasily for twelve days when a second, longer meeting took place. This time Illescas brought a host of Amerindian chieftains and the leaders of another maroon faction, the brothers Arobe (also called Mangaches), and fifty Amerindians in tow. It was at once a feast, a show of force, and a demonstration of Illescas's influence among the local villages. But more important, it gave Illescas an opportunity to utilize Cabello's authority to confirm his appointment as *gobernador* (governor) of the region. Before this crowd of native leaders and especially the brothers Arobes, Illescas tried to enhance his leadership by acknowledging Spanish legitimation. Notably, Illescas refused to bring Cabello to the maroons' settlement (although he asked repeatedly to visit), stating that the place was unhealthy. And more important, inland was Illescas's safe dominion, unlike the coastland, which was neutral territory where the parties could meet on more equal terms. The beach was thus a utile space suitable to an enactment of colonial authority. It could represent the initial point of Spanish subjugation, but also the limit of Spanish authority. The coastland belonged to no specific group and was accessible to all. However, it was the only space regularly claimed by Spanish colonizers and their location of choice for a settlement in the region.

Cabello spent the day in conversation with Illescas and conveyed how impressed he was by his knowledge, his confidence of speech, and his upbringing in Spain:

> It was as though he left only yesterday and he had good memories of strumming and playing songs on a guitar, the playing of swords and bucklers, and many other experiences. He can speak of and recount the great happenings of his times with a certitude that is admirable. In other things, he is so ladino as he affirms that he was born in a Spanish house in Cape Verde, and raised in Seville until he was twenty-five years of age.[32]

Illescas spent two nights there with the chieftains, maroons, and their followers. At their departure, Cabello once more described the trepidation and desolation felt by the Spaniards. This time Illescas allowed one of them, Juan de Caceres Patíno, to visit his village, or palenque, although it was well hidden in the hills.[33] Caceres described how they journeyed four leagues upriver, stowed their canoes, and then traveled on foot another six leagues. He described the terrain as *montaña* (wooded hill country). Here Illescas, his Portuguese lieutenant Gonzalo de Avila, and their followers each had agricultural plots, or *ranchos*. Caceres explored the locale during his six-day stay noting their fields of corn, yucca, and plantains.

Back at Atacames, an incident occurred during Caceres's absence when they discovered a ship anchored in the bay one morning. While it pleased Cabello and his companions, they did nothing, worried that the maroons might think this part of a plan to attack them. The next day Gonzalo de Avila arrived with Illescas's sons Henrique and Sebastian as well as two Amerindian chiefs and fourteen or fifteen of their followers. Avila waived a white cloth to the ship. The captain and crew came ashore. As it was late in the day, they agreed to meet the next morning. This time the sailors brought plenty to trade. The Esmeraldeños purchased provisions, odd goods, and wine. For payment, by Cabello's account, the maroons gave them more than seven hundred pesos in high quality gold.[34]

What they had witnessed was a not so well-kept secret on the coast. The maroons had gold to trade and profits could be made supplying their community. We don't know how often this occurred, but the familiarity of the encounter indicates that it was not infrequent. Like much commerce in colonial Peru, it was contraband, a common enough occurrence throughout the Spanish empire.[35] In this instance the ship was probably from Guayaquil.[36] To complicate matters even more Cabello met the ship's master, a "fulano Martinez," sometime later in Lima and was told of how one of the crew, a Portuguese and friend of Gonzalo de Avila delivered a letter written by an unnamed person living among them, to a Mateo de Párraga, who resided in Puerto Viejo. The letter invited Párraga and his wife, said to be like family (*parientes*) to Avila, to visit Atacames so that they might act as *compadres* (godparents) to an upcoming wedding and baptism.[37] This invite, for Spanish residents to visit Esmeraldas, indicates ongoing relationships, especially between Avila—as well as other Europeans who might be living among the maroons—with residents of Puerto Viejo and possibly Manta as well. Although the evidence is of this one instance, it points to possible ties between the maroons and their coastal Spanish neighbors. The coastland, rather than merely providing a line of geographic continuity between the different regions, also nurtured social connections and commerce between maroons and the outside world.

Cabello's expedition never succeeded in transferring the maroon communities and their allied peoples to the Bay of San Mateo. Just as the Africans were set to leave their hidden village, rebellion broke out in the land. Upon investigation, Cabello's people found a great number of rafts made in preparation for the move destroyed upriver from the bay.[38] With heavy hearts, they were forced to embark on a monthlong trek down the coast to Puerto Viejo.

Though Cabello had seen the signs of disunity and rebellion among the Esmeraldeños, the longer report of his expedition emphatically claimed that they did not really know the cause of Illescas's failure to settle at San Mateo. They were perplexed that his enthusiasm to be legitimized was followed by his failure to deliver. However, a reasonable explanation that fits with the evidence of the destroyed rafts is that the Esmeraldeños deemed the coastal borderland as too dangerous a place to reside. Spanish ships regularly landed there, and the titles granted Illescas might not protect them from abuse and exploitation by Spanish settlers. Finally, moving to the coast would increase their vulnerability to attacks by outsiders (as would later occur at the Spanish towns of Guayaquil and Manta.) The coastland might be healthier in terms of its air, rainfall, and wildlife, but their well-hidden village in the hills provided greater security and protection.

Piracy, Provisioning, and Salvage

In September 1578 a new, but not unexpected, dimension of the coastal borderland arrived when Francis Drake (called "*el Draque*") made his way to the Pacific seaboard of South America. Passing through the Strait of Magellan, he sailed north to Valdivia in Chile and on to Lima, searching out Spanish treasure along the way. Although his activities did not affect the Esmeraldas maroons, the greatest prize of his journey, the silver laden (with more than 26 tons) *Nuestra Señora de la Concepción,* also called the *Cacafuego*, was taken off the Esmeraldas coast, near the Cape of San Francisco.[39] Drake's presence sowed chaos in Quito and Guayaquil and the fear of a possible English landing terrorized royal authorities. It turned out to be the first of several English and Dutch expeditions to raid the coastal settlements in search of riches and ransoms. Piracy and privateering, which had been common enough in the Caribbean Sea, would become a factor of life on the Pacific coast.[40]

In the decades that followed, privateers sought to emulate the achievements of Drake in the Pacific. Thomas Cavendish and Richard Hawkins followed el Draque's path through the Strait of Magellan and up the western coast of South America. Cities like Valdivia, Lima, Trujillo, and Guayaquil were attacked, but Esmeraldas became a rest stop: a stopping point for fresh water and provisions where seaborne marauders established relations with maroons and Amerindians.[41] Unlike Drake and Oxenham's expedition to Panama in the 1570s where they allied with maroons, the Esmeraldeños did not partner with the English to attack Spanish settlements. However, sources indicate that they engaged in regular trade. Possibly the maroon leaders wanted to discourage Spanish retribution. More likely, Esmeraldas was too far removed from sources of ready wealth. Quiteños, however, feared the possibility of an overland attack. Such an assault never materialized. The northern coastland remained not just the borderland of encounter and trade but a critical buffer to foreign incursions.

Thomas Cavendish entered Pacific waters in March 1587.[42] His depredations near Quito centered on the Island of Puná off the coast of Guayaquil and were highlighted by several pitched skirmishes against Spanish residents.[43] He seems to have passed Esmeraldas without notice on his way to intercept the Manila galleons in New Spain.

In 1594 Richard Hawkins, a nephew of Francis Drake, appeared to seek fortune as his uncle had off the Cape of San Francisco when he captured the *Cacafuego*. In *The Observations of Sir Richard Hawkins*, he left a description of Atacames, the Cape of San Francisco, and the Bay of San Mateo. As Kris Lane points out, privateers' detailed accounts of geography and navigation demonstrated an interest in things other than marauding. Accurate information for future voyages was highly regarded and esteemed by the crown. To Hawkins's misfortune, his crew chose to go up against Spanish ships spotted off the Cape of San Francisco where they were defeated. His captors hauled Hawkins off to Lima and then to Seville. He was ransomed and returned to England in 1602.

Mixing his own observation with what he surely learned from the Spanish, Hawkins penned his own narrative of the Esmeraldeños:

> [At the] the bay of San Mathew. It is a goodly harbour, and hath a great fresh river, which higheth fifteene or sixteene foote water, and is a good countrey, and well peopled with Indians: they have

store of gold and emeralds. Heere the Spaniards from Guayaquill made an habitation, whilst I was prisoner in Lyma, by the Indians consent; but after, not able to suffer the insolencies of their guests, and being a people of stomacke and presumption, they suffered themselves to bee perswaded and led by a Molato [Mulatto—a person of mixed African and European ancestry]. This leader many yeares before had fled unto them from the Spaniards: him they had long time held in reputation of their captaine generall, and was admitted also unto a chiefe office by the Spaniardes, to gaine him unto them.

But now the Indians uniting themselves together, presuming that by the helpe of this Molato, they should force the Spaniards out of the countrey, put their resolution into execution, drove their enemies into the woods, and slue as many as they could lay hands on; some they killed, few escaped with life; and those who had that good happe, suffered extreame misery before they came to Quito, the place of neerest habitation of Spaniards.[44]

In Hawkins's interpretation, the Esmeraldeños were not partners but enemies of the Spaniards. Perhaps the English once again hoped to utilize maroon allies as Oxenham and Drake had done in Panama (and their countrymen would later in Nicaragua)—as associates that they could depend upon for sustenance and aid.[45]

The Spanish managed a defensive response to Hawkins's attempt to befriend the Esmeraldeños. In 1599–1600, through a series of treaties promoted by Audiencia president Juan Barrio de Sepulveda, chieftains along the coast from Esmeraldas to Barbacoas (today southern Colombia) agreed to refrain from associating with foreign interlopers.[46]

In 1680 Bartholomew Sharpe's expedition crossed Panama, captured ships to maraud the South Sea coast, and famously captured a *derrotero*, a book of Pacific seaboard nautical charts, with descriptions of the coastline and maps. Ironically it was on the coast of Esmeraldas, at Cabo Pasao, where Sharpe captured the *Santa Rosario* and the *derrotero* was found in the captain's possession. Later it would be published by William Hacke and renamed the *Buccaneers Atlas*. Its description of San Mateo Bay made clear that Esmeraldas might be a haven to foreign ships. Commentary by Basil Ringrose cautioned, however, that the Esmeraldeños would respond only to fair treatment.

The Bay of St Matheo at SW & SWRS at 5 or 6 leagues distance apears as it here is described; in this bay 2 leagues up the river on the larboard shore is very good sweet water; you will find Indian warriors here but they will not hurt a stranger; in this bay is good trees fit for ships masts & all sorts of provisions which is sold by the Mulato's; if com to this-bay in necesity I do give you important advice viz't not to jest with theire women nor debauch them, 2dly not threaten them with armes nor otherwise; but treat them with humility you may have what you please, you may rode where the anchor is set.[47]

Over the course of the seventeenth century, privateers and pirates, English, Dutch, and French alike, would employ the same knowledge marked out in the *Buccaneers Atlas* to determine the best locations to land their ships and refill their stores along the Pacific coast. Long used sites such as Isla Gorgona, Isla de Gallo, Atacames, and the Bay of San Mateo were frequented by foreign privateers bound from Peru to Panama. Established settlements like Guayaquil and Tumaco fell victim to their predations, but as with Hawkins and Sharpe, they approached the Esmeraldas coast as a safe harbor.

Examples from two such expeditions, the first undertaken by Captain William Dampier and William Funnell in 1703, describe an abandoned village near the shore at Atacames where twenty of his men found a bark laden with wood planks (perhaps of the shipbuilding variety). In addition, they mention Indian villages two leagues (about seven miles) upriver that furnished Spanish ships with coconuts, plantains, bananas, and other fruits.[48]

Although plans for a Spanish settlement at Esmeraldas failed repeatedly for more than a century, the region's native peoples and African maroon descendants successfully created a borderland trading post where both Spanish and foreign ships stopped for provisions.[49] However, the Esmeraldeños continued to largely avoid residing on the coast. This strategic treatment of geographic space, where the forested interior provided refuge and safety from enemies and the coastal borderland acted as the place for meeting and trading, served the Afro-Amerindians well.

Relations between the Esmeraldeños and the English were further enhanced just a few years later when Woodes Rogers visited in August 1709 after pillaging his way across the Atlantic and stopping at the island of Juan Fernandez where he picked up Alexander Selkirk, a true-life castaway thought to have inspired Daniel Defoe's *Robinson Crusoe* (1719).[50] The two ships of his expedition, the *Duke* and *Duchess*, spent time searching for provisions and careening on *Isla Gorgona*. They visited Atacames, which Rogers describes as a place "where the Indians are free." Encountering the Esmeraldeños was tricky as the insecurity of the coast led an entire village to flee upon their arrival. According to Rogers, they traded with the approval of a local priest and were careful to provide gifts: "We sent them three large wooden saints to adorn their church, which they took as a great present; and I sent a feathered cap to the wife of the chief which was well accepted."[51] Bartering their plunder, Rogers notes that they were able to fill their stores with cattle, hogs, and plantains "very cheap" before heading for the Galapagos Islands.[52]

The age of buccaneers came to a close in the decades after Woodes Rogers's landing at Atacames.[53] However, the life of the coastland was just beginning. Over the course of the eighteenth century, with naval aggressions in the Pacific subsiding, Atacames developed a small permanent population, numbering thirty households, and the city of Esmeraldas was already established when William Stevenson traveled there in 1825.[54] He noted the strong character and customs of the "zambos" (ethnically mixed African and native people) descended from the sixteenth-century shipwrecks. While centuries of trade with passing vessels still provided livelihood for the Esmeraldeños of the coastland, the days when the shoreline divided the people of the interior lands from those of the sea appeared to have faded.

It is not uncommon for maroon communities and marginalized borderlands to appear static in the long mix of colonial history. The complaints of the distant past in Esmeraldas (lack of development, need for closer communication, the creation of

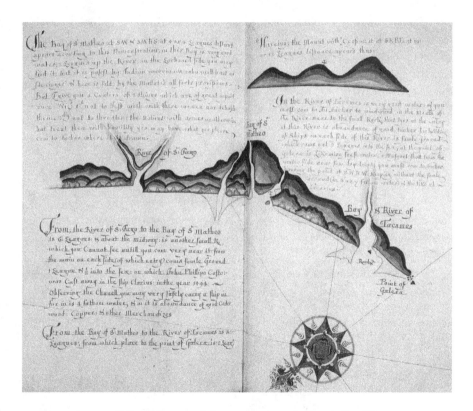

FIGURE 13. Image of San Mateo and Atacames shore in South Sea Waggoneer. Source: Alamy.

a port) can seem like the same complaints two and even three centuries later. What is harder to see in this dynamic are the transformations that conditioned lifeways in these regions over time. From its sixteenth-century beginnings as a populated beachhead of Amerindian communities, the Esmeraldas coast became a jumping off point for the conquest of the Incan Empire. In the wake of Spanish conquest and repeated incursions, it transitioned to a semibarren but critical interstitial zone, a neutralized territory where Spaniards, maroons, and their followers could meet, exchange, and develop relationships with outsiders who might gain entrance to the interior lands. While still a precarious place for settlement, the seventeenth- and eighteenth-century coastland became an ad-hoc trading post where Spanish and foreign ships put in for provisions and repairs along the lengthy and sometimes difficult journey along the Pacific seacoast. With the worries brought on by privateers and interlopers diminished by the mid-eighteenth century, the coastland once again became a place of settlement and population growth.

At the shoreline of Esmeraldas, the periphery at the center reflected transformations in the broader colonial world. Esmeraldeños adapted to local conditions and changes in social makeup and political authority. The African maroons and "free Indian" authorities diminished as Spanish priests, traders, and soldiers made inroads among the population. By Stevenson's time the coastal peoples, Zambos, Cayapas, and Malabas, had come to an understanding with Spanish authorities in which they maintained their histories and lifeways even as the empire that brought the coastal borderland into existence had come to an end.

Notes

1. Robert Cushman Murphy, "The Littoral of Pacific Colombia and Ecuador," 1.

2. Carlos M. Larrea, "Geographical Notes on Esmeraldas, Northwestern Ecuador," 373.

3. Murphy, "The Earliest Spanish Advances Southward," 15–19 passim.

4. Cieza de León, *The Discovery and Conquest of Peru*, chaps. 6, 7, 8. Cieza also described the region as full of "frightful forests" and "hellish because even the birds and the beasts shied away from living there" (48–49).

5. Kris E. Lane examines the lure of emeralds and their cultural significance in Europe and Asia in *Colour of Paradise: The Emerald in the Age of Gunpowder Empires*. See chapter 2, "Conquistadors." True to the picaresque imagination, Esmeraldas was not a source of the green gems. It was a market for mined emeralds that probably originated in the Muisca highlands of Colombia (Lane, 47).

6. Games, "Atlantic History," 747. Far from implying a neat division, however, there are complex parochial issues relating to oceanic history (for want of a better term). Inevitably, there are methodological gray areas, especially when one considers that Atlantic privateers, for instance, were eager to capture Manila galleons and sometimes continued their Pacific coast activities in Asian waters. See Mapp, "Atlantic History from Imperial, Continental, and Pacific Perspectives."

7. There are a number of important exceptions, studies that focus on the coastal complex as the principal loci of historical development and change. Outstanding examples include Camilla Townsend's *Tale of Two Cities*. The African Atlantic coast also stands out in this regard as it often formed the boundary point of European integration to local economies and politics. Of many excellent studies, Randy Sparks's captures these richly complex borderland societies. See Sparks, *The Two Princes of Calabar: An Eighteenth-Century Atlantic Odyssey*.

8. For prime examples see Columbus voyages for the former and Bernal Díaz's chapters describing landing on the coast of Yucatan and later Vera Cruz for the latter. Columbus, *The Diario of Christopher Columbus's first voyage to America, 1492–1493*; Díaz, *The Conquest of New Spain*.

9. Millet, "Defining Freedom in the Atlantic Borderlands of the Revolutionary Southeast," 367–94.

10. Millet, "Borderlands in the Atlantic World," 268.

11. Nicholas Rogers cites sources that claimed Miskito raids captured two thousand natives from Costa Rica between 1700–1720, thus playing a significant role in the circum-Caribbean Indian slave trade. See Rogers, "Caribbean Borderland," 122.

12. See Bushnell, "Gates, Patterns, and Peripheries," 20.

13. This notion of a peripheral frontier refers to interior regions and areas further removed from Western contact like those comprising today's western Canada, Alaska, and the interior of Brazil. Europeans, in some cases, traveled to these vast regions, but few settled there before the eighteenth century, and sometimes much later than that.

14. Philip Steinberg notes in his study of oceanic territorialization that every historical period "besides having a particular spatiality on land, has had a complementary—if often contrapuntal—spatiality at sea." Steinberg, *The Social Construction of the Ocean*, 4–5. Additionally, J. C. Sharman concludes that early European expansion into Asia and Africa primarily consisted in attempts to monopolize seaborne trade and control of territory was minimal. While Spain enjoyed larger territorial claims in the Americas, large areas in both peripheral and core regions remained outside of colonizer control. See the introduction and chapter 1 of Sharman, *Empires of the Weak*. Michael Pearson's work on the Indian Ocean examines how European claims to control oceans, seas, and coastlines affected the circum-Indian Ocean world in the Early Modern period. See Pearson, *The Indian Ocean*.

15. The Treaty of Tordesillas, for example, outlined the division of territories between Spain and Portugal and also contained provisions giving Portugal exclusive rights to fisheries off the African coast. See *Tratados de Tordesillas I–II*.

16. Steinberg, *The Social Construction*, 76–79. As Steinberg asserts, the interpretations or views of the ocean are created by actors who reproduce a "construction of the ocean as unclaimable transport surface, claimable resource space, a set of discrete places and events, and a field for military adventure." He further asserts that these competing and "contradictory constructions . . . shift from time to time, as the power of the actors varied and as the need for certain ocean uses waxed and waned" (4).

17. Its northern half is described by Murphy in dire terms: "This is the maritime Choco, a flooded lowland of perpetual rains, of selva and morasses, of hundreds of streams, many or

most of which pour into the Pacific through multiple mouths. The line between earth and ocean becomes tenuous, for the greater part of the shore is fringed with a maze of mangrove-covered flats and islands, separated by a network of esteros and grading into shifting bars and shallows, which in many places extend for miles offshore." Closer to Buenaventura he notes, "Violent tidal currents, rips, white-water shoals, and a dangerous flotsam of forest wreckage, which includes countless trunks of large trees, give the whole area a well-earned sinister repute." See Murphy, "The Littoral of Pacific Colombia," 14.

18. See Markham, *Reports on the Discovery of Peru*, 3–8.

19. Markham, *Reports*, 7–8

20. Porras Berrenechea describes Jerez's chronicle as "the most precise and detailed narrative of the initial phase of the conquest." Barrenechea, *Los cronistas del Perú, 1528–1650*, 1:206.

21. See Guinea, "Diferentes mecanismos de articulación hombre-entorno en la costa norte de Ecuador," 53. Guinea further notes that the Esmeraldas River serves as a break to the coastal mangrove forests found in regions to the north of the river, and although the region is classified as tropical rainforest (between 800 and 1,000 mm average rainfall), Atacames to the south and west possesses a microclimate enclave similar to many parts of the southern half of the Esmeraldas coast called "very dry tropical" (48). Murphy provides an even more dramatic comparison for the region: "Close to the great bend at Cape San Francisco comes this second and more abrupt physiographic and biotic break, which is also a famous climatic landmark. It divides the Chocó from the more southern district of seasonal rainfall, the annual pattern of which, however, is the reverse of that at Panama. The general altitude of the land rises, and the shore becomes cliffy; the waves are studded with dark, bald rocks. The trees are smaller than in Colombia; arborescent ferns, lianas, and orchids and other epiphytes thin out; Euphorbiaceae become prominent, and cactus makes its appearance. Bare banks and ledges are conspicuous from the sea: the white cliffs of 'Tacames' are much mentioned in eighteenth-century British literature, and Cape San Francisco was likened by the buccaneers to Beachy Head, in Sussex." Murphy, "The Littoral of Pacific Colombia," 17–18.

22. See Chardon, "The Elusive Spanish League," 294–302. These were possibly fully grown American crocodiles (*Crocodylus acutus*) currently endangered but historically common to the Ecuadorian coast.

23. Coaque's wealth was taken as an augury of more to come and numerous chroniclers mentioned it, including Pedro Cieza de León, Cristóbal de Mena, Francisco de Jerez, and Juan Ruiz de Arce.

24. See Benzoni, *The History of the New World: Benzoni's Historia del Mondo Nuovo*, 84.

25. Benzoni, *The History of the New World*, 83.

26. For a comprehensive list of expeditions see Franch, *Penetración española en Esmeraldas*.

27. Benzoni also describes the hamlets as somewhat fantastical "houses in the tops of trees." See Benzoni, *The History of the New World*, 82.

28. DeBoar's description of the wetter Santiago Cayapas region north of the Esmeraldas River ("small settlements dispersed along interfluvial ridge tops") exemplifies one type of dispersed settlement pattern found in the region and, according to DeBoar, associated with a "defensive strategy." See Deboar, *Traces Behind the Esmeraldas Shore*, 170–71.

29. See Ponce Leiva, *Relaciones histórico-geográficas de la Audiencia de Quito*, 92.

30. Benzoni describes several issues sailing south from Panama. The months from January through April were the best for travel due to the winds and currents. During the rest of the year, the voyage could last months. Additionally, ships typically had to navigate a hundred miles or more west before turning south and east to catch a strong current. Finally, boats utilized in the Pacific did not have shelters, exposing passengers to the elements and often causing onboard illnesses. See Benzoni, *The History of the New World*, 81–83.

31. Cabello Balboa, *Obras*, chaps. 7–8 passim.

32. Cabello Balboa, *Obras*, 43–44.

33. Caceres Patiño provided testimony of the expedition in a court case where he states that Illescas and the Amerindian chiefs spent two days with them and left on the third. AGI-Esc922b.2.39r-42r (Archivo General de Indias).

34. Cabello Balboa, *Obras*, 47–48.

35. As Lawrence Clayton points out, trade along the Pacific coast of the Viceroyalty of Peru "evolved quite apart and under different influences from the Atlantic world." His study also notes the widespread practice of contraband commerce along the coast of colonial Ecuador and the existence of a lively, robust trade economy. See Clayton, "Trade and Navigation in the Seventeenth-Century Viceroyalty of Peru," 1.

36. See Rumazo, *Documentos para la Historia de la Audiencia de Quito*, 3:393. Cabello notes the ship was returning to Guayaquil.

37. Cabello Balboa, *Obras*, 48, 52–53.

38. Cabello Balboa, *Obras*, chap. 11. Rumazo, *Documentos*, 3:389–96. Juan Caceres Patiño testimony in AGI-Escribania 922b.

39. This was in stark contrast to Drake's activities in 1572 and 1573 when he and John Oxenham made allies of the Panama maroons to engage in a number of daring attacks. See Lane, *Pillaging the Empire*, 43–47.

40. Lane's chronology of early modern piracy notes eight major expeditions undertaken by the English and Dutch into the Pacific between 1577 and 1690. Lane, *Pillaging the Empire*, xxi–xxiv.

41. Lane, *Pillaging the Empire*, 41.

42. Lane, *Pillaging the Empire*, 53–56.

43. Lane, *Quito 1599*, 199–203.

44. Hawkins, *The Observations of Sir Richard Hawkins*, 181–82.

45. See Pike, "Black Rebels," 243–66; and Rogers, "Carribbean Borderland."

46. Lane, "Buccaneers and Coastal Defense in Late-Seventeenth-Century Quito," 149–50.

47. Hacke, *An accurate description of all the harbours riuers ports islands sands rocks and dangers*, 77. A nearly identical passage is also noted by Lane, *Bucaneers and Coastal Defense*, 157.

48. Funnell, *A voyage round the world*.

49. See Lane, *Buccaneers and Coastal Defense*, 157.

50. Lane, *Pillaging the Empire*, 182.

51. Rogers, *A Cruising Voyage Around the World*, 180.

52. Rogers, *A Cruising Voyage Around the World*, 182.

53. Lane, *Pillaging the Empire*, 198. Rogers, though a privateer, would be commissioned on an antipirate expedition to the Bahamas in 1718 (185).

54. Stevenson, *A historical and descriptive narrative*, 398.

CHAPTER NINE

FUGITIVE TIME, SPACE, AND REFUSAL IN THE PACIFIC ANDES

Rachel Sarah O'Toole

IN 1657, Agustín Balanta negated the criminal accusations leveled by the Trujillo magistrate. According to the notary who transcribed his mandatory confession, Balanta said "that he did not go about stealing or assaulting" but only asked for food from indigenous Andeans.[1] His companion, Domingo Angola, likewise disputed the gendered and racist charges that included sexual assault of indigenous Andean women and armed robbery of Spanish men.[2] Witnesses disagreed, calling on circulating tropes of dangerous Black men to describe how the two had resisted arrest armed with bows and arrows and then continued four months of fugitivity. Unsurprisingly, both men would be sentenced and punished for two crimes including absence from enslavement, or *cimarronaje*, and assault of travelers on the royal road that connected the towns and ports on the northern Peruvian coast of the Pacific Andes. Nonetheless, the men from Senegambia and West Central Africa disrupted a colonial judicial narrative that cast them as thieves and resistant fugitives from slavery. By refusing to confess to the accusations, Balanta and Angola challenged enslavement and refused colonial authority.

Enslavers attempted to contain Africans and their descendants geographically and judicially. On the Peruvian northern coast, indigenous Andeans and enslaved Black laborers worked on sugar and wheat estates, transporting crops along roads to Pacific ports.[3] In contrast to a perception of rural disorder, Spanish colonizers imagined that the literacy and law represented in their cities constructed as well as maintained racial, class, and gendered hierarchies.[4] White Spaniards enacted their colonial superiority by marking uncultivated hillsides and desolated deserts, or *monte*, as dangerous places inhabited by criminals, fugitives, vagabonds, and others resistant to the civilizing order of urban empire.[5] Enslavers and colonial officials attempted to police these environments and their inhabitants. Estate owners and local officials sponsored a regional armed patrol and required legal documentation of manumitted status from Black men who moved among colonial cities.[6] Fugitives from slavery were especially targeted. Colonial authorities, with the consent of enslavers, tortured, beat, shackled, and jailed fugitives whose testimonies were recorded as formulaic responses to predetermined questions. Through these material and discursive acts of enclosure, enslavers elaborated racial ideologies of anti-blackness to categorize Africans and their descendants as requiring surveillance and erasure from written representation.[7] Slavery in colonial Spanish America, therefore, was created through material and paper means as enslavers melded documentation of enslaved laborers with the physical actions of enslavement and enforcement.

Enslaved men and women on the northern Peruvian coast, however, contested legal enslavement and colonial authority that radiated from the Spanish colonial city. On coastal estates, enslaved people insulted enslavers as well as their proxies, refused to work as ordered, and burned the means of production. As vendors, muleteers, and artisans, enslaved men and women crisscrossed the plazas, markets, and streets of the northern cities, towns, and villages to negotiate, trade, and worship. Fugitives from slavery, known as maroons or *cimarrones,* claimed landscapes such as swamps, mountains, and *montes*—remote from enslavers—while also establishing settlements and creating social pathways, often in plain sight of enslavers' estates, cities, and households.[8] The Spanish colonial city, as a legal concept, was claimed, rejected, and reformed by enslaved people and fugitives from slavery who recentered borderlands by setting their own timetables, establishing fugitive communities, and militarily resisting capture. In effect, enslaved people claimed and created what historian Stephanie Camp theorized was a "rival geography" to the one imposed by enslavers (discussed by Christina Marie Villareal in this volume). While Spanish enslavers employed the irrigated fields of the northern coast as sites of capitalized agriculture, enslaved people and fugitives from slavery experienced sugar and wheat estates in "alternative ways" that "conflicted planters' [enslavers'] ideals and demands."[9] Geographies created by enslaved people, but fugitives in particular, help us to see how borderlands were not marginal spaces but sites where Africans and their descendants developed communities, politics, and ideologies. Rather than spaces solely of confinement, exploitation, and punishment, enslaved people and fugitives from slavery, according to Camp, repossessed what colonial authorities referred to as *monte* and historians as borderlands through the very actions of their mobility and refusals.

Mobile enslaved people and fugitives from slavery, however, did not contest Spanish rule. As Camp explains, a rival geography "did not threaten to overthrow American slavery, nor did it provide slaves with autonomous spaces."[10] Truly dangerous places where enslavers hunted fugitives from slavery, rival geographies were conflictual spaces where fugitives could engage in their own practices of family, ritual, respite, and freedom.[11] Enslaved people and fugitives from slavery understood the possibilities of these times and places that Katherine McKittrick theorizes as Black women's geographies that simultaneously bind and release. McKittrick challenges us to imagine a "geographic trick" created by the motions of enslaved and fugitive people where a person is "both inside and outside, captive and free."[12] The key to fugitive time and space was, as Stephanie Camp explains, that enslaved people and fugitives from slavery engaged in activities "without reference to their owners."[13] In this chapter, therefore, I employ fragmentary and suppressed evidence of enslaved and fugitive testimony from criminal trials that began and ended in Trujillo's regional court to illuminate how fugitives from slavery made their own meanings in the *monte*. Multilingual and highly conversant in colonial laws, and intent on multiprong strategies of freedom, enslaved people and fugitives from slavery negated, refused, and transformed the racist, sexist, and criminalizing narrative of colonial authorities to articulate locations apart from enslavers.[14] Rather than turning toward the Spanish hegemony, this chapter employs borderlands conceptually to follow how Africans and their descendants activated fugitive practices that turned away from the lettered city.

Fugitive Time and Space

African and African-descent women and men on the northern Peruvian coast created fugitive geographies by claiming time and space from enslavers. Enslaved people worked to sustain themselves whenever possible by engaging in tasks not assigned or approved, or taking moments dedicated to self, including those with kin and companions.[15] At the same time, enslavers both feared and depended on enslaved mobility since enslaved people ran local markets, conducted business in ports, and worked independently to submit daily or weekly wage payments to enslavers. To counter fugitive practices, enslavers employed a rural guard (Santa Hermandad) that monitored provincial urban areas and disciplined enslaved people who exceeded enslavement's regulations of mobility.[16] Enslaved and free people, wisely, monitored their disclosures of fugitive time, of themselves and others, even in provincial criminal cases. In these judicial texts, fugitives from slavery were attentive to how Spanish royal mandates, and Trujillo's colonial authorities, dispensed punishment according to the length of time absent from an enslaver. The accused and witnesses also knew when local authorities desired to ferret out accomplices. Their fragmented interventions and coerced narratives in mostly criminal trials also reveal how fugitives transformed landscapes into refuges, homes, and meeting points.

Provincial magistrates and Trujillo's *alcaldes*, for example, punished fugitives from slavery according to the time they had been reportedly absent from their enslaver. Enslavers and colonial authorities wished to penalize fugitives from slavery for their lack of laboring time.[17] Trujillo officials, in their short formulaic cases, made sure to include royal mandates that disciplined fugitives according to the days or months an enslaved person had been absent. In an economy where enslaved laborers' hours were calculated in pesos and enslaved people could rent their labor time for wages, time away meant stolen funds. Most commonly, crown regulations increased physical beatings from two hundred to four hundred lashes when an enslaved person had been absent for more than four months.[18] The location or the activity of fugitives from slavery was secondary to the criminal charge that defined removal from slavery in increments of time.[19] In Trujillo, colonial authorities followed crown law and on paper charged fugitives from slavery according to the number of absences from their enslaver.[20] Authorities articulated, measured, and justified judicial violence against Africans and their descendants as criminals according to royal law.

In the next step of the criminal cases, Trujillo authorities required accused fugitives to confess to the specific time of their absence. Municipal notaries recorded the questions posed to incarcerated fugitives that were often lengthy accusations of crimes, including the specific number of months absent from an enslaver's control.[21] Shackled in Trujillo's city jail, held in the hacienda stocks, or detained in an indigenous Andean village, fugitives seemingly gave formulaic responses to the notary's questions. Enslaved fugitives certainly would have been coerced in these moments, suffering from hunger, wounds from their capture, and imprisonment. The responses suggest that the notary recorded the required evidence to fit the official accusation, matching the criminal charges and the royal mandates that equated punishments with specific periods of absenteeism.[22] Bernaldo Criollo's confession detailed how he spent one month at the Chicama River, another near the indigenous village of Magdalena de Cao, and two months in the hillsides above Trujillo for a tidy total of four months of absenteeism.[23] In another case, Juan, a native of Cabo Verde, was recorded as confessing to exactly one month of absence.[24] The municipal notary recorded fugitive Joseph Jiron's confession that he sought refuge in the Franciscan convent for no less than two months.[25] Colonial authorities, therefore, demonstrated their adherence to crown mandates through the recorded confessions from fugitives from slavery that precisely matched the regulated amount of time absent with the prescribed severity of the punishment.[26] Time, in recorded accusations against fugitives, was made to fit the required specifications of cimarron criminalization.

Enslaved men, however, claimed their own version of time and space. Juan de la Cruz solicited indigenous muleteers on Lima's infamous Malambo street for the chance to travel to Trujillo. Initially the experienced travelers rejected Cruz, suspecting his criminalized fugitive status, and they refused to be slowed down by a passenger on foot. Persistent, Cruz acquired a horse and crashed the mule train on its way north, declaring that he was a free man and paying his passage.[27] When captured and charged for absenteeism from his enslaver, Cruz confessed to Trujillo's magistrate that he was enslaved to a Lima merchant. Clearly, Cruz was practiced in the economies and negotiations of coastal transportation and even planned to return to his home of Quito once arriving in Trujillo. Enslaved men like Cruz had gained reputations as adept fugitives, in effect inhabiting transitional spaces of their own making.[28] Cruz had been caught, but his attempt suggests that he and others knew how to work human and physical geographies to successfully arrive at their destinations.

Enslaved people understood that colonial authorities policed and punished their mobility according to an imperial standard of what constituted absenteeism, or *cimarronaje*. As a son of an Andean indigenous man and a Black woman, Pedro de Calpe was well known in the Chicama Valley, where he was born, and easily hid (or was hidden) from his enslaver.[29] Criminalized as a fugitive from slavery, Calpe challenged his enslaver by boldly declaring that he was free.[30] Within the legal colonial apparatus as well as outside in the time and space of fugitivity, Calpe made public—and even confronted—his enslaver's inability to control his body but also his perception of self. Calpe's claims, however, were met with severe retaliation. The enslaver received the magistrate's permission to brand the young man with a sign of his surname on his forehead and cheeks to reassure that wherever and whenever Calpe moved his status as enslaved would be known. Calpe was not alone. Trujillo's magistrate ordered public lashings, held accused fugitives for months in the city jail, and displayed the severed bodies of deceased fugitives throughout the region. The physical punishments for absenteeism, therefore, were what Marisa Fuentes explains as quintessential "technologies of . . . enslaved surveillance" that, on the Peruvian northern coast, included the measurement of time.[31] Simultaneously, Calpe's and others' persistent attempts at removal reveal a fugitive vision of time and space rooted in bodily control.

Additionally, time, specifically the concept of time, could be defied. In contrast to the official calculation of months, enslaved people marked time according to moon cycles, community festivals, and the passing of the sun.[32] As a result, when Juan de la Cruz, the hitchhiker from Lima, contested charges of absenteeism, he explained that his journey with indigenous Andean muleteers to Trujillo took twenty-two days.[33] Exceeding the official four days that marked a legal charge of absenteeism, but less than the one month equated with physical punishment, Cruz's lengthy confession was further supported by the indigenous Andean muleteers who had, allegedly unknowingly, facilitated his journey. Together, the travel companions explained that a flooded river, promises of payment on arrival, and a shared interest in potential stolen goods had bound their temporary fellowship along the coastal road.[34] Their justifications must have worked since Trujillo's magistrate did not sentence or punish Juan de la Cruz.

Enslavers and officials also attempted to police the spaces of supposed known fugitive activities. Throughout the seventeenth century and into the early eighteenth century, colonial authorities sought out fugitives from slavery where robberies were reported. In 1642, the magistrate declared that two fugitive groups, each with their captain, descended from the hills near Trujillo to assault and rob highland indigenous travelers on the royal road.[35] In 1725, Trujillo's city officials headed to an infamous group of small white hills to capture fugitives, a place known even today as a dangerous curve just before the road leaves the coastal valley.[36] Authorities, therefore, associated fugitives from slavery with the landscapes of the inner valleys. There, steep coastal canyons provided cover for bandits to quickly descend on travelers, and then escape from authorities.[37] Trujillo's authorities, then, created fugitive locations in supposed borderlands that were distant from the provincial city. In these criminal records, colonial authorities described fugitives from slavery engaged in repeated attacks and forays, thus requiring the attention of regular rural patrols.[38] By mapping fugitives from slavery onto narrow canyons, steep ravines, and overlooks, colonial authorities generated an expected cimarron geography.

In contrast, enslaved fugitives created homes on lands considered hacienda borderlands. In 1642, Trujillo's authorities did not find fugitives from slavery on the royal road but in the irrigation canal of an estate.[39] At the supposed edge of the slavery economy's landscape, Blas Angola and Anton Congo gathered snails, a well-known coastal food source, to feed their community.[40] The two men from the established *palenque*, or settlement of fugitives from slavery, were not raiding travelers as commonly accused in *cimarronaje* judicial trials, but transforming the infrastructure of a colonial hacienda into collective sustenance.[41] In another location, Bernaldo Criollo explained that his group—including Francisco Folupo, Silvestre Angola, and Catalina, a young *mulata* woman—spent time along the Chicama river banks where they may have been able to gather foodstuffs and hunt small prey.[42] Considered marginal to colonial authorities and regional enslavers, fugitives from slavery targeted the dry arroyo for regular meals. Similarly, fugitives from slavery established homes in the interstitial spaces of colonial estates and ranches, or *monte* in areas that Villareal (in this volume) suggests would have made fugitives aware of each other. María, of Bañol land, was found in a cave that she had probably made into her home.[43] In the 1640s, communities numbering up to forty or fifty lived in established *ranchos* with livestock and fields in the uncultivated hills near Trujillo.[44] In the 1690s, a smaller group built a *rancho* in the forest near the central valley haciendas of Chicama.[45] Considered marginal by enslavers and colonial authorities, fugitives made these borderlands central to their sense of home, family, and community.

Enslaved fugitives, therefore, created and marked their kinship in the supposed marginal lands of the *monte*. When describing fugitives, enslavers and colonial authorities gestured to the *monte*, a catch-all term on the Peruvian northern coast for the uncultivated lands that surrounded haciendas, farms, and estates including arid hillsides and stretches of desert.[46] When reporting their activities, Trujillo's rural patrols did not name particular locations on the landscape but described their pursuit of enslaved fugitives as movement through "different places" or along nameless hillsides.[47] Fugitives from slavery could be equally opaque in their testimonies and confessions recorded in criminal cases. Josepha de Ibarra explained that she fled to the *monte* but did not disclose the location of a rendezvous with a *mulato* man who, in solidarity, took off her shackles.[48] For Ibarra, the location of the *monte* could be what Marisa Fuentes names as a "useful disguise" that was both geographical as well as archival.[49] To colonial authorities and enslavers, fugitives from slavery did not point to specific places to protect communities, networks, and themselves. Clearly, men and women who removed themselves from slavery knew the *monte* that they marked according to the location of friends, allies, and kin.[50] Joseph Jiron hid in a *rancho* of an indigenous Andean man outside of the city walls, while Juan Negro, a native of Cabo Verde, took refuge in the house of his friend, Isabel, an enslaved Black woman.[51] More specifically, María of Bañol land met and spent a year with Juanillo, a Black man, in the *monte*, while Susana of *casta angola* fled to her husband in the *monte*.[52] Clearly, the responses reflect repeated demands of colonial authorities that the arrested name their accomplices. Regardless of their careful deflection, enslaved people and fugitives from slavery created deep kinship connections in the lands dismissed by enslavers that we might call borderlands.

In both their movement through the northern coastal landscape and in the recorded archival testimonies, the witnesses and the accused mapped out fugitive geographies. On their own time, fugitives from slavery expanded, and exceeded, the mobility afforded by enslavers. Enslaved people and those accused of *cimarronaje* visited households of free people, and traveled by horseback along royal roads.[53] Hardly contained, in these spaces, fugitives recentered geographies of slavery focused on the movement of sugar, wheat, and other commodities toward urban and external markets.[54] Instead, fugitive geographies connected to centers of sustainable exchange.[55] The small fugitive group that included Francisco Folupo, Bernaldo Criollo, Silvestre Angola, and Catalina lived near the indigenous Andean village of Magdalena de Cao, the site of a regular market as well as villagers eager to trade.[56] Likewise, Juan Negro, a native of Cabo Verde, hid for a month on the large estate of Facala where enslaved and free friends must have provided food, shelter, and a watchful eye.[57] In sites unnamed by colonial authorities as well as locations of enslavement, fugitives from slavery built communities that, in turn, created families and relationships that could not be captured or contained by legal means.

Fugitive Refusal

When possible, northern Peruvian fugitives engaged in a politic of refusal that included rejecting the geographic confines and the labor rhythms of slavery. Like other fugitives from slavery throughout the Atlantic world, northern Peruvian African and African-descent men and women claimed forests, the banks of scrub surrounding waterways, and urban environments as opposed to the estates, ports, and roads devoted to slavery's economies.[58] To steal time and labor away from enslavers, enslaved people as well as fugitives gathered in taverns and households during festivals and market days to trade, exchange news, and celebrate kin.[59] More pointedly, in the 1630s and 1640s more than forty men and women removed themselves from enslavement to join a hillside community led by two Congo men named Gabriel and Domingo. Their settlement, or *palenque*, was targeted, attacked, and prosecuted by enslavers, the rural guard, and Trujillo's judiciary, leaving a series of criminal records that largely obscured the perspectives of the Africans and their descendants.[60] Still, by reading how members created their settlement apart from the geography and labor of slavery and enslavers, I underline how the *palenque* was a site of refusal.[61] Through local cooperation and a decided military response, settlement members articulated a politic that did not solely reference or resist Iberian or enslavers' authority.

Colonial authorities aggressively targeted fugitives from the settlement. As aforementioned, following the crown's orders, Trujillo's magistrate accused fugitives from slavery of stealing their labor time from enslavers and measured their crime in days and months. Repeatedly, colonial authorities criminalized Gabriel and Domingo's settlement, issuing special orders that the fugitives associated with the infamous location in the *monte* return to "the houses and masters," or sites of enslavement.[62] The magistrate was losing his patience. For years the repetitive assaults on the settlement led by Gabriel and Domingo had been unsuccessful. To justify expenses of the rural guard's multiple *entradas* (military ventures) against the fugitive settlement, I suspect the northern coastal magistrate also trumped up charges by accusing members of Gabriel and Domingo's settlement of assaulting indigenous travelers.[63] According to the highest colonial authority on the Peruvian northern coast, Gabriel and Domingo directed their members to rob chickens, sheep, and clothing from the "Indians" in the surrounding valley.[64] The persistent accusations and the equally standardized responses of witnesses and the accused, therefore, reflect the magistrate's clear intent to punish these fugitives.

Reading the same testimonies for evidence of how West Central African *palenque* inhabitants sustained their community reveals a collaboration, not a conflict, with local indigenous villagers. Fugitives in the criminal trials were less clear about the location of their supposed thefts, perhaps to protect themselves. Often, the accused narrated eating maize or meat "from the fields" or explained "their friends" gave them food to eat.[65] The West Central African settlement members, however, practiced a particular acuity in trade and barter. In 1639, Anton Malamba agreed that at one point he had stolen hens and pigs with the settlement members but denied doing "any other bad thing to the Indians." Familiar with barter, he confessed to "coming to the fields of the Indians for maize to eat." Moreover, Anton Malamba explained that he wore pants "given to him by an Indian" when he descended to the valley with another member of the settlement.[66] West Central Africans such as Anton Malamba were commercially proficient, having been sold through trade networks from regions where rural people employed currency at local markets and traded for cloth or metal with long-distance merchants.[67] Settlement members frequented indigenous villages and homes on Spanish estates as the rural guard arrested Nicolas Malamba in the home of an indigenous laborer.[68] There, Malamba may have been engaged in the vibrant trade among enslaved people, fugitives from slavery, and indigenous laborers as suggested by Villareal in this volume. Suggestively, deviating from the script provided by the magistrate's questions, Malamba and other settlement fugitives discussed their trade, barter, and exchange with enslaved allies and indigenous neighbors.

The hillside settlement led by Gabriel and Domingo, then, coexisted with their indigenous neighbors and acted with an ethic of fair exchange. Targeted by the rural guard and sought by enslavers, the West Central African fugitives were dependent on local allies to secure items not made in the settlement. To acquire tobacco, settlement members visited indigenous homes or asked their enslaved ally Domingo to ascend the hillside with the coveted good.[69] A man named as Anton of *casta malemba* explained in his confession that the leader Gabriel Congo regularly asked two indigenous neighbors to purchase tobacco and bread for the settlement.[70] To prove the criminal accusations, colonial authorities secured the testimonies of two indigenous Andean men who reported that when they did not return the fugitives' money or the goods, Gabriel reportedly stole their pig.[71] Yet, indigenous witnesses reported the incident only when colonial authorities targeted the fugitive settlement for attracting enslaved laborers from the provincial city. In other words, we do not know how long indigenous neighbors shopped for the settlement. Moreover, the indigenous men had not independently reported Gabriel's theft. Read in the time and space of a neighborhood economy, and one informed by a creolized West Central African market ethic, Gabriel redeemed his investment from his trading peers when he seized the valuable farm animal.[72] Even through the distortion of colonial condemnation of Black men, combined with the patronizing tone toward indigenous men, their testimonies reveal a cooperative relationship among neighbors and an act of restorative justice on the part of the fugitive leader Gabriel.

The fugitives were able to demand payment from their indigenous trading partners in part because of their advanced military skills. Municipal officials of Trujillo dismissed the activities of Gabriel and Domingo's group as "raids" conducted by a "band" of Black *cimarrones*. Yet, Trujillo's amateur rural guard (largely motivated by bounty payments) described a highly trained military organization that was even more organized than the well-hidden maroon community of San Maló on the Spanish Gulf Coast discussed by Villareal in this volume. Along with Angolan men who had experienced the tumultuous West Central African conflicts of the 1620s and 1630s, the men led by Gabriel and Domingo could have included trained soldiers from the Angolan *guerra preta* (African auxiliaries) or the Kongo military.[73] Like the two leaders, members of the settlement also were named as Congo, suggesting that they had been traded into the transatlantic and Pacific slave trades due to the civil war in the Kingdom of Kongo.[74] Multiple witnesses explained how the settlement men expertly wielded machetes, swords, daggers, lances, knives, and clubs much like Kongolese troops.[75] Following West Central African armies, the settlement employed firearms sparingly, but expertly, as the rural guardsmen detailed how Simon Congo and Juanillo Congo shot at them to defend the settlement.[76] Moreover, a year later, a member of the rural guard described how the fugitive men attacked in military formation, or in three *quadrillas* of fifteen men each with four additional fugitive soldiers in the advance.[77] While hardly the same size, West Central African Ndongo's armies organized into three units when going into battle, including forward detachments of skilled soldiers.[78] In a similar trained maneuver of an organized army, Gabriel directed his men to conduct actions only at night, moving in two *quadrillas*, each with its own captain.[79] The settlement, then, included West Central African soldiers who, as armed and trained men of the fugitive *quadrillas*, defended their territory and challenged their foe's invasion.

The hillside *palenque* was never collectively defeated by Trujillo's colonial authorities. The rural guard was only able to seize individual settlement members who had been caught unaware. For example, armed officials came across Blas Angola and Anton Angola inside an irrigation canal where they were probably foraging. Cornered within the narrow channel of water, the two West Central African men were not able to execute their form of combat that required sufficient room to leap and twist.[80] In another moment, the rural guard surprised and captured members of the settlement who were unable to reach their weapons and had been forced into a narrow ravine.[81] Most accounts regarding the hillside settlement report that members escaped by descending the hillside, fording a river, and then meeting at a location higher in the foothills a few days later.[82] Armed, trained, and coordinated, the fugitives from slavery who formed the hillside settlement repeatedly bested Trujillo's colonial forces by returning to and rebuilding the hillside location.[83] Critically, there is no record of Gabriel and Domingo or their *Malemba* lieutenants' capture. Apparently for decades, the hillside *palenque* members coordinated their refusal.

Highly regulated and carefully organized, the settlement attracted men and women who sought community outside of enslavement. Three *ladina* women identified as "from Congo land" provide the most intimate assessment of life among the houses, gardens, and patios in the settlement. Captured, interrogated, and probably tortured by the rural guard, Isabel, Inés, and María confessed that settlement members had forcefully abducted them.[84] It is possible that the captured women attempted a legal strategy to avoid criminal charges by emphasizing their victimhood against supposed predatory criminal *cimarrones*.[85] Isabel, Inés, and María also could have been captured by the settlement members as laborers and perhaps unwilling companions, much like military forces would have done in West Central Africa.[86] Indeed, all three women explained that their main task in the settlement was to garden, grind maize, and prepare food such as *sango*, a thick porridge of West Central Africa, and *chicha*, a corn beer commonly consumed throughout the Andes.[87] All three women, however, appear to have incorporated the settlement into their own fugitive goals. Prior to their capture, Isabel, a skilled market woman, had left an abusive Trujillo enslaver, while Inés escaped from her enslaver multiple times in search of her husband.[88] Another possibility, especially as understood among Kongo people (including Isabel, Inés, and María), was that as captured people they were to marry and establish households in their adoptive new home.[89] However disciplined and strict, the settlement leadership appeared to be assimilating new members since in West Central Africa, strangers were transformed into junior relatives by intermarriage, but also through the public acts of patronage and redistribution.[90] Indeed, in the settlement, while members recounted food scarcity and constant work, none of the witnesses described the physical abuse and sale of members that characterized Spanish colonial slavery. The settlement also allowed people to leave. As María explained, at one point Gabriel could not provide for the settlement, so members left the *palenque*, descending the hillside in search of new fugitive spaces.[91] Highly regimented, definitively hierarchical, and certainly patriarchal, the settlement did not replicate a colonial Spanish ownership of humans as property.

Turning away did not mean a lack of threat as Gabriel and his settlement challenged the sovereignty of Spanish colonial authorities and regional enslavers. West Central Africans and others were drawn to the settlement not solely due to the members' military skills but also to the organizational capabilities of Gabriel whom, Isabel noted, "all obeyed."[92] Settlement members named Gabriel as their captain and his *compañero* Domingo as his lieutenant, but also his magistrate.[93] The civic title suggests that fugitives from slavery, such as Juan Mosanga, sought a ruler because, in contrast, outside of the settlement "he did not have a captain nor who to govern him."[94] Gabriel's governance style may have taken cues from a seventeenth-century West Central African lord, or a *soba*—who though required to pay tribute to Iberians, still regulated the incursion of enemy combatants and mediated trade while protecting their subjects.[95] Pointedly, the *ladina* Congo women of the settlement described how Gabriel was engaged "in the war of the Spanish."[96] More than a mere skirmish, Gabriel and Domingo mounted a defense of their sovereign space by playing drums "like in battle," communicating orders to their soldiers and ordering civilians to take cover.[97] Lords of the fugitive settlement, Gabriel and Domingo intimidated the rural guard militarily and opposed the political hegemony of Trujillo's Spanish authorities.

In the narrow valley and rugged hillsides outside of Trujillo, Gabriel and Domingo communicated their positions as powerful military and political leaders, clearly refusing the category of slave. Women from the settlement recalled the stirring image of their leaders, noting that Domingo wore a blue cape while Gabriel sported a fashionable slashed and padded black taffeta shirt.[98] Among the *palenque* community, this clothing marked both men's command. Like Trujillo's militiamen, Domingo wore a uniform of a steadfast lieutenant but also the color reserved for a king's regalia in West Central Africa's Ndongo.[99] Gabriel's luxurious attire reminded his community of his prowess, defiance, and skills since he had won the shirt from a Spaniard during a raid, but also because West Central Africans commonly employed imported cloth to visibly mark prestige, honor, and authority.[100] In the criminal cases against *palenque* members, Trujillo's enslavers simultaneously recognized and dismissed Gabriel's leadership, as one Spanish *vecino* claimed that Gabriel was a "captain [who wore] a fake garment of Señor Santiago saying that he was *governador* and *caudillo*."[101] Clearly, as the undisputed *palenque* leader, Gabriel dressed as other West Central African elites who wore hats, capes, and stockings as well as displayed buttons, umbrellas, and other European apparel to mark their prestige.[102] In their attempt to dismiss a rival and competitor, Trujillo's enslavers interpreted Gabriel's creolized Kongo Catholicism as fake and his clothing as a disingenuous proof of leadership. Yet, by employing the insignias and colors of Saint James, a long-standing patron of Iberian soldiers, Gabriel invoked a powerful tool intended to bring him victory in battle.[103] Indeed, Afonso, Kongo's king, had called on Saint James to defeat his half-brother.[104] Gabriel's clothing, then, worked in several registers. To indigenous Andeans and West Central Africans, he clearly communicated his superiority, and to colonial enslavers, he and his followers articulated a politic that refused to obey colonial authority.

Fragmented evidence from criminal accusations illuminates how fugitives from slavery created a community politic that did not reference enslavement at all. Trujillo's rural guard repeatedly reported that settlement members hurled "many shameful words" toward those who attempted to roust them.[105] It is plausible that the narrow valley provided the right acoustics for *palenque* members to shout down to their enemies below. Given their fluency in Iberian languages, members of Gabriel and Domingo's settlement knew which words and phrases would be offensive.[106] What is notable is why the rural guard would bother to report these incidents of wordplay. Clearly, the rural guard was insulted by words that should only be traded in Iberian society by peers.[107] By insulting their attackers, the fugitives from slavery clearly inverted the expected hierarchy of enslaved deference to colonial authorities. Additionally, in 1641 the rural guard also captured fugitives from slavery who were not a part of Gabriel and Domingo's settlement. Instead, Pasqual, a *ladino* man "who says he is of Congo land" reported that he had joined with a Black man called Xinga who led eight fugitives from slavery.[108] Rather than using a Christian name, the infamous leader was known by the name of a people living in the area of Matamba, the location of the last capital of Queen Njinga (also called Zinga or Xinga), a powerful warrior and astute political leader of Ndongo in West Central Africa.[109] Among West Central Africans traded through Luanda into the Atlantic and Pacific, Xinga could have been associated with military might, esteemed royalty, and a claim to the legitimate rule of Ndongo or Angola.[110] Trujillo's authorities attempted to dismiss the group as a band of thieves. Still, the West Central African men resisted capture with expert use of swords and guns to literally disappear into the uncultivated hillsides.[111] For the historian, the archival shard of Xinga's name suggests that West Central Africans in colonial Peru signaled to each other independent polities, leadership hierarchies, and claims to independence outside of Iberian colonial comprehension.

Enslavers, in turn, struggled to retain patriarchal control of fugitive men and women, who they considered to be dependents within their extended households as well as valuable property. Fugitives from slavery, especially those who formed cohesive and long-lasting communities, defied enslavers. Wearing feathers, signaling attacks with drums, and singing their defiance, fugitive soldiers militarily refused enslavement in a manner that was only partially understandable to enslavers and colonial authorities. By illustrating to enslavers that they were soldiers, perhaps better ones than the rural guard, and with a home to defend, *palenque* members communicated their place in relation to the Spanish lettered city, or legal hegemony.

First, fugitives established a peer equivalence between themselves and enslavers that, though denied in Spanish measurements of race and slavery, was made plain in terms of fugitives' military might. Second, in the distinct space of the *palenque* and the repeated defenses, fugitives suggested a larger vision of what constituted freedom on the northern Peruvian coast that, while coexisting with slavery, was not bound by it. Moving apart from enslavers and refusing Spanish authority, fugitive leaders claimed positions of patronage and rulership that presented a range of political choices to Africans and their descendants not bound by the lettered city.

Conclusions

Enslavement in the early modern Iberian world categorically denied, and in practice circumscribed, the abilities of enslaved people and fugitives from slavery to live with their kin, claim bodily sovereignty, or organize labor according to their community's standards. Regardless, fugitives understood, practiced, and articulated a politic and a practice of freedom. Fugitives from slavery counted time according to their own interests, moved toward spaces inhabited by their kin, and defended their communities. By claiming time and space, fugitives refused to labor when and where it was desired by enslavers. Moving freely, fugitives challenged the boundaries marked by enslavers between the territory of the hacienda and "uncontrolled" *monte* settled by West Central Africans. These borderlands were constructed by the Spanish against the pull of fugitives who conceptualized a sovereignty separate from enslavers. The challenge has been how to extract fugitive geographical articulations from colonial archives. I have worked, in this chapter, to employ archival fragments to reveal how enslaved men who armed themselves and fugitive women who built kinship allegiances demonstrated autonomous politics and practices viewable through an African diasporic lens. Rather than think of fugitives in relation solely to Spanish justice or colonial enslavers, how did fugitive claims of time and space as well as refusal defy our own classifications of center or periphery?[112] By building a narrative of fugitive practices from the fragments of the archives and the pieces of official testimony that do not fit into colonial Spanish narratives and geographies, I suggest what may have been possible for fugitives in their hard-won spatial and conceptual territories.

Notes

I thank Kristen Block, Joan Bristol, Rebecca Earle, Cameron Jones, Ann Kakaliouras, and Tamara Walker for their exceptional critique. Participants and audiences during presentations at the May 2021 Latin American Studies Association and January 2012 American Historical Association meetings provided critical comments. Research funding was provided by the University of California, Irvine's Humanities Center.

1. Archivo Regional La Libertad (Trujillo, Peru) (ARLL). Corregimiento (Co). Causas Criminales (Cr). Legajo (Leg.) 247. Expediente (Exp.) 2583 (1657), 6.

2. For more discussion of how criminal charges against Black men were racialized and gendered, see Aidoo, *Slavery Unseen*, 6; Blumenthal, *Enemies and Familiars*, 168; Finch, *Rethinking Slave Rebellion*, 151.

3. Macera, *Los Jesuitas y la agricultura*, 202, 206; Ramírez, *Provincial Patriarchs*, 84, 110.

4. Rama, *Lettered City*, 11, 22; Rappaport and Cummins, *Beyond the Lettered City*, 20, 113–14.

5. Avilez Rocha, "Maroons in the *Montes*," 17. For Spanish colonizers' identification of fugitives from slavery with the *monte*, see J. Gutiérrez Rivas, "Disconformes con su destino," 73; Tardieu, *Cimarrones de Panama*, 197.

6. Commonly, regional authorities questioned how long captured fugitives had been absent from their owners but also where and with whom they had hidden. See the testimony of Gaspar, of *casta angola*, ARLL. Co. Cr. Leg. 245. Exp. 2493 (1638), 2v. In 1639, the magistrate issued a decree against "any person of any *estado, calidad*, or condition" hiding a Black fugitive, suggesting that enslavers as well as enslaved and freed people were working together in fugitive activities. ARRL. Co. Asuntos de gobierno (Asuntos). Leg. 267. Exp. 3129 (1639), 1.

7. Camp, *Closer to Freedom*, 15–17; Trouillot, *Silencing the Past*, 51.

8. Thompson, *Flight to Freedom*, 133, 181.

9. Camp, *Closer to Freedom*, 7. Camp explains that the term *rival geography* was first employed by Edward Said and continues to be used by geographers of colonial occupation.

10. Camp, *Closer to Freedom*, 7.

11. Gomes, "Other Black Atlantic Borders," 274, 275; Roberts, *Freedom as Marronage*, 15, 77.

12. McKittrick, *Demonic Grounds*, 41, 42.

13. Camp, *Closer to Freedom*, 7.

14. Fuentes, *Dispossessed Lives*, 7, 127; Johnson, *Wicked Flesh*, 14.

15. Camp, *Closer to Freedom*, 41, 44, 48; Walker, *Exquisite Slaves*, 52–53, 59.

16. For more on the work of exceeding, see Campt, *Listening to Images*, 98.

17. For more on how to read judicial archives cognizant of violence against enslaved people, see Fuentes, *Dispossessed Lives*, 108–9.

18. *Recopilacion de Leyes*, Titulo Quinto, Ley xxi, Ley xxii.

19. Sherwin Bryant discusses how colonial regulations of enslaved fugitives were associated with crimes such as robbery as well as murder. Bryant, "Enslaved Rebels," 15–17.

20. ARRL. Co. Cr. Leg. 245. Exp. 2493 (1638), 1v–2v; ARRL. Ca. Cr. Leg. 80. Exp. 1380 (1647), 15–17v; ARRL. Co. Cr. Leg. 249. Exp. 2676 (1692), 1v–4v; ARRL. Ca. Cr. Leg. 82. Exp. 1454 (1704), 3v–5; ARRL. Ca. Cr. Leg. 83. Exp. 1485 (1725), 6v–8.

21. ARRL. Ca. Cr. Leg. 82. Exp. 1440 (1697), 1; ARRL. Ca. Cr. Leg. 80. Exp. 1380 (1647), 16; ARRL. Ca. Ords. Leg. 17. Exp. 364 (1637); ARRL. Ca. Cr. Leg. 78. Exp. 1314 (1616), 1v.

22. Hartman, *Scenes of Subjection*, 12.

23. ARRL. Ca. Cr. Leg. 82. Exp. 1440 (1697), 8.

24. ARRL. Ca. Cr. Leg. 79. Exp. 1325 (1618), n/f.

25. ARRL. Ca. Cr. Leg. 83. Exp. 1485 (1725), 7.

26. For more on how the colonial archive follows the logic of enslavers, see Fuentes, *Dispossessed Lives*, 114.

27. ARRL. Co. Cr. Leg. 247. Exp. 2587 (1660), 2.

28. Roberts, *Freedom as Marronage*, 15.

29. ARRL. Co. Ords. Leg. 194. Exp. 1261 (1653), 2, 3v.

30. ARRL. Co. Ords. Leg. 194. Exp. 1261 (1653), 3.

31. Fuentes, *Dispossessed Lives*, 111.

32. ARRL. Co. Cr. Leg. 245. Exp. 2500 (1639), 12v.

33. ARRL. Co. Cr. Leg. 247. Exp. 2587 (1660), 1v.

34. ARRL. Co. Cr. Leg. 247. Exp. 2587 (1660), n/f.

35. ARRL. Co. Cr. Leg. 246. Exp. 2533 (1642), 1.

36. ARRL. Ca. Cr. Leg. 83. Exp. 1485 (1725), 3v.

37. Espinosa, *Cimarronaje y palenques*, 31.

38. Bryant, "Enslaved Rebels," 15.

39. For more on the dangerous locations of official and unofficial space, see Camp, *Closer to Freedom*, 50.

40. ARRL. Co. Cr. Leg. 246. Exp. 2533 (1642), 1v; Thompson, *Flight to Freedom*, 249.

41. Avilez Rocha, "Maroons in the *Montes*," 22.

42. ARRL. Ca. Cr. Leg. 82. Exp. 1440 (1697), 8.

43. ARRL. Ca. Cr. Leg. 78. Exp. 1314 (1616), 1; Thompson, *Flight to Freedom*, 191.

44. ARRL. Co. Cr. Leg. 246. Exp. 2533 (1642), 4; Espinoza, "Cimarronaje y palenques," 36; Santos Gomes, "Peasants, Maroons," 378; Thompson, *Flight to Freedom*, 253.

45. ARRL. Ca. Cr. Leg. 82. Exp. 1440 (1697), 2.

46. ARRL. Protocolos. Cortijo Quero. Leg. 117, #32 "Carta de poder," (1707), 71.

47. ARRL. Ca. Cr. Leg. 82. Exp. 1440 (1697), 2; ARRL. Co. Cr. Leg. 246. Exp. 2533 (1642), 1.

48. ARRL. Ca. Cr. Leg. 82. Exp. 1434 (1693), 2v. Likewise, Domingo Angola explained that he fled to the *monte*. ARRL. Ca. Cr. Leg. 80. Exp. 1380 (1647), 17v.

49. Fuentes, *Dispossessed Lives*, 29.

50. For more on the distinction between the *monte* and what enslaved people knew, see Finch, *Rethinking Slave Rebellion*, 63. For fugitive practices that built kinship connections, see Camp, *Closer to Freedom*, 44.

51. ARRL. Cr. Leg. 83. Exp. 1485 (1725), 7; ARRL. Ca. Cr. Leg. 79. Exp. 1325 (1618).

52. ARRL. Ca. Cr. Leg. 78. Exp. 1314 (1616), 1v; ARRL. Ca. Ords. Leg. 17. Exp. 364 (1637), n/f.

53. Camp, *Closer to Freedom*, 42; Finch, *Rethinking Slave Rebellion*, 64–65.

54. Avilez Rocha, "Maroons in the Montes," 18. For more on the refusal of containment, see Campt, *Listening to Images*, 43.

55. Gaspar, "Material Culture," 238; Thompson, *Flight to Freedom*, 259.

56. ARRL. Ca. Cr. Leg. 82. Exp. 1440 (1697), 8; Gomes, "Africans and *Petit Marronage*," 76; Thompson, *Flight to Freedom*, 65.

57. ARRL. Ca. Cr. Leg. 79. Exp. 1325 (1618); Camp, *Closer to Freedom*, 39, 47–48; Finch, *Rethinking Slave*, 64, 74; Fraga, *Crossroads of Freedom*, 58; Gomes, "Other Black Atlantic Borders," 260; Thompson, *Flight to Freedom*, 139.

58. Gomes, "Africans and *Petit* Marronage," 76; Thompson, *Flight to Freedom*, 191; Wilson, "The Performance of Freedom," 65.

59. Finch, *Rethinking Slave*, 64–65; Gaspar, "Material Culture," 238; Santos Gomes, "Peasants, Maroons," 386; Thompson, *Flight to Freedom*, 259.

60. Fuentes, *Dispossessed Lives*, 29.

61. Avilez Rocha, "Maroons in the *Montes*," 17, 18.

62. ARRL. Co. Cr. Leg. 244. Exp. 2472 (1634), 1; ARRL. Co. Asuntos de Gobierno. Leg. 267. Exp. 3129 (1639), 1.

63. ARRL. Co. Cr. Leg. 245. Exp. 2500 (1639), 3, 4, 5v; ARRL. Ca. Cr. Leg. 79. Exp. 1353 (1642), 2v.

64. ARRL. Co. Cr. Leg. 244. Exp. 2472 (1634), 2; ARRL. Co. Cr. Leg. 245. Exp. 2494 (1638), 3; ARRL. Co. Cr. Leg. 245. Exp. 2500 (1639), 5v, 7, 9v, 26.

65. ARRL. Co. Cr. Leg. 245. Exp. 2494 (1638), 3; ARRL. Ca. Cr. Leg. 79. Exp. 1353 (1642), 15.

66. ARRL. Co. Cr. Leg. 245. Exp. 2500 (1639), 16.

67. Caldeira, "Angola and the Seventeenth-Century," 115–16; Heywood and Thornton, *Central Africans*, 40–41, 55, 127; Thornton, *The Kingdom of Kongo*, 23, 25, 32, 33.

68. ARRL. Ca. Cr. Leg. 79. Exp. 1351 (1641), 2v.

69. ARRL. Ca. Cr. Leg. 79. Exp. 1350 (1641), 5; ARRL. Ca. Cr. Leg. 79. Exp. 1350 (1641), 18v.

70. Gabriel controlled the accession and distribution of tobacco, underlining what West Central Africans would have expected from their leader. Hilton, *The Kingdom of the Kongo*, 43; Miller, *Way of Death*, 49.

71. ARRL. Co. Cr. Leg. 245. Exp. 2500 (1639), 13v.

72. For a discussion of the West Central African "ongoing process of creolization," see Candido, *An African Slaving Port*, 52.

73. ARRL. Ca. Cr. Leg. 79. Exp. 1350 (1641), ff. 1v, 2, 11, 11v, 13, 14; Thornton, "Art," 362–63; Merolla da Sorrento, "A to Voyage Congo," 710, 732.

74. Heywood and Thornton, *Central Africans*, 142.

75. Thornton, *Warfare in Atlantic*, 105, 106.

76. Thornton, *Warfare in Atlantic*, 108.

77. ARRL. Co. Cr. Leg. 246. Exp. 2532 (1643), 2.

78. Thornton, *Warfare in Atlantic*, 107.

79. ARRL. Co. Cr. Leg. 246. Exp. 2533 (1642), 1.

80. Thornton, "Art," 363–64.

81. ARRL. Ca. Cr. Leg. 79. Exp. 1350 (1641), f. 2, 6v.

82. Retreating and regrouping was a tactic employed by Angola commanders and members of Cuban *palenques* with a strong Congo membership. Thornton, "Art," 368; La Rosa Corzo, *Runaway*, 19–20.

83. Years after the 1639 attack by the rural guard, the magistrate reported a settlement with *ranchos* in the same hillside location. ARRL. Co. Asuntos de gobierno. Leg. 267. Exp. 3147 (1646), 2.

84. ARRL. Ca. Cr. Leg. 79. Exp. 1350 (1641), 21v, 25, 28v.

85. McKnight, "Confronted Rituals," para. 44. For an example of an enslaver arguing in court to lessen the charges against an enslaved person accused of *cimarronaje*, see ARRL. Ca. Cr. Leg. 79. Exp. 1345 (1637), 6v.

86. Miller, *Way of Death*, 386.

87. All Spanish-speaking, the women of the settlement may have translated their name for grain beer that was usually brewed by women in the drier coastal areas or savanna plains of West Central Africa. Curto, *Enslaving Spirits*, 36–38. ARRL. Ca. Cr. Leg. 79. Exp. 1350 (1641), 18v. Common foods for West Central Africans and their enslaved neighbors, these ingredients were very much like the mealies prepared in Luanda or the *nfundi* made by Kongo women in the seventeenth and eighteenth centuries. ARRL. Ca. Cr. Leg. 79. Exp. 1350 (1641), f. 18v; Miller, *Way of Death*, 394; Thornton, *Kingdom of Kongo*, 30; Knight, *Working the Diaspora*, 43. By this period maize had become a staple item among Kongo commoners. Guattini, "A Curious and Exact Account," 620, 629; ARRL. Co. Asuntos. Leg. 267. Exp. 3147 (1646), 1, 2; ARRL. Ca. Cr. Leg. 79. Exp. 1350 (1641), f. 22v; Hilton, *Kingdom of Kongo*, 6; Thornton, *The Kingdom of Kongo*, 29; Broecke, *Pieter Van Den Broecke*, 59. For other examples of provision grounds within fugitive settlements, see Lokken, "A Maroon Moment," 51; Sheridan, "The Maroons of Jamaica," 164.

88. ARRL. Ca. Cr. Leg. 79. Exp. 1350 (1641), 21–21v, 25.

89. Thornton, *The Kingdom of Kongo*, 22.

90. Miller, *Way of Death*, 49.

91. ARRL. Ca. Cr. Leg. 79. Exp. 1350 (1641), 30.

92. ARRL. Ca. Cr. Leg. 79. Exp. 1350 (1641), 22.

93. ARRL. Ca. Cr. Leg. 79. Exp. 1350 (1641), 19, 22.

94. ARRL. Ca. Cr. Leg. 79. Exp. 1350 (1641), 32v.

95. Candido, *An African Enslaving Port*, 52–53.

96. ARRL. Ca. Cr. Leg. 79. Exp. 1350 (1641), f. 23v, "andaba apretado con la guerra de los españoles." Another captured witness, Inés of Congo land, stated that "Gabriel andaba ocupado en la guerra de los españoles." I am correcting my own translation in O'Toole, "'In a War,'"

50–51.

97. Captured witnesses explained that noncombatants hid when the settlement's soldiers went to war. ARRL. Ca. Cr. Leg. 79. Exp. 1350 (1641), 23v, 27v. For examples of other fugitives employing drums in battle, see La Rosa Corzo, *Runaway Slave Settlements*, 107. During battle, West Central African armies communicated with each other through drum signals, and military leaders directed the battle with sounds such as bells. Thornton, "Art," 366; Thornton, "African Dimensions," 1111; Battell, *The Strange Adventures*, 15, 21; Birmingham, *Trade and Conflict*, 101.

98. ARRL. Ca. Cr. Leg. 79. Exp. 1350 (1641), 19.

99. Fromont, "Common Threads," 846; Walker, *Exquisite Slaves*, 160.

100. Fromont, "Common Threads," 857; Candido, "Women's Material," 83–84.

101. ARRL. Co. Cr. Leg. 246. Exp. 2533 (1642), f. 8v. For another example of fugitives from slavery invoking Santiago, see Aguado, *Historia de Venezuela* in *African Maroons*, 53, 56.

102. Walker, *Exquisite Slaves*, 53. Guattini, "A Curious and Exact Account," 628; Hilton, *The Kingdom of Kongo*, 109; Heywood and Thornton, *Central Africans*, 218; Merolla da Sorrento, "A Voyage to Congo," 695; Broecke, *Pieter Van Den Broecke*, 58.

103. For an example of other fugitive Africans adapting Santiago in battle, see F. Rodríguez, "Cimarrón Revolts," 138. For a discussion of the adaptive powers of Santiago, see Silverblatt, "Political Memories," 187.

104. Heywood and Thornton, *Central Africans*, 62.

105. ARRL. Ca. Cr. Leg. 79. Exp. 1350 (1641), 6v.

106. The Kongolese could have been familiar with Portuguese, and all captured fugitives spoke Spanish so well that they did not require translators. Last, many in the fugitive community were quite knowledgeable of enslavers and their proxies having escaped several times from their owners. Thornton, "African Dimensions," 1107; Guattini, "A Curious and Exact Account," 628. ARRL. Co. Cr. Leg. 245. Exp. 2500 (1639), 11v.

107. For inversion of colonial authority within subaltern insults, see Lipsett-Rivera, "*De Obra y Palabra*," 530.

108. ARRL. Ca. Cr. Leg. 79. Exp. 1350 (1641), 34.110.

109. Heywood, *Njinga of Angola*, 157, 274. By the 1620s, her army had adopted an aggressive warfare practice of Imbangala, and by the 1650s, her son, Njinga Mona, was the senior commander. Anguiano, *Vida, y Virtvdes*, 216; Thornton, "Legitimacy and Political Power," 32; Birmingham, *Trade and Conflict*, 92–95; Hilton, *The Kingdom of Kongo*, 111–12. It is also plausible that the reference was Jinga, another polity involved in the slaving wars. Miller, *Way of Death*, 121, 145.

110. Heywood, *Njinga of Angola*, 178, 201.

111. ARRL. Ca. Cr. Leg. 79. Exp. 1350 (1641), ff. 34–34v.

112. Sweeny, "Market Marronage," 198.

CHAPTER TEN

AQUEOUS AND DRY BORDERLANDS

Africans and Their Descendants in Colonial Rio de la Plata

Alex Borucki

DURING THE 250-year history of the traffic of captive Africans and Afro-Brazilians to the Río de la Plata, from about the 1580s to the 1830s, free and enslaved Black men and women were both agents and subjects in the process of constructing borderlands.[1] In the littoral of this region, Buenos Aires and Montevideo were the most significant Spanish ports of the South Atlantic, located in lands claimed by both the Spanish and Portuguese empires. The Río de la Plata was a region of Amerindian frontiers as well, where indigenous societies adopted European horses and weaponry to resist the expansion of Spanish colonialism. Itinerant indigenous groups organized as *tolderías* held different degrees of control over the territory in the hinterland of Buenos Aires, Montevideo, and other towns.[2] The Spanish and Portuguese colonists and their descendants had to negotiate passage with Amerindian groups in the countryside as well as through the Paraná and Uruguay Rivers even during the late colonial era. Effective Spanish rule stretched just a few miles south of Buenos Aires, and large pockets of Amerindian control existed in the Gran Chaco region of what is today Northern Argentina, Western Paraguay, and Eastern Bolivia. The Guarani missions, headed by the Jesuits up until 1767 on the shores of the Paraná and Uruguay Rivers north from Buenos Aires and East from Asunción (Paraguay), also buffered Spanish and Portuguese imperial claims, even as they were under Spanish rule. The Río de la Plata was also a maritime edge of empire, where an invading army could disembark and march toward Upper Peru, the main silver-producing region of South America.[3] While coastal shipping bringing both legal and illegal commerce linked Buenos Aires with Brazilian ports since the late sixteenth century, this traffic increased notably during the viceregal era (1777–1810), when these maritime interactions could be examined as a waterscape frontier or a maritime borderland.[4]

The definitive fall of the Portuguese town of Colonia del Sacramento, across the Río de la Plata from Buenos Aires, to Spanish hands in 1777 led Afro-Brazilians living in this town to move as free-Black men and women to Montevideo and Buenos Aires, where they became significant for Black social organizations such as Black Catholic confraternities and free-Black militias in the 1780s. In the following years, Afro-Brazilians knowledgeable of the countryside alongside indigenous men and women shaped strategies of resistance that facilitated the escape of enslaved people from Montevideo to the borderlands between Iberian powers in what is today's northern Uruguay and southern Brazil. This social practice led to a collective slave escape from Montevideo to the borderlands in 1803, the most important coordinated action of resistance by the enslaved in the history of Uruguay. Afro-Brazilians living in the Portuguese-Spanish borderlands also became agents of the transimperial politics in the roles of contrabandists, defectors, spies, and military scouts.[5]

These were not the only type of interactions defining the borderlands for people of African ancestry. To expand this register of social practices and interactions, this chapter examines strategies of autonomy of people of African ancestry in relation to the indigenous-Spanish frontier. Africans and their descendants could modify the terms of their enslavement and even liberate themselves when interacting with indigenous groups. While doing this, Africans and their descendants brought an additional meaning to the construction of borderlands in the region. This chapter also focuses on maritime experiences, as free Africans and Afro-Brazilians could be enslaved if they found themselves in the maritime borderland of the South Atlantic littoral during war as examined in the last section. Crossing imperial boundaries for enslaved people during wartime usually entailed freedom, as illustrated by slaves living in Brazil who liberated themselves by joining Spanish troops during wartime. However, the encounters of free Africans and Afro-Brazilians with privateers (merchant ships outfitted and armed to capture enemy property) illustrate a different pattern. The survey of claims of freedom in the maritime routes connecting Brazil with Montevideo and Buenos Aires also reveals seafaring communities supporting the claims of Africans and their descendants, which leads to a rethinking of these ports as a maritime borderland as well.

In Buenos Aires and Montevideo as well as far inland from these towns, indigenous peoples, Africans, Spaniards, Portuguese, and their mixed descendants had mature knowledge of each other by the late eighteenth century. To a certain extent, each group knew how to operate under different sovereignties—including indigenous rule—to make sense of the borderland. Fabrício Prado's understanding of the Rio de la Plata as an *interaction zone* is useful here to examine a mature colonial society where European and European-descended elites and commoners interacted with indigenous peoples, Africans, and their mixed ancestry—all of them shaping narratives and definitions of borderlands. In interaction zones, descriptions of the borderlands were mediated by contacts among unequal social groups, both living in the region and originating from the larger Atlantic.[6] When seeking autonomy and freedom, Africans and their descendants strategically defined the borderlands of the Río de la Plata to their own advantage. While different communities held knowledge of each other, still uncertainty defined interactions in the borderlands both at sea and overland. This was a space of dangers and possibilities. As Jeffrey Erbig presents, the late colonial indigenous communities controlled the Rio de la Plata by differing degrees, forcing the Spanish and Portuguese to obtain indigenous authorization to cross the landscape when traveling between towns. We should, however, also consider the waterscape, the coastal connections between the Portuguese and the Spanish with a degree of uncertainty, particularly for free Africans and their descendants who sailed from the coastlines connecting South American Atlantic ports.[7]

National Archives and Spaces

While the historiography on the borderlands in the Río de la Plata usually centers on spaces limited by the contours of national archives located in cities such as Asunción, Buenos Aires, and Montevideo, which limits the space by national boundaries and keyword searches by national identity in these repositories, people living in colonial times experienced the borderlands before the creation of the nineteenth-century republics. Their lives highlighted connections from Upper Peru (today's Bolivia), Paraguay, Argentina, and Uruguay and their shared colonial borderland with Portuguese Brazil. Colonial sources provide information beyond the nations under which later national archives were organized. In addition, materials from national archives tend to showcase claims of autonomy, freedom, and sovereignty in the borderland, as well as those related to trade and contraband, given that representatives of colonial rule in the borderland, or the subjects of these cases themselves, asked for a resolution to these claims in colonial centers such as Buenos Aires. The human experiences and interactions were more complex than the genre of cases produced by colonial authorities and preserved by national archives.

This movement of both people and paper (the files or *expedientes*) across regions is illustrated by the case of Antonio (his last name is nowhere in his case), a free Black man from São Paulo, Brazil, who was captured by Paraguace Indians and sold into slavery in Asunción, Paraguay, in the early 1730s. According to those who rescued Antonio, the Paraguace captured him from Portuguese forces who were intending to attack Spanish Paraguay. Antonio disagreed about his participation in the military. Maria Roxas bought ("rescued") Antonio from the Paraguace, and later, a Portuguese resident in Asunción, José de Silva, bought Antonio from her. José told Antonio that he would liberate him after working two years for him, for Antonio to be able to save money to pay his travel from Buenos Aires to Brazil. After two years, both José de Silva and Antonio made it to Buenos Aires. While Antonio thought he was going to be embarking to Brazil, José tried to sell Antonio as a slave, which sparked the actions of Antonio to pursue his freedom by presenting his case to colonial authorities.[8] This story was not unique, given that the Spanish subjects in Asunción asked the colonial authorities to declare "slaves" all Black men and women that their indigenous allies captured from the Portuguese in 1734, which colonial authorities declined. Thus, a number of free Afro-Brazilians were probably held as slaves in Asunción. Their claims were heard as far as in Buenos Aires. The rejection of colonial authorities to declare this group of people "slaves" may be one of the reasons why José de Silva took Antonio from Asunción to Buenos Aires, to avoid his liberation. In 1742 the governor of Buenos Aires set Antonio free with the obligation of remaining enslaved five years after his rescue from the Paraguace, which Antonio had already done by serving Maria Roxas and José de Silva. Thus, he walked free.[9]

Spanish authorities in Buenos Aires eagerly tried to extract information about Portuguese settlements and troop movements from free and enslaved Black men and women across this vast region and as far north from the viceregal capital as in today's Bolivia. In 1782, the Angolan-born Miguel Alves Ferreira provided knowledge to the colonial authorities in the Moxo Missions and Santa Cruz de la Sierra (today's Bolivia) about the Portuguese in Mato Grosso. While born in Africa, Miguel lived in Mato Grosso most of his life. According to his narrative, he crossed to the Spanish settlements because his enslaver had failed to fulfill a promise to release him from slavery even though Antonio had saved money to that end. Antonio provided extended reports of the advance of the Portuguese on the Paraguay River north and to the west of Spanish towns. He declared that there were many (muchísimos) "Blacks and Portuguese extracting mineral," which was the reason why Portuguese merchants were venturing there too.[10] The Spanish trusted Miguel Alves Ferreira as they described him as a "quite rational Black," and his testimony was one of the very first in a lengthy file sent from Santa Cruz to Buenos Aires, then the capital of the viceroyalty of the Rio de la Plata.

Colonial sources produced in this region commonly place indigenous people in the borderland, but they remain relatively silent about those living in towns like Buenos Aires and Montevideo. In a long report about the defenses of the city, and in response to the question of the quantity of provisions needed to warehouse in order to feed the population during a military siege, the governor of Montevideo Joaquin del Pino mentioned "Blacks, Mulattos, Indians, and Mestizos" who were unaccounted for by colonial censuses or viceregal authorities, but lived in the city and were essential to move the artillery.[11] By 1800, a section outside of Montevideo's walls was indeed known as "cuartel de los indios" (neighborhood of the Indians).[12] Thus, when examining interactions between people of African and indigenous ancestry in the borderlands, scholars should note that these shared experiences may have originated in the towns and then extended to rural areas or vice versa. Indigenous people as well as enslaved and free Black men and women were part of the floating populations in these towns as well.[13]

Autonomy in Indigenous and Black Interactions

Indigenous-Spanish, indigenous-Portuguese, and both overland and maritime interactions between the Spanish and Portuguese overlapped with each other in the experiences of Africans and their descendants. Free and enslaved Black men and women found themselves sailing from Rio de Janeiro to Buenos Aires, joining indigenous groups (both coerced and by their own free will) from Patagonia to Paraguay, and participating in the Portuguese-Spanish military conflicts in the Río de la Plata. Take the case of the free *pardo* (man of mixed African and European ancestry) from Buenos Aires, Agustin Rodriguez. In 1753, colonial authorities ordered all free Black and *pardo* able-bodied men of Buenos Aires to join the Spanish forces against the Guarani missions, located east of the Uruguay River, which had rebelled against a Spanish-Portuguese treaty ceding the missions to Portugal. Agustin marched to what is today Rio Grande do Sul (southern Brazil) following the troops fighting against these Guarani groups. In 1762, the governor of Buenos Aires, Pedro Cevallos, ordered all free Black and *pardo* men into militia service to support the Spanish attack against the Portuguese town of Colonia del Sacramento, which the Spanish took over but then returned to Portuguese rule in 1764. As a result, Agustin lived two years in Colonia fighting alongside Guarani militias against the besieged Portuguese. While Agustin had fought Guarani groups in 1753, now he was in the same army with other Guarani troops besieging Colonia. When he returned to Buenos Aires, Agustin became a worker in the royal carts (*carretas del rey*), which had him transporting goods along the route to Mendoza in the foot of the Andes mountains. Probably because of this experience, in 1778, a militia captain selected Agustin to join a large expedition to Salinas Grandes, a salt pan in today's La Pampa province located south and well beyond Spanish control at the time, to extract salt for Buenos Aires and explore a region under indigenous control. After surviving two borderland conflicts and now noting the prospect of war, given that Agustin penned down in his plea the phrase "invasion of the Indians," he sent a petition to the viceroy mentioning that he had never been paid by the crown for his service. Agustin noted he was naked, which was not only a figure of speech defining poverty but also a concrete request given that he predicted encountering cold weather and strong winds in the southern Pampa.[14] Agustin's life experiences, which were not unique given the participation of other men in nonwhite militias, ranged from war against widely different indigenous groups beyond the northern and southern extent of Spanish rule to allying Guarani troops to besiege the Portuguese town of Colonia, located a few miles from Buenos Aires.

Enslaved and free Black men held strategic knowledge for Spanish authorities by knowing the language and customs of indigenous communities as well as the terrain of the borderlands. As they were knowledgeable of how to move through the landscape, pathways, and shortcuts, they became guides or *baqueanos*. Sometimes this knowledge provided Africans and their descendants with an edge to gain autonomy from Spanish authorities. Furthermore, their knowledge of the workings of Spanish society, both countryside and city, could provide people of African ancestry with certain privileges when they sought autonomy within indigenous groups. Ventura, an enslaved man who lived in Rio Negro, the southernmost permanent Spanish post in the mid-eighteenth century, in today's northern Patagonia and southern tip of the Province of Buenos Aires, experienced different degrees of slavery, captivity, and freedom as he lived both under Spanish and indigenous rule. At some point in his life, Ventura was captured by a Pampa indigenous group (or he escaped to this group). In one skirmish with the Pampas in 1779, the Spaniards recaptured Ventura and returned him to his enslaver in Rio Negro. However, since then, Ventura worked for the colonial authorities as a *lenguaraz*, an interpreter between the Spaniards and Pampa *tolderías* (itinerant groups).[15] In 1787, Commander Francisco Viedma asked viceregal authorities for two hundred pesos to free Ventura from Magdalena Guzman in order to recruit Ventura into the royal service officially as a *lenguaraz*, with salary and uniform, given that Ventura was indispensable for continuous communication with the Pampas as he understood their "customs and ideas." This petition went all the way to the High Court of Buenos Aires, the Real Audiencia, which approved the measure by 1791, thus freeing Ventura. He now was supported by the royal treasury with rations and a uniform, though without salary.[16]

This knowledge of both the people and the land was useful to maintain peace, but of course it became essential during war. In 1804, Portuguese troops from the Seven Eastern Missions (former Jesuit Missions on the eastern shore of the Uruguay River occupied by the Portuguese in 1801) stole some six hundred horses from the Spanish in the indigenous town of Belen, south of the Seven Missions (and now in Uruguay). According to Spanish authorities, the Portuguese killed fourteen people and injured nine more. The surprise was such that "Commander Rondeau escaped thanks to the skills and fast thinking of the Black Domingo Guzman, *baqueano* of the troop."[17] This commander was Jose Rondeau, who later became one of the leaders of the independence movement and director of the United Provinces of the Rio de la Plata in the 1810s. Perhaps Domingo Guzman received a commendation or some material benefit for his service, but he surely continued serving in the northern Amerindian frontier between the Spanish and the Portuguese given his unique knowledge of the area.

Knowledge of indigenous society may have sparked enslaved men, and perhaps women, to escape to the borderland to secure autonomy. In 1789, Juan Gallardo requested to the colonial authorities in Buenos Aires that an enslaved man, Damian, about eighteen to twenty years old, be returned to him. Damian had escaped to Chascomus (south of Buenos Aires) "to live among the Indians."[18] Now Gallardo knew that Damian had been captured by the Spanish garrison in Chascomus and requested his return. Damian was born in this region and thus he may have had contacts with indigenous people. A network of small forts (*fortines*) peppered the southern and western hinterland of Buenos Aires, frequently reporting to the city news of free and enslaved Black men and women who were among indigenous groups, some of them willingly like Damian, and others against their will as captives. Spanish garrisons sent lists of captives living among the indigenous *tolderías* to Buenos Aires. For instance, in 1782, colonial authorities received two lists of captives, one with those returned to Spanish control and another listing captives still held by two caciques that included a "free mulatta girl of about nine years old."[19] The recovered captives, Spaniards who lived in between this network of small forts from Lujan to Chascomús and Magdalena, provided additional intelligence of the captives still held by the *tolderías*.[20]

While free Afro-Brazilians were usually present as petty traders and contrabandists in the Spanish-Portuguese border of what is today Uruguay, they were uncommon in the southern frontier of Buenos Aires. The garrison of Fortín Navarro, southwest of Buenos Aires, captured an unnamed free-Black Portuguese man in 1790. He was sent to Buenos Aires and subsequently to Montevideo, probably to be deported in a ship to Brazil, as the Spaniards did with other foreigners who lacked family in the region.[21] He was not among the lists of captives living in *tolderías*; thus, he was willingly in the borderland and perhaps attempting trade with indigenous groups.

Recently arrived Africans also ran away to the indigenous frontier, located near internal slave routes linking Buenos Aires overland to Chile via the Andes, as well as in the Patagonian littoral where ships from Buenos Aires and Montevideo went to cross the Straits of Magellan to reach the Pacific. These ships, in their sailing up the Pacific, stopped in the Chilean port of Valparaiso before their final passage to Lima. Shipwrecks close to the Patagonian coast washed the survivors into indigenous-controlled areas. Manuel Piedra was a slave trader who sold captives in the route from Buenos Aires to Chile via Mendoza. In 1802, an enslaved African boy who suffered this route ran away from a group near Corral de Bustos, in today's province of Cordoba. Later that year, Piedras heard of a young African captured in a Spanish raid against indigenous groups southeast of Buenos Aires, in Salinas, who allegedly matched the clothing that the fugitive was wearing. Piedras asked for his return to Spanish authorities, which, after he provided witnesses about his claim, agreed to comply.[22] In April 1806, in Chascomus, located south from Buenos Aires, the Pampa indigenous leader Manquetripay showed up with others to deliver to the Spanish commander a gravely sick African man. Upon interrogation through a translator, the ill man told the Spaniards that he was among a group of enslaved Africans embarked two years previously from Buenos Aires to Lima, but the vessel shipwrecked in Patagonia, and since then they lived with Manquetripay. It seems that Manquetripay brought this African man to Chascomus to find a cure for him. Both Manquetripay and the unnamed African were sent to Buenos Aires, where the priest of the San Nicolas church baptized the African with the name José before he died. The priest noted that the African was named José because he was known with this name before, and that from his communication with him, the priest believed José was enslaved by the Pampa chief Manquetripay.[23] In this case, the difference between captivity and slavery seemingly blurs, as this story leaves us to wonder about the relationships between Manquetripay and this African man, whether as one of dependency, captivity, or slavery.

The garrisons of the borderland south of Buenos Aires were also places of militarization and punishment, where the authorities of the city deported populations they deemed dangerous. This was an additional reason for Africans and their descendants to be forcibly displaced there. In 1795, Rosa Robles asked the authorities in Buenos Aires to send Mariano to the fort of Barracas for "correction and disciplining."[24] She claimed that the carpenter Mariano was her slave, but after her husband died, she could no longer control him given that there was no other man in the house. Robles added that Mariano saw himself as free now and suffered from mental illness that made him dangerous to others. As the documents include only the petition from Rosa Robles, we lack a response from Mariano. The authorities agreed with Rosa Robles, arrested Mariano, and sent him to Barracas, so that Mariano could serve as carpenter in public works. Thus, these forts could become sites of punishment for, in the opinion of enslavers, intractable slaves. Other enslaved men and women lived in these forts as prisoners as well. While Africans and their descendants tried to escape slavery in the borderlands, or to gain certain autonomy within the conflicts between the Spanish authorities and the indigenous *tolderías*, these forts also served to reinforce captivity for them as sites of exile and deportation.

Securing Freedom in Aqueous Borderlands

Military conflicts constituted an opening of possibilities for enslaved people in Brazil to liberate themselves by escaping to Spanish troops in the Río de la Plata. However, this was always tentative, given that some of those who housed these fugitives also sought to receive service from them and even enslave them again. The fugitives' freedom was in dispute even after decades of settling under Spanish rule. Manuel Olivera was enslaved in the Portuguese fort of San Miguel located in the borderlands, in today's Uruguay, when the Seven Years War led Spanish troops to advance on this fort and later occupy the Portuguese town of Rio Grande in 1762 (in today's Rio Grande do Sul, Brazil). Manuel explained that he fled his enslaver to "be welcomed by the flags of Spain," which was a commonly used phrase by colonial officers in the borderland to convey these situations to their superiors in Buenos Aires and Montevideo. He found Spanish troops led by Commander José de Molina, who consigned Manuel to Captain Joaquin Morote as an auxiliary to serve this officer up to the end of the war. As he was very *baqueano*, knowledgeable of the countryside, Manuel gathered cattle from neighboring Portuguese ranches to feed the Spanish troops on the move. After the war, Manuel continued serving Morote as a free man in Buenos Aires. Later he married a free Black woman as well as established a small farm in lands belonging to Morote. But after twenty years, in 1787, Marina Lara, the widow of Morote, tried to sell him as an enslaved man. In the end, Marina Lara recognized that Manuel's story was true, but he had to ask his support network to testify about the last twenty-five years of his life.[25]

Another case coming from the Seven Years War, and from the same region as well, took place in 1783, when Francisco Chaves tried to re-enslave a woman named Luisa by pointing out that she lacked papers proving her freedom. Luisa argued that in the war of 1762 her mother, enslaved by the Portuguese, joined the Spanish camp of José de Molina in Rio Grande, which made both Luisa and her mother free. Luisa asserted that José de Molina gave her to Francisco Chaves and his wife in the town of San Carlos (in today's eastern Uruguay), but as a free child, only to take care of her up to adulthood. But Chaves countered this version with the testimony of a soldier, arguing that the mother of Juana arrived in Buenos Aires as a prisoner instead, to be sold as a prize of war. Chaves mentions that the enslaved people found in Rio Grande when the Spanish troops arrived were transferred by Molina to the Royal Treasury and some of them were given to military leaders and officials in 1763. The case is truncated, without further witnesses nor verdict, which may suggest an extra-judicial understanding between Luisa and Chaves or that one of the parties ceased litigation. Yet these cases illustrate that men and women who escaped slavery in Brazil could be subjected to re-enslavement after twenty years of living among the Spanish. Thus, they had to keep track of a network of contacts who could support their stories before colonial authorities.[26]

Free Afro-Brazilians also avoided the dangers of re-enslavement by crossing the borderlands during peace. In 1785, Luis Antonio, a free man of mixed ancestry born in Rio de Janeiro, was sent from the Spanish garrison in Yaguarón (in the same borderland that Manuel and Luisa crossed above), alongside other men, to Montevideo.[27] Luis Antonio claimed that he initially was accompanying the Portuguese Sargent José Joaquim Rodrigues from Rio de Janeiro to Rio Grande, the southernmost Portuguese town. Luis Antonio suspected that the Sergeant wanted to take advantage of him, to sell him into slavery in Rio Grande, where Luis Antonio was a stranger lacking the networks of support to vouch for his freedom. This misgiving led Luis Antonio to cross the borderland. He was not alone in his journey to the Spanish garrisons as he was captured with four other men, a Portuguese surgeon, a Peninsular Spaniard, an "Indian from Montevideo," and another indigenous man from Viamão. All of them had previously met in the hemp factory in Rio Grande, where they worked and eventually decided to move to Spanish dominions.[28] While all of these men had different reasons for escaping the hemp factory, all of them vouched for the freedom of Luis Antonio. All of them, as a group, presented themselves to the commander of the countryside (*Comandante de Campaña*), Felix de la Rosa, in the Yaguarón River with the hope to settle under Spanish jurisdiction. The commander sent this group to Montevideo, which put the fate of these men in the hands of the governor. While these types of cases sometimes end with an order of deportation to Brazil, or a communication to Rio Grande to extract information about the enslavers of the fugitives, no such order is found in this file, which may suggest that this group probably was jailed for some time in Montevideo and then released.

The slave trade between Brazilian ports and the Río de la Plata, with extensions all the way to Lima, provided a venue to re-enslave people in Brazil by selling them to Spanish American markets. Cayetana was born in Rio de Janeiro, where she was enslaved in the late eighteenth century. She managed to buy her freedom from Jose Gonzales Fontes, with Luis Pereira de Melo paying for her manumission in exchange for installments with added interest, not an uncommon arrangement. But when the transaction was to be conducted, Gonzales Fontes claimed that Melo's money came from illegal means, and instead of freeing Cayetana he forced her to embark a ship sailing to Buenos Aires to be sold in Lima in 1800. He was trying to sell her outside of Rio de Janeiro as punishment. Once in Buenos Aires, Cayetana was able to seek support from sailors from the ship that carried her, and ultimately, she got the defender of slaves (a city council position) to ask to stop her travel to Lima.[29] The defender blocked the sale as he could not confirm that she had indeed been enslaved. He noted that the recent declaration of war between Spain and Portugal stopped communication between Buenos Aires and Rio de Janeiro, which made it impossible to send a request for information to Cayetana's enslaver. This is another truncated case, but I assume that Cayetana either stayed in Buenos Aires or returned to Rio de Janeiro given that there is no sentence for her to continue embarkation to Lima.[30] War provided Cayetana with some time to at least stop her removal from Buenos Aires and make her case before the authorities there. For others, finding war at seas endangered their freedom as French and Spanish privateers attacked Portuguese ships crossing the South Atlantic.

Free Africans and Afro-Brazilians living in Rio de Janeiro knew about the dangers of kidnapping and maritime re-enslavement, which could forcibly bring them to the Rio de la Plata. Maximiano Francisco Gomes was born enslaved in Rio de Janeiro, where he married Isabel Rebola from West Central Africa and had a daughter also born in slavery, all during the second half of the eighteenth century. His enslaver promised to free Maximiano and his family in his will, which went into effect after his death in 1796. For instance, Maximiano enrolled in the free-Black militia of the Henriques in Rio de Janeiro after his enslaver died. However, neither Maximiano nor his family received freedom papers confirming their status. In his petition to the Prince Regent João VI, which Maximiano seemingly delivered personally in Lisbon in 1804, he explains that he traveled with viceregal approval but without freedom papers from Rio to Angola, where he worked as a mason, before his arrival in Lisbon. In the petition, Maximiano mentions that it was common to "secretly transport slaves" from Rio de Janeiro to southern Brazil and Montevideo, which probably implied the kidnapping of free Black men, women, and children. He attached to his petition a copy of the testament of his deceased enslaver, which probably was the only documentary evidence of his freedom allowing him to travel. Thus, Maximiano requested to secure a notarized copy of his manumission.[31]

Maritime war endangered the status of free Africans and Afro-Brazilians who toiled in the ships connecting the South Atlantic littoral. In January 1799 the French privateer ship *Républicaine* arrived in Montevideo bringing a Portuguese slave vessel as a prize, the brigantine *Rainha dos Anjos*, which was a large ship intending to bring captives from Luanda to Rio de Janeiro.[32] Not all Africans in the *Rainha dos Anjos* were enslaved, as free Black crewmen were common in the Luso-Brazilian slave vessels.[33] Rosa Maria was a free servant, a cook, working on the ship. She was born in Benguela and sold into slavery in Luanda. According to Captain José Antônio de Santana, he freed Rosa Maria in 1798 because of the care she gave to him when he was gravely ill. Rosa Maria wanted to travel as a free woman to Rio de Janeiro, for which she also brought papers proving her status. However, after disembarkation in Montevideo, Rosa Maria was housed alongside the captives in the quarantine site for recently arrived enslaved Africans, surely for the purpose of auctioning her. By mid-January, Portuguese sailor Manuel Alfonso, while walking on the beach outside of Montevideo, eventually made it to the quarantine site, where he recognized Rosa Maria. She gave him the freedom papers to prove she was free before the Spanish authorities. The court took declarations from the ship's captain, Santana. Then the authorities tried to contact the French captain of the *Républicaine*, Pierre Marie Le Bozec, but he had gone to Buenos Aires. This put Rosa's case on hold for his response. Le Bozec returned to Montevideo in March and thus authorities sent him the case of Rosa Maria, the paper *expediente*, for his response. However, he stonewalled the case by not returning the file back to the authorities. A free *pardo* woman, Teresa Petrona Marquez, took Rosa's side and waited in front of the house where Le Bozec was staying many times to get the papers back. Teresa's petition provides details of how Le Bozec avoided her in repeated occasions. She described that she had been chasing Le Bozec for a month, but the French captain was resisting returning the case. She threatened him with the costs of the case. In four other instances a member of the court also visited the French ship without result. Finally, on April 22, 1799, infantry captain Jose Merlo retrieved the file from the ship before the *Républicaine* headed out of the bay, in addition to receiving permission from Le Bozec to consider Rosa as free, four months after her arrival and imprisonment in Montevideo. It is unclear if Rosa stayed in the quarantine site during these months given that we lack information of where she was housed later. Perhaps Teresa met Rosa in this site, as Teresa may have worked there. Later Teresa may have provided Rosa with housing for the duration of the case, given that it was Teresa who persisted before the authorities to recover the file from the French captain.[34]

The brief war between the Spanish and Portuguese in 1801 brought more cases like this, given that it was common for Portuguese shipping to have both enslaved and free-Black people serving as crewmembers. On November 13, 1801, the defender of slaves in Buenos Aires, José de la Oyuela, issued a petition on behalf of four Black Portuguese men, Jose Martins, João da Silva, and Zeferino and Marcelino Jose. They were crewmembers of a Portuguese ship sailing from Rio Grande to Rio de Janeiro, which was captured by the Spanish privateer *Pilar*.[35] Geronimo Merino, who outfitted the *Pilar*, wanted to sell these men into slavery in Buenos Aires while disregarding the evidence they provided about their freedom. Merino claimed the documents lacked authentication. The case shows the geographical stretch of the lives of these men. According to his testimony, Marcelino Jose was a free-Black man born in Rio de Janeiro. His mother was also a free woman, Juana Maria de la Concepcion, who freed Marcelino from Manuel Josef Duarte Braga in 1799 in exchange for two ounces of gold. Juan da Silva, born in Angola, testified that his enslaver Domingo da Silva freed him in his will. José Martins, from Villa Rica (Ouro Preto, in Minas Gerais) was a shoemaker and testified that he was free from birth. Finally, Zeferino Josef, from Salvador de Bahia, testified that he had been enslaved by the priest Bento Texeira, who had died. Zeferino became free when he went with his enslaver to Porto, Portugal, given the Portuguese law that all enslaved persons passing to Europe became free. He was given such freedom papers in Porto and later he received a copy in Lisbon. After these testimonies, Merino recognized that Zeferino's papers were official and that he should be free, but he insisted that the rest should be enslaved. After the claimants provided copies in Spanish of all their documents, in March 1802, they were declared free by the authorities. After the sentence, Jose Martin requested his documents back because he didn't want to embark another ship and risk re-enslavement again. During the case these men were not under the power of Merino, but instead, they were housed probably by other Portuguese residents in Buenos Aires, who seemingly supported their claims of freedom.

In 1802, Francisco Telechea litigated against the same Geronimo Merino in order to get the payment back from his purchase of three enslaved individuals, who themselves were also suing Merino in a separate case for their own freedom. These were not the same men discussed in the previous paragraph, which points out that Merino took advantage of the war to indiscriminately sell Black crewmen captured in Portuguese vessels by his privateer ship.[36] Two of these men were Ilario Correa and Jose Acosta, whose names were not listed in the third case related to the privateer *Pilar*, examined next. When considering these three cases together, it emerges that Merino was trying to sell at least fifteen free people captured from three different ships as slaves in Buenos Aires.

The third claim against Merino came from Josef Janairo del Espiritu Santo, Manuel Vicente, and Josef Ignacio, all of whom had free status from birth, and Vicente Ferreyra, Domingo Gomez, Pedro Martin, Fabian de Cristo, Antonio Gomez, and Josef Antonio, who were freed by manumission. In Buenos Aires, the defender of slaves stated that Merino wanted to "sell them as slaves without more evidence than their color." He argued that the freedom papers of Fabian de Cristo, Antonio Gomez, and Josef Antonio were thrown overboard by the captain of the privateer ship *Pilar*, Luis Goytia. In his response, Goytia argued that these three men did not present documents but a single paper with fresh ink, which he thought was a ruse and trashed. The first testimony on behalf of the claimants came from Juan Antonio Gonzalez, from Galicia, who was a sailor on the Portuguese ship *Santa Rita* with Josef Januario. This vessel was based in Rio de Janeiro and sailed the route to Porto, Portugal. Gonzalez attested that Josef received salary and forwarded part of his money to his parents in Pernambuco, Brazil. Another witness, Manuel Tomas Soares from Porto, attested that he knew Josef Januario was free and worked in vessels connecting Porto and Rio de Janeiro and that he met him also on a warship. Dozens of declarations from Portuguese mariners, captains, and merchants living in Buenos Aires, as well as some Spaniards like the Galician Gonzalez, attested knowledge about all of the free-Black and *pardo* men with individual stories for each of them spanning from Bahia and Rio de Janeiro to Rio Grande and neighboring towns and islands, all the way to Portugal through the shipping lanes. Witnesses provided two or three itineraries for each of the free-Black and *pardo* men before their capture by the privateers, always pointing out each time that these men were considered free and paid as such for their work. Some of the witnesses aboard the ship confirmed the destruction of freedom papers by the captain. After the first round of these declarations, Merino acknowledged the freedom of four men in this group, and then colonial authorities left another one free, but still four other men were not declared free by the last page of this case. They were not declared slaves either as the case was left truncated. Perhaps the four other men eventually were liberated by Merino to save him additional economic and social burdens—the costs of being involved in three seemingly simultaneous litigations and the pressure from Portuguese merchants and mariners living in Buenos Aires who were significant in the local maritime community.[37]

Manuel de la Pasion, Antonio Mina, Joaquin Santa Ana, Francisco Joaquin, Josef Francisco Vieira, and Francisco Pires were crewmembers of the Portuguese schooner *Santisimo Sacramento*, captured by the privateer vessel from Buenos Aires *San Juan Baptista* in 1801.[38] The privateer captain, Juan Bautista Egaña, disembarked them in Montevideo and later consigned them to a merchant of Buenos Aires, Juan Antonio Lezica, to be sold in the viceregal capital as slaves. But these men protested, which led Lezica to put them in jail. Their case was taken by Defender of Slaves Manuel Ortiz de Basavilbaso in January 1802. Lezica and Egaña were defended by the representatives of the merchant guild, who asserted that the captured Black men had been one month in Montevideo without telling the authorities they were free, which they only did after arriving in Buenos Aires. Captain Egaña argued that all Black crewmembers in this ship were enslaved and, thus, part of the prize. He added the testimony of the owner of the ship and cargo, Francisco Jose de Sousa, who claimed that five of these men were slaves of the vessel, his slaves, but he could not provide documents because the papers were in another judicial case in which he was seeking restitution for the cargo, a result of the peace between Portugal and Spain. Yet, the Portuguese captain of the ship testified that Manuel de la Pasion was free, which was confirmed by authorities. The fate of the five other men remains unclear as the case finished without a sentence, though these men were still jailed. The next step for the defense of these men was providing witnesses, as we examined in the previous case. Perhaps this step became unnecessary if Lezica and Egaña stopped pursuing the sale of these five men as slaves.

Francisco Carvalho was serving in the ship *Nuestra Señora de Monserrat*, sailing from Portugal to Brazil, when this ship was captured by the privateer *Carolina*, which had been outfitted by the merchant guild of Buenos Aires. As a result, he arrived as a prisoner in Montevideo, but then he was set free and sent to Buenos Aires to register there with the rest of the crew. Once in Buenos Aires, Joaquin Silva, captain of the schooner *Rivera Nova*, asserted that Francisco was his slave and shackled Francisco in chains to prevent his escape. Francisco received 350 lashes for attempting to liberate himself. Another free-Black sailor, Juan Jose Manzano, from the same ship, asserted Francisco was free. Sailors from the privateer ship *Carolina* attested that Francisco was the free cook of the vessel *Nuestra Señora de Monserrat* and not enslaved. Others specified that he was the assistant to the cook, personally serving the captain and the notary of the ship, but not enslaved either. When the privateer captured this ship, Francisco was imprisoned with the free people, and he was not sold with the enslaved individuals. While Francisco was eventually liberated from the ship and released from Silva, Silva's lawyer kept the file for three months in 1803, delaying the case's conclusion. One of the arguments against Francisco's liberation was that Silva had made a pact with Francisco (as an enslaved man) to declare to the privateers that Francisco was free so he would not be captured by the Spaniards.[39] After his liberation, Francisco tried to get reparations from Silva because of the torture he suffered, but Silva had left for Rio de Janeiro.

Pleas regarding freedom for Africans and Afro-Brazilians crossing the borderland of the Iberian empires in what is today Uruguay and southern Brazil are common in the archives through the late colonial period, and they continued even after independence given that slavery expanded in Rio Grande do Sul during the first half of the nineteenth century.[40] In contrast, the petitions of freedom coming from Africans and Afro-Brazilians arriving by sea to Buenos Aires and Montevideo were only produced, seemingly, during the war of 1801 and its aftermath, with the exception of a couple litigations concerning French privateering against Portuguese ships. The cases involving freedom in the maritime routes are a unique window to visualize the participation of free people of African ancestry in the waterscape connecting Brazil with the Rio de la Plata, which otherwise would remain invisible. These cases also reveal maritime communities living, in an itinerant manner, in Buenos Aires and Montevideo, who could vouch for these Africans and Afro-Brazilians if they were enslaved as happened in 1801. Thus, they uncover a certain degree of belonging of these free-Black men and women to these communities. Finally, these cases sketch a waterscape that could be understood as a borderland too, challenging our definitions of land-bound frontiers.

Conclusion

Africans and their descendants lived in different types of borderlands in late colonial Buenos Aires and Montevideo, as exemplified by the relations of this population with Amerindians who lived outside Spanish colonial rule, by the encounters of Africans and their descendants with the imperial politics of the Spanish-Portuguese borderlands, and by their experience in ships connecting Brazilian ports with Buenos Aires and Montevideo, which constituted a maritime borderland.

Freedom and military intelligence were some of the main keywords in the colonial archive preserving records of the experiences of Africans and their descendants in the borderlands. However, widely different interactions fell under these categories, in regions under different degrees of indigenous control stretching from Patagonia to Paraguay, and in the imperial frontiers with the Portuguese from the Atlantic littoral to the heart of South America. These files only recorded fragments of a larger participation of Africans and their descendants in the constructions of borderlands, both overland and maritime. The scholarship of the Rio de la Plata usually limits the focus of examinations of the borderlands to indigenous people, the Spanish, and the Portuguese, but Africans and their descendants should be included. The unequal encounters of human groups with different conceptions of sovereignty and space defined the borderlands; thus, we should also include these types of definitions coming from Africans and their descendants. For instance, we may wonder how the perceptions of water and aquatic culture of Africans and Afro-Brazilians shaped the waterscape connecting Brazil and the Rio de la Plata, and how their experience of laboring in the cattle ranches and agriculture of this region shaped their interactions with indigenous groups in the vast countryside.[41]

The presence of Africans and their descendants among indigenous groups with different degrees of control over the borderlands challenges conceptions of slavery, captivity, and dependence, and leaves us to wonder about the process of incorporation of these men and women into indigenous *tolderías*—something that was unstable as the stories in this chapter attest. On the other side, the cases about the re-enslavement of free Africans and Afro-Brazilians in the maritime borderland show a great degree of communication between the Spanish and Portuguese South Atlantic ports and the creation of itinerant maritime communities that could act as a living archive of freedom.[42] The narrow period in which these cases appeared (1799–1803) suggests that the existence of the maritime connections between Brazil and the Rio de la Plata needed some degree of security for the freedom of Africans and their descendants in this coastal shipping, because these men, and sometimes women, were central to manning the ships connecting these ports.

Notes

1. Africans and their descendants are largely missing in the foundational comparison between

the US Southwest and the Rio de la Plata, the two edges of the Spanish empire in the Americas, published a quarter century ago; see Guy and Sheridan, *Contested Ground.*

2. The term *toldería* designated a group of indigenous people that migrated from place to place in the region. These groups were held together by conceptions of identity and authority based on kin. The *toldería* was also a physical site defined by the *toldos* or ephemeral constructions made of cattle hides and wood branches, similar to the *rancherías* of the US Southwest but itinerant. Erbig, *Where Caciques and Mapmakers Met,* 184, n41. On the relations of Africans and their descendants with indigenous groups in other borderlands, see the contributions of Mark Lentz, Christina Villarreal, and Cameron Jones in this volume.

3. The fears of a maritime seizure materialized for the Spanish with the British invasions of Buenos Aires and Montevideo in 1806–1807. On Africans and their descendants in other transimperial borderlands, see the contributions of Mark Lentz, Christina Villarreal, and Cameron Jones in this volume.

4. On definitions of "waterscape," see Dawson, *Undercurrents of Power,* 4.

5. Borucki, "Across Imperial Boundaries."

6. Prado, *Edge of Empire,* 10–11, 112–13. See Erbig, *Where Caciques and Mapmakers Met,* on the significance of indigenous peoples for European mapmaking and imperial territorial claims.

7. Apart from Erbig, *Where Caciques and Mapmakers Met,* see for the historiography of the Iberian borderlands, Herzog, *Frontiers of Possession.*

8. Archivo General de la Nación, Argentina (hereafter AGN-A), IX, 42–1–1, "Autos sobre la libertad de Antonio Negro," 1739.

9. On African and indigenous interactions in Paraguay, and how indigenous encomienda shaped free-Black men tribute obligations, see Austin, *Colonial Kinship.*

10. AGN-A, IX, 31–4–1, "Sobre introducción de portugueses en Chiquitos," 1782, f. 28–30.

11. AGN-A, IX, 2–5–5, Governor of Montevideo Joaquin del Pino to Viceroy Loreto, February 25, 1788.

12. Archivo General de la Nación, Uruguay (hereafter AGN-U), Archivos Judiciales, "Criminal sobre averiguacion," exp. 52, 1800.

13. On the itineraries between cities and borderlands in southern Argentina in this period, see Mandrini, *Vivir entre dos mundos,* 21–42.

14. AGN-A, Sala IX, 12–9–9, Agustin Rodriguez, f. 98.

15. *Lenguaraz* comes from *lengua* (tongue) and was the term used to describe not only translators but also go-betweens facilitating interactions of different groups.

16. Viedma wrote that Ventura "comprendia sus costumbres e ideas era fiel y leal interprete," AGN-A, IX, 12–9–6, Francisco Viedma to Viceroy, Nov 9, 1787; and Archivo de la Real Academia de Historia, Madrid, Colección Mata Linares, II, 3791, and LXXVIII, f. 1332, November 8, 1791.

17. AGN-A, IX, 2–10–5, "Expediente sobre conquista de los portugueses," 1804, f. 2.

18. AGN-A, IX, 12–9–12, Juan Gallardo, 1789.

19. AGN-A, IX, 30–1–2, Bernardo Miranda to Teniente del Rey, January 8, 1782.

20. On the historiography of captivity by indigenous groups, see Socolow, "Spanish Captives in Indian Societies."

21. AGN-A, IX, 2–6–7, January 31, 1790.

22. AGN-A, IX, 23–5–3, "Expediente promovido por Dn Manuel de la Piedra," 1802.

23. AGN-A, IX, 27–6–4, "El oidor proctector de naturales . . ." April 21, 1806.

24. AGN-A, IX, 12–9–9, Rosa Robles to Viceroy, April 13, 1795, f. 96.

25. AGN-A, IX, 35–6–2, "Expediente promovido por el esclavo Manuel de Olivera," 1787.

26. AGN-A, IX, 38–2–3, "Dn Joaquin Ortuño sobre que Luisa Marin parda esclava le exige la declare libre," 1783. Historian Arturo Bentancur provides additional cases of free Afro-Brazilian women who were considered slaves by Portuguese visitors in Montevideo, which forced these women to request papers and witnesses about their status. Bentancur and Aparicio, *Amos y Esclavos en el Río de la Plata*, 49.

27. AGN-A, IX, 2–4–5, June 11, 1785.

28. Hemp was essential for cords and ropes for navigation.

29. On the City Council (Cabildo) Office of the Defender of Slaves, see Johnson, "'A Lack of Legitimate Obedience and Respect'"; and Rebagliati, "Entre las aspiraciones de libertad y el derecho de propiedad."

30. AGN-A, IX, 23–4–7, January 10, 1801.

31. Arquivo Histórico Ultramarino (Lisbon), Rio de Janeiro, cx. 302, doc. 130, "Requerimento do escravo Maximiano Francisco Gomes, ao príncipe regente [D. João]." I thank John Marquez for pointing out this document to me. On this subject, see Marquez, "Freedom's Edge."

32. AGN-A, IX, 35–3–5, "La negra Rosa María, procedente del bergantín portugués La Reina de los Ángeles," 1799. Voyage #8411 in the Transatlantic Slave Trade Database, Slave Voyages website, www.slavevoyages.org.

33. See Rodrigues, *De Costa a Costa*.

34. On the case of the *Republicaine* and how Rioplatense slave traders tried to prevent further actions by French privateers, as these privateers preyed upon Portuguese ships, see Secreto, "Territorialidades fluidas." Some of these cases were examined by Johnson, "'A Lack of Legitimate Obedience and Respect.'"

35. AGN-A, IX, 23–4–7, "Expediente promovido por Dn Josef de la Oyuela," 1801. I thank Gustavo Fabían Alonso, at the Argentine National Archives, for providing me a copy of this file.

36. AGN-A, IX, 23–5–5, "Expediente sobre la devolución de tres esclavos," July 6, 1802.

37. AGN-A, IX, 30–6–9, "Expediente promovido por Dn. Jose de la Oyuela." For testimony of Juan Antonio Gonzalez, see f. 19v.

38. AGN-A, IX, 23–5–3, "El regidor defensor de pobres a nombre de seis pardos," 1802.

39. AGN-A, IX, 23–5–6, "Francisco, negro libre, sobre quererle esclavizar el capitán," 1803.

40. Grinberg, *As Fronteiras da Escravidão e da Liberdade no Sul da America.*

41. Garavaglia, "The Economic Role of Slavery in a Non-Slave Society"; Sluyter, *Black Ranching Frontiers.*

42. On illegal enslavement and petitions of freedom within the Luso-Angolan-Brazilian South Atlantic, see Marquez, "Witnesses to Freedom"; Candido, *An African Enslaving Port and the Atlantic World.*

BIBLIOGRAPHY

Adelman, Jeremy, and Stephen Aron. "From Borderlands to Borders: Empires, Nation-States, and the Peoples in Between in North American History." *American Historical Review* 104, no. 3 (June 1999): 814–41.

Aguado, Pedro de. *Historia de Venezuela*. 2 vols. Madrid: Real Academia de la Historia, 1919.

Aidoo, Lamonte. *Slavery Unseen: Sex, Power, and Violence in Brazilian History*. Durham, NC: Duke University Press, 2018.

Alcina Franch, José. "Penetración española en Esmeraldas tipología del descubrimiento." *Revista de Indias* 143–144 (1976): 65–121.

Althouse, Aaron. "Contested Mestizos, Alleged Mulattos: Racial Identity and Caste Hierarchy in Eighteenth Century Pátzcuaro, Mexico." *Americas* 62, no. 2 (2005): 151–75.

Altman, Ida. "The Revolt of Enriquillo and the Historiography of Early Spanish America." *Americas* 63, no. 4 (2007): 587–614.

Álvarez Macías, Diana Lucía. "Transformaciones de la identidad social en Los Altos de Jalisco (1926–1990)." *Mediaciones Sociales* 16 (2017): 27–41.

Andrews, George Reid. "The Afro-Argentine Officers of Buenos Aires Province, 1800–1860." *Journal of Negro History* 64, no. 2 (Spring 1979): 85–100.

Anguiano, Fr. Mateo de. *Vida, y Virtvdes del Capvchino español, el Venerable Siervo de Dios Fray Francisco de Pamplona, Religioso Lego de la Sagrada Orden de Menores Capuchinos de N. Padre San Francisco, y primer Missionario Apostolico de las Provincias de España, para el Reyno del Congo en Africa, y para los Indios infieles en la America*. Madrid: Lorenzo Garcia, 1685.

Anonymous. "Compendiosa noticia del actual estado de la provincia de Novitá." *Cespedesia* 45–46, suppl. 4 (1983): 449–59.

———. "Descripción de la provincia de Zitará u curso del río Atrato, 1777." In *Colección de documentos inéditos sobre la geografía y historia de Colombia*. Vol. 2, *Geografía, geografía y viajes*. Edited by Antonio B. Cuervo, 306–24. Bogotá: Casa Editorial de J. J. Pérez, 1892.

———. "Descripción superficial de la provincia del Zitará, con sucinto relato de sus poblaciones, establecimientos de minas y ríos de mayor nombre." *Cespedesia* 45–46, suppl. 4 (1983): 425–46.

Ansell, Amy. "Critical Race Theory." In *Encyclopedia of Race, Ethnicity, and Society. Vol. 1*. Edited by Richard T. Schaefer, 344–46. Los Angeles: SAGE, 2008.

Argumaniz Tello, Juan Luis. "El lapso de sobremortalidad de 1785–1786 en Guadalajara y sus alrededores." In *Epidemias y rutas de propagación en la Nueva España y México (Siglos xviii–xix)*, edited by Mario Alberto Magaña Mancillas, 178–210. Mexicali, Baja California, México: Universidad Autónoma de Baja California, Instituto de Investigaciones Culturales-Museo; La Paz, Baja California Sur: Instituto Sudcaliforniano de Cultura, Archivo Histórico Pablo L. Martinez, 2013.

Arias Ortiz, Teri Erandeni. "El caso del mulato Juan Thomas y la Conquista de El Petén (1695–1704)." *Indiana* 30 (2013): 173–98.

Arrom, José Juan, and Manuel Antonio García Arévalo. *Cimarrón.* Santo Domingo, República Dominicana: Ediciones Fundación García-Arévalo, 1986.

Arrubla, José Manuel. "Descripción de la provincia del Zitará u curso del río Atrato por autor desconocido, 1777." *Boletín de la Sociedad Geográfica Colombia* 8, no. 1 (1948): 17–39.

"Art. IX–1. Correspondence with the British Commissioners relating to the Slave-Trade. 1825, 1826." *Quarterly Review* 34, no. 68 (1827): 585.

Austin, Shawn. *Colonial Kinship: Guaraní, Spaniards, and Africans in Paraguay.* Albuquerque: University of New Mexico Press, 2020.

Bannon, John Francis, ed. *Bolton and the Spanish Borderlands.* Norman: University of Oklahoma Press, 1964.

Barnwell, Cherron A. "Anti-Slavery Press." In *Encyclopedia of African American History, 1619–1895: From the Colonial Period to the Age of Frederick Douglas,* edited by Graham Russell Hodges, 87–92. New York: Oxford University Press, 2006.

Barona, Guido. "Problemas de la historia económica y social colonial en referencia a los grupos negros, Siglo XVIII." In *La participación del negro en la formación de las sociedades Latinoamericanas,* edited by Alexander Cifuentes, 61–80. Bogotá: Instituto Colombiano de Antropología, 1986.

Barona, Guido, and Camilo Domínguez Ossa. Geografía física y política de la Confederación Granadina, Vol I. Estado de Cauca: Tomo 2, Provincias del Chocó, Buenaventura, Cauca y Popayán, Obra dirigida por el general Agustín Codazzi. Vol. 1. Cali: Colciencias, Grupo de Estudios Ambientales, GEA, Universidad del Cauca, 2002.

Barr, Juliana. "Geographies of Power: Mapping Indian Borders in the 'Borderlands' of the Early Southwest." *William and Mary Quarterly* 68, no. 1 (2011): 5–46.

———. *Peace Came in the Form of a Woman: Indians and Spaniards in the Texas Borderlands.* Chapel Hill: University of North Carolina Press, 2007.

Barragan, Yesenia. "Free Black Women, Slavery, and the Politics of Place in Chocó, Colombia." *Revista de Estudios Colombianos* 47 (2016): 57–66.

———. "Gendering Mastery: Female Slaveholders in the Colombian Pacific Lowlands." *Slavery & Abolition: A Journal of Slave and Post-Slave Studies* 39, no. 1 (2018): 1–26.

Battell, Andrew. *The Strange Adventures of Andrew Battell of Leigh, in Angola and the Adjoining Regions.* London: Hukluyt Society, [1625] 1991.

Becerra Jiménez, Celina G. *Indios, españoles, y africanos en los Altos de Jalisco: Jalostotitlán, 1650–1780.* Lagos de Moreno, Jalisco, México: Centro Universitario de Ciencias Sociales y Humanidades, 2015.

Bennett, Herman L. *Africans in Colonial Mexico: Absolutism, Christianity, and Afro-Creole Consciousness, 1570–1640.* Bloomington: Indiana University Press, 2005.

———. *Colonial Blackness: A History of Afro-Mexico.* Bloomington: Indiana University Press, 2009.

Bense, Judith Ann. *Archaeology of Colonial Pensacola*. Gainesville: University Press of Florida, 1999.

———. "Presidio Santa María de Galve (1698–1719): A Frontier Garrison in Spanish West Florida." *Historical Archaeology* 38, no. 3 (2004), 47–65.

Bentancur, Antonio, and Fernando Aparicio. *Amos y Esclavos en el Río de la Plata*. Montevideo: Planeta, 2006.

Benzoni, Girolamo. *The History of the New World: Benzoni's Historia Del Mondo Nuovo*. Edited by Robert C. Schwaller and Jana Byers. Translated by Jana Byers. Latin American Originals. University Park: Penn State University Press, 2017.

Berlin, Ira. *Many Thousands Gone: The First Two Centuries of Slavery in North America*. Cambridge, MA: Harvard University Press, 1998.

Birmingham, David. *Trade and Conflict in Angola: The Mbundu and their Neighbours Under the Influence of the Portuguese, 1483–1790*. Oxford: Clarendon, 1966.

Block, Kristen. *Ordinary Lives in the Early Caribbean: Religion, Colonial Competition, and the Politics of Profit*. Athens: University of Georgia Press, 2012.

Blumenthal, Debra. *Enemies and Familiars: Slavery and Mastery in Fifteenth-Century Valencia*. Ithaca, NY: Cornell University Press, 2009.

Bolland, O. Nigel. *Colonialism and Resistance in Belize: Essays in Historical Sociology*. Benque Viejo del Carmen, Belize: Cubola, 1988.

Bolton, Herbert Eugene. *Athanase de Mézières and the Louisiana-Texas Frontier, 1768–1780: Documents published for the first time, from the original Spanish and French manuscripts, chiefly in the archives of Mexico and Spain*. Vol. 1. Cleveland: A. H. Clark, 1914.

Borucki, Alex. "Across Imperial Boundaries: Black Social Networks Across the Iberian South Atlantic, 1760–1810." *Atlantic Studies* 14, no. 1 (2017): 11–36.

Borucki, Alex, David Eltis, and David Wheat. "Atlantic History and the Slave Trade to Spanish America." *American Historical Review* 120, no. 2 (2015): 433–61.

Boucher, Philip P. *France and the American Tropics to 1700: Tropics of Discontent?* Baltimore: Johns Hopkins University Press, 2008.

Boyd-Bowman, Peter, and William Frederick Sharp. *Description of the Province of Zitará and Course of the River Atrato*. Critical Edition. Buffalo: Council on International Studies, State University of New York at Buffalo, 1981.

Brásio, António. *Monumenta Missionaria Africana: África Ocidental*. Vol. 9. Lisboa: Agéncia Geral do Ultramar, [1643–1646] 1952.

Brasseaux, Carl A. "The Administration of Slave Regulations in French Louisiana, 1724–1766." *Louisiana History* 21, no. 2 (1980): 139–58.

Bristol, Joan Cameron. *Christians, Blasphemers, and Witches: Afro-Mexican Ritual Practice in the Seventeenth Century*. Albuquerque: University of New Mexico Press, 2007.

Broecke, Pieter Van Den. *Pieter Van Den Broecke's Journal of Voyages to Cape Verde, Guinea and Angola (1605–1612)*. London: Hakluyt Society, [1605–1612] 2000.

Bryant, Sherwin. "Enslaved Rebels, Fugitives, and Litigants: The Resistance Continuum in Quito." *Colonial Latin American Review* 13, no. 1 (2004): 7–46.

Burton, Sophie H., and F. Todd Smith. "Slavery in the Louisiana Backcountry: Natchitoches, 1714–1803." *Louisiana History: The Journal of the Louisiana Historical Association* 52, no. 2 (2011): 133–88.

Bushnell, Amy Turner. "Gates, Patterns, and Peripheries." In *Negotiated Empires: Centers and Peripheries in the Americas, 1500–1820*, edited by Christine Daniels and Michael V. Kennedy, 15–28. New York: Routledge, 2002.

Cabello Balboa, Miguel. *Obras*, vol. 1. Quito: Editorial Ecuatoriana, 1945.

Caldeira, Arlindo Manuel. "Angola and the Seventeenth-Century South Atlantic Slave Trade." In *Networks and Trans-Cultural Exchange: Slave Trading in the South Atlantic, 1590–1867*, edited by David Richardson and Filipa Ribeiro da Silva, chapter 4. Leiden: Brill, 2014.

Calendar of State Papers Colonial, America and West Indies: Volume 11, 1681–1685. Edited by J. W. Fortescue. London: Her Majesty's Stationery Office 1898. British History Online, accessed June 24, 2022. http://www.british-history.ac.uk/cal-state-papers/colonial/america-west-indies/vol11.

Camp, Stephanie M. H. *Closer to Freedom: Enslaved Women & Everyday Resistance in the Plantation South*. Chapel Hill: University of North Carolina Press, 2004.

———. "The Pleasures of Resistance: Enslaved Woman and Body Politics in the Plantation South, 1830–1861." *Journal of Southern History* 68, no. 3 (2002): 533–72.

Campt, Tina. *Listening to Images*. Durham, NC: Duke University Press, 2017.

Candido, Mariana. *An African Enslaving Port and the Atlantic World: Benguela and Its Hinterland*. Cambridge: Cambridge University Press, 2013.

———. "Women's Material World in Nineteenth-Century Benguela." In *African Women in the Atlantic World: Property, Vulnerability & Mobility, 1660–1880*, edited by Mariana Candido and Adam Jones, chapter 4. Suffolk: James Currey, 2019.

Cantor, Erick Werner. "Extracción de oro. Encuentro de emberá, afroamericanos, y europeos en la cuenca del Atrato, Siglo XVIII." In *Construcción territorial en ell Chocó*. Vol 1, *Historias Regionales*, edited by Patricia Vargas Sarmiento, 67–96. Bogotá: Programa de Historia Local y Regional del Instituto Colombiano de Antropología, 1999.

———. *Ni aniquilados ni vencidos. Los Embera y la gente negra del Atrato bajo el dominio español, Siglo XVIII*. Bogotá: Instituto Colombiano de Antropología e Historia, 2000.

Carbajal López, David. "Reflexiones metodológicas sobre el mestizaje en la Nueva España. Una propuesta a partir de las familias del Real de Bolaños, 1740–1822." *Letras Históricas* 1, no. 1 (2009): 13–38.

Carroll, Patrick J. *Blacks in Colonial Veracruz*. 2nd ed. Austin: University of Texas Press, 2010.

Carroll, Patrick J., and Jeffrey N. Lamb. "Los mexicanos negros, el mestizaje y los fundamentos olvidados de la 'Raza Cósmica': una perspectiva regional." *Historia Mexicana* 44, no. 3 (1995): 403–38.

Castillo-Palma, Norma A. "Calidad socio-racial, condición estamental, su variabilidad en el mestizaje novohispano: ¿Familias plurietnicas?" In *Familias Pluriétnicas y Mestizaje en la Nueva España y el Río de la Plata*, edited by David Carbajal López, 173–210. Guadalajara: Universidad de Guadalajara, 2014.

Chalmers, George. *A Collection of Treaties Between Great Britain and Other Powers,* vol. 2. London, 1790.

Chambers, Douglas B. "'My Own Nation': Igbo Exiles in the Diaspora." *Slavery and Abolition* 18, no. 1 (1997): 72–97.

Chance, John K., and William B. Taylor. "Estate and Class in a Colonial City: Oaxaca in 1792." *Comparative Studies in Society and History* 19 (July 1977): 454–87.

Chardon, Roland. "The Elusive Spanish League: A Problem of Measurement in Sixteenth-Century New Spain." *Hispanic American Historical Review* 60, no. 2 (1980): 294–302.

Chipman, Donald E., and Harriett Denise Joseph. *Spanish Texas, 1519–1821.* 2nd ed. Austin: University of Texas Press, 2010.

Cieza de León, Pedro de. *The Discovery and Conquest of Peru.* Edited and translated by Alexandra Parma Cook and Noble David Cook. Durham, NC: Duke University Press, 1998.

Clark, J. M. H. *Veracruz and the Caribbean in the Seventeenth Century.* New York: Cambridge University Press, 2023.

Clavin, Matthew J. *Aiming for Pensacola: Fugitive Slaves on the Atlantic and Southern Frontiers.* Cambridge, MA: Harvard University Press, 2015.

Clayton, Lawrence A. "Trade and Navigation in the Seventeenth-Century Viceroyalty of Peru." *Journal of Latin American Studies* 7, no. 1 (1975): 1–21.

Clune, John J., R. Wayne Childers, William S. Coker, and Brenda N. Swan. "Settlement, Settlers, and Survival: Documentary Evidence." In *Presidio Santa Maria de Galve: A Struggle for Survival in Colonial Spanish America,* edited by Judith A. Bense, 25–82. Gainesville: University of Florida Press, 2003.

Colmenares, Germán. *Historia económica y social de Colombia.* Vol. 2, *Popayán. Una sociedad esclavista, 1680–1800.* 2nd ed. Bogotá: Tercer Mundo Editores, 1997.

———. *Relaciones e informes de los gobernantes de la Nueva Granada.* 3 vols. Bogotá: Fondo de Promoción de la Cultura del Banco Popular, 1989.

Columbus, Christopher. *The Diario of Christopher Columbus's first voyage to America, 1492–1493 / abstracted by Fray Bartolomé de las Casas; transcribed and translated into English, with notes and a concordance of the Spanish by Oliver Dunn and James E. Kelley, Jr.* Norman: University of Oklahoma Press, c1989.

Cope, R. Douglas. *The Limits of Racial Domination: Plebeian Society in Colonial Mexico City, 1660–1720.* Madison: University of Wisconsin Press, 1994.

Cornell, Sarah E. "Citizens of Nowhere: Fugitive Slaves and Free African Americans in Mexico, 1833–1857." *Journal of American History* 100, no. 2 (2013): 351–74.

Cromwell, Jesse. "More than Slaves and Sugar: Recent Historiography of the Trans-Imperial Caribbean and Its Sinew Populations." *History Compass* 12, no. 10 (2014): 770–83.

———. *The Smuggler's World: Illicit Trade and Atlantic Communities in Eighteenth-Century Venezuela.* Chapel Hill: University of North Carolina Press, 2018.

Curto, José C. *Enslaving Spirits: The Portuguese-Brazilian Alcohol Trade at Luanda and Its Hinterland, c. 1550–1830.* Leiden: Brill, 2004.

Dawdy, Shannon Lee. *Building the Devil's Empire: French Colonial New Orleans.* Chicago: University of Chicago Press, 2008.

Dawson, Kevin. *Undercurrents of Power: Aquatic Culture in the African Diaspora.* Philadelphia: University of Pennsylvania Press, 2018.

de la Fuente, Alejandro. *Havana and the Atlantic in the Sixteenth Century.* Chapel Hill: University of North Carolina Press, 2008.

de la Guardia, Roberto. *Los cimarrones del maniel de Neiba: Historia y etnografía.* Santo Domingo: Banco Central de la República Dominicana, 1985.

———. *Los guerrilleros negros.* Santo Domingo: Fundación Cultural Dominicana, 1989.

———. *Los negros del Istmo de Panamá.* Panama: Ediciones INAC, 1977.

de la Teja, Jesús F. *Faces of Béxar: Early San Antonio and Texas.* College Station: Texas A&M University Press, 2016.

———. "Why Urbano and María Trinidad Can't Get Married: Social Relations in Late Colonial San Antonio." *Southwestern Historical Quarterly* 112, no. 2 (October 2008): 121–46.

Deagan, Kathleen. "Eliciting Contraband Through Archaeology: Illicit Trade in Eighteenth-Century St. Augustin." *Historical Archaeology* 41, no. 4 (2007): 98–116.

Deboar, Warren. *Traces Behind the Esmeraldas Shore.* Tuscaloosa: University of Alabama Press, 1996.

DeCorse, Christopher. "Oceans Apart: Africanist Perspectives of Diaspora Archaeology." In *"I Too, Am America": Archaeological Studies of African-American Life,* edited by Teresa Singleton, 132–55. Charlottesville: University Press of Virginia, 1999.

Deive, Carlos Esteban. *La esclavitud del negro en Santo Domingo.* 2 vols. Santo Domingo: Museo del Hombre Dominicano, 1980.

———. *Los cimarrones del maniel de Neiba: Historia y etnografía.* Santo Domingo: Banco Central de la República Dominicana, 1985.

———. *Los guerrilleros negros.* Santo Domingo: Fundación Cultural Dominicana, 1989.

del Castillo Mathieu, Nicolás. *Esclavos negros en Cartagena. Sus aportes léxicos.* Bogotá: Instituto Caro y Cuervo, 1982.

Departamento Administrativo Nacional de Estadística (DANE). *Colombia: Una nación multicultural. Su diversidad étnica,* 2007.

Díaz, Bernal. *The Conquest of New Spain.* Translated with an introduction by John M. Cohen. Baltimore: Penguin Books, 1963.

Díaz, María Elena. *The Virgin, the King, and the Royal Slaves of El Cobre: Negotiating Freedom in Colonial Cuba, 1670–1780.* Stanford, CA: Stanford University Press, 2001.

Diez Castillo, Luis A. *Los cimarrones y los negros antillanos en Panamá.* Panama: Impresora R. Mercado Rudas, 1981.

Din, Gilbert C. "'Cimarrones' and the San Malo Band in Spanish Louisiana." *Louisiana History: The Journal of the Louisiana Historical Association* 21, no. 3 (Summer 1980): 237–62.

———. *Spaniards, Planters, and Slaves: The Spanish Regulation of Slavery in Louisiana, 1763–1803.* College Station: Texas A&M University Press, 1999.

Diouf, Sylviane A. *Slavery's Exiles: The Story of the American Maroons.* New York: New York University Press, 2014.

Dubcovsky, Alejandra. *Informed Power: Communication in the Early American South*. Cambridge, MA: Harvard University Press, 2016.

———. "The Testimony of Thomás de la Torre." *William and Mary Quarterly* 70, no. 3 (July 2013): 559–80.

Dunn, William Edward. "The Spanish Search for La Salle's Colony on the Bay of Espiritu Santo." *Southwestern Historical Quarterly* 19, no. 4 (April 1916), 323–69.

Earle, Rebecca. "The Pleasures of Taxonomy: Casta Paintings, Classification, and Colonialism." *William and Mary Quarterly* 73, no. 3 (July 2016): 427–66.

The Early California Population Project: A Database Compiled and Developed at the Huntington Library. Edition 1.0. General Editor, Steven W. Hackel. Lead Compiler, Anne M. Reid. The Henry E. Huntington Library, San Marino, California, 2006.

Edwards, Laura F. *Gendered Strife & Confusion: The Political Culture of Reconstruction*. Urbana: University of Illinois Press, 1997.

Ekins, Richard, and David King. *Blending Genders: Social Aspects of Cross-Dressing and Sex Changing*. New York: Routledge, 1995.

Erbig, Jeffrey. *Where Caciques and Mapmakers Met: Border Making in Eighteenth-Century South America*. Chapel Hill: University of North Carolina Press, 2020.

Eschbach, Krista L. "Mechanisms of Colonial Transformation at the Port of Veracruz and the Northwest Florida Presidios." PhD diss., Arizona State University, 2019.

Espinosa Cortés, Luz María. "'El año del hambre' en Nueva España, 1785–1786: escasez de maíz, epidemias y 'cocinas públicas' para los pobres." *Diálogos: Revista de Historia* 17, no. 1 (2016): 89–110.

Espinosa, Victoria. *Cimarronaje y palenques en la costa central del Perú: 1700–1815*. Lima, Peru: Consejo Nacional de Ciencia y Tecnología, 1988.

Ferreira, Roquinaldo. *Cross-Cultural Exchange in the Atlantic World: Angola and Brazil During the Era of the Slave Trade*. New York: Cambridge University Press, 2014.

Finch, Aisha K. *Rethinking Slave Rebellion in Cuba: La Escalera and the Insurgencies of 1841–1844*. Chapel Hill: University of North Carolina Press, 2015.

Fisher, Damany M. *Discovering Early California Afro-Latino Presence*. Berkeley, CA: Heyday, 2010.

Florescano, Enrique. *Los precios del maíz y crisis agrícolas en México, 1708–1810*. Rev. ed. México: Editorial Era, 1986.

Flórez Bolívar, Roicer, Sergio Paolo Solano D., and Jairo Álvarez Jiménez. "Liberalismo, ciudadanía y vecindad en Nueva Granada (Colombia) durante la primera mitad del siglo XIX." *Tempo* 18, no. 32 (2012): 163–92.

Foreman, P. Gabrielle, et al. "Writing about Slavery/Teaching About Slavery: This Might Help." Community-sourced document, June 28, 2021, https://docs.google.com/document/d/1A4TEdDgYslX-hlKezLodMIM71My3KTN0zxRv0IQTOQs/mobilebasic.

Fortune, Armando. "Bayano, precursor de la libertad de los esclavos." *Revista Lotería* no. 234 (1975): 1–15.

———. "El esclavo negro en el desenvolvimiento económico del Istmo de Panamá durante el descubrimiento y la conquista (1501–1532)." *Revista Lotería* no. 228 (1975): 1–16.

———. "Los primeros negros en el Istmo de Panama." *Revista Lotería* no. 144 (1967): 56–84.

Fraga, Walter. *Crossroads of Freedom: Slaves and Freed People in Bahia, Brazil, 1870–1910*. Durham, NC: Duke University Press, 2016.

Franco, José Luciano. *La diaspora africana en el nuevo mundo*. Havana, Cuba: Editorial de Ciencias Sociales, 1975.

Fromont, Cécile. "Common Threads: Cloth, Colour, and the Slave Trade in Early Modern Kongo and Angola." *Art History* 41, no. 5 (2018): 838–67.

Fuentes, Marisa J. *Dispossessed Lives: Enslaved Women, Violence, and the Archive*. Philadelphia: University of Pennsylvania Press, 2016.

Funnell, William. *A Voyage Round the World. Containing an Account of Captain Dampier's Expedition into the South-Seas in the Ship St George, in the Years 1703 and 1704. . . . Together with the Author's Voyage from Amapalla . . . By William Funnell*. London: W. Botham, for James Knapton, 1707. http://name.umdl.umich.edu/004904317.0001.000.

Galván, Melisa Catarina. "From Contraband Capital to Border City: Matamoros, 1746–1848." PhD diss., University of California, Berkeley, 2013.

Games, Alison. "Atlantic History: Definitions, Challenges, and Opportunities." *American Historical Review* 111, no. 3 (June 2006): 741–57.

Garavaglia, Juan C. "The Economic Role of Slavery in a Non-Slave Society: The River Plate, 1750–1860." In *Slavery and Antislavery in Spain's Atlantic Empire*, edited by Josep M. Fradera and Christopher Schmidt-Nowara, 74–100. New York: Berghahn, 2013.

García de León, Antonio. *Tierra adentro, mar en fuera: el puerto de Veracruz y su litoral sotavento, 1519–1821*. Fondo de Cultura Ecónomica, 2011.

García, Octavio. "African Slavery and the Impact of the Haitian Revolution in Bourbon New Spain: Empire-Building in the Atlantic Age of Revolution, 1750–1808." PhD diss., University of Arizona, 2015.

Garrido, Margarita. "'Free Men of All Colors' in New Granada: Identity and Obedience before Independence." In *Political Cultures in the Andes, 1750–1950*, edited by Nils Jacobsen and Cristobal Aljovín de Losada, 165–83. Durham, NC: Duke University Press, 2005.

Gaspar, María Dulce. "Material Culture, Daily Life, and Archeological Possibilities in the Plantation Borders of the Guanabana Bay Region." *Review* (Fernand Braudel Center), *Rethinking the Plantation: Histories, Anthropologies and Archaeologies* 34, no. 1–2 (2011): 217–43.

Gerhard, Peter. "Un censo de la diócesis de Puebla en 1681." *Historia Mexicana* 30, no. 4 (April–June 1981): 530–60.

Germeten, Nicole von. *Black Blood Brothers: Confraternities and Social Mobility for Afro-Mexicans*. Gainesville: University of Florida Press, 2006.

Gharala, Norah L. A. *Taxing Blackness: Free Afromexican Tribute in Bourbon New Spain*. Tuscaloosa: University of Alabama Press, 2019.

Gomes, Flávio. "Africans and Petit Marronage in Rio de Janeiro, ca. 1800–1840." *Luso-Brazilian Review* 47, no. 2 (2010): 74–99.

_____. "Other Black Atlantic Borders: Escape Routes, 'Mocambos,' and Fears of Sedition in Brazil and French Guiana, Eighteenth to Nineteenth Centuries." *New West Indian Guide* 77, no. 3–4 (2003): 253–87.

Gómez, Pablo F. *The Experiential Caribbean: Creating Knowledge and Healing in the Early Modern Atlantic.* Chapel Hill: University of North Carolina Press, 2017.

Goode, Kenneth G. *California's Black Pioneers: A Brief Historical Survey.* Santa Barbara, CA: McNally & Loftin, 1974.

Graubart, Karen. "Lazos que unen. Dueñas negras de esclavos negros en Lima, siglos XVI–XVII." *Nueva Corónica* 2 (2013): 625–40.

Grinberg, Keila, ed. *As Fronteiras da Escravidão e da Liberdade no Sul da America.* Rio de Janeiro: 7 Letras, 2013.

———. "Illegal Enslavement, International Relations, and International Law on the Southern Border of Brazil." *Law and History Review* 35, no. 1 (2017): 31–52. doi:10.1017/S0738248016000547.

Guattini, Michele Angelo. *A Curious and Exact Account of a Voyage to Congo.* London, 1732.

Guillot, Carlos F. *Negros rebeldes y negros cimarrones: perfil afroamericano en la historia del Nuevo Mundo durante el siglo XVI.* Buenos Aires: Librería y Editorial El Ateneo, 1961.

Guinea, Mercedes. "Diferentes Mecanismos De Articulación Hombre-Entorno En La Costa Norte De Ecuador: La Desembodadura Del Esmeraldas Del Principio De Nuestra Era Al Año 1527." In *Primer Encuentro De Investigadores De La Costa Ecuatoriana En Europa*, edited by Aurelio Álvarez, Silvia G. Álvarez, Carmen Fauría, and Jorge G. Marcos, 47–58. Barcelona: Asociacion Centro de Estudios y Cooperacion Para America Latina, 1996.

Gutiérrez, Ramon. *When Jesus Came, the Corn Mothers Went Away: Marriage, Sexuality, and Power in New Mexico, 1500–1846.* Stanford, CA: Stanford University Press, 1991.

Gutiérrez Rivas, Julissa "Disconformes con su destino: una revuelta de esclavos en el paraje de Vicus (Piura, 1707)." *Mercurio Peruano* [Piura] 524 (2011): 67–79.

Guy, Donna, and Thomas Sheridan, eds. *Contested Grounds: Comparative Frontiers on the Northern and Southern Edges of the Spanish Frontier.* Tucson: University of Arizona Press, 1998.

Hacke, William. *An Accurate Description of All the Harbours Riuers Ports Islands Sands Rocks and Dangers between the Mouth of Calafornia & the Straghts of Lemaire in the South Sea of America as Allso of Pepys's Island in the North Sea near to the Magellan Straghts / by William Hack Hydrographer.* London, after 1698.

Hackett, Charles W., ed. *Pichardo's Treatise on the Limits of Louisiana and Texas.* Vol. 4. Austin: University of Texas Press, 1946.

Hackle, Steven W. "Early California Population Project Report." *Journal of California and Great Basin Anthropology* 26, no. 1 (2006): 73–76.

Hall, Gwendolyn M. *Africans in Colonial Louisiana: The Development of Afro-Creole Culture in the Eighteenth Century.* Baton Rouge: Louisiana State University Press, 1995.

———. *Louisiana Slave Database*. 2000. www.ibiblio.org/laslave.

Hall, N. A. T. "Maritime Maroons: 'Grand Marronage' from the Danish West Indies." *William and Mary Quarterly* 42, no. 4 (October 1985): 476–98.

Hanger, Kimberly S. "Avenues to Freedom Open to New Orleans' Black Population, 1769–1779." *Louisiana History: The Journal of the Louisiana Historical Association* 31, no. 3 (1990): 237–64.

———. *Bounded Lives, Bounded Places: Free Black Society in Colonial New Orleans, 1769–1803*. Durham, NC: Duke University Press, 1997.

Hardin, Monica L. *Household Mobility and Persistence in Guadalajara, Mexico, 1811–1842*. Lanham, MD: Lexington Books, 2017.

Hartman, Saidiya V. *Scenes of Subjection: Terror, Slavery, and Self-Making in Nineteenth-Century America*. New York: Oxford University Press, 1997.

Hawkins, Richard. *The Observations of Sir Richard Hawkins, Knt in His Voyage into the South Sea in the Year 1593*. Edited by C. R. Drinkwater Bethune. London: Hakluyt Society, [1622] 1847. https://www.gutenberg.org/files/57502/57502-h/57502-h.htm.

Herrera, Marta. "En un rincón de ese imperio en que no se ocultaba el sol: Colonialismo, oro, y terror en Barbacoas, Siglo XVIII." *Anuario Colombiano de Historia Social y de la Cultura* 32 (2005): 31–49.

———. "Las divisiones político-administrativas del virreinato de la Nueva Granada a finales del período colonial." *Historia Crítica* 22 (2001): 76–98.

Herzog, Tamar. *Defining Nations: Immigrants and Citizens in Early Modern Spain and Spanish America*. New Haven, CT: Yale University Press, 2008.

———. *Frontiers of Possession: Spain and Portugal in Europe and the Americas*. Cambridge, MA: Harvard University Press, 2015.

Heywood, Linda M. *Njinga of Angola: Africa's Warrior Queen*. Cambridge, MA: Harvard University Press, 2017.

Heywood, Linda M., and John K. Thornton. *Central Africans, Atlantic Creoles, and the Foundation of the Americas, 1585–1660*. New York: Cambridge University Press, 2007.

Hilton, Anne. *The Kingdom of Kongo*. Oxford: Clarendon, 1985.

Hoonhout, Bram, and Thomas Mareite. "Freedom at the Fringes? Slave Flight and Empire-building in the Early Modern Spanish Borderlands of Essequibo–Venezuela and Louisiana–Texas." *Slavery & Abolition* 40, no. 1 (March 2018): 61–86.

Hurtado, Albert. *Herbert Eugene Bolton: Historian of the American Borderlands*. Berkeley: University of California Press, 2012.

Ibarra, Antonio. *La organización regional del mercado interno novohispano. La economía colonial de Guadalajara, 1770–1804*. México: Universidad Autónoma de Puebla/Universidad Nacional Autónoma de México, 2000.

Iberville, Pierre. *Iberville's Gulf Journals*. Translated and edited by Richebourg McWilliams. Tuscaloosa: University of Alabama Press, 1981.

Ingersoll, Thomas N. "Free Blacks in a Slave Society: New Orleans, 1718–1812." *William and Mary Quarterly* 48, no. 2 (1991): 173–200.

―――. *Mammon and Manon in Early New Orleans: The First Slave Society in the Deep South, 1718–1819*. Knoxville: University of Tennessee Press, 1999.

Ireton, Chloe. "'They Are Blacks of the Caste of Black Christians': Old Christian Black Blood in the Sixteenth- and Early Seventeenth-Century Iberian Atlantic." *Hispanic American Historical Review* 97, no. 4 (2017): 579–612.

Jaramillo Uribe, Jaime. "La economía del virreinato 1740–1810." In *Historia Económica de Colombia*, edited by José Antonio Ocampo, 49–85. Bogotá: Siglo Veintiuno Editores de Colombia, Fedesarrollo, 1987.

Jiménez Gonzalez, Carlos Alberto. "Ecología de los Pastos Nativos de los Altos de Jalisco." Master's thesis, University of Guadalajara, 1976. http://repositorio.cucba.udg. mx:8080/xmlui/bitstream/handle/123456789/1941/Jimenez_Gonzalez_ Carlos_Alberto.pdf?sequence=1.

Jiménez Meneses, Orián. *El Chocó. Un paraíso del demonio: Nóvita, Citará y el Baudó, Siglo XVIII*. Medellín: Facultad de Ciencias Humanas y Económicas, Editorial Universidad de Antioquia, 2004.

Jiménez Meneses, Orián, and Edgardo Pérez Morales. *Voces de esclavitud y libertad. Documentos y testimonios Colombia, 1701–1833*. Popayán: Editorial Universidad del Cauca, 2013.

Johnson, Jessica M. *Wicked Flesh: Black Women, Intimacy, and Freedom in the Atlantic World*. Philadelphia: University of Pennsylvania Press, 2020.

Johnson, Lyman L. "'A Lack of Legitimate Obedience and Respect': Slaves and Their masters in the Courts of Late Colonial Buenos Aires." *Hispanic American Historical Review* 87, 4 (2007): 631–51.

―――. "Dangerous Words, Provocative Gestures, and Violent Acts: The Disputed Hierarchies of Plebeian Life in Colonial Buenos Aires." In *The Faces of Honor: Sex, Shame, and Violence in Colonial Latin America*, edited by Lyman L. Johnson and Sonya Lipsett-Rivera, 127–51. Albuquerque: University of New Mexico Press, 1998.

Johnson, Rashauna. *Slavery's Metropolis: Unfree Labor in New Orleans During the Age of Revolutions*. Cambridge: Cambridge University Press, 2016.

Jopling, Carol F., ed. *Indios y negros en Panamá en los siglos XVI y XVII: selecciones de los documentos del Archivo General de Indias*. Antigua: Centro de Investigaciones Regionales de Mesoamérica, 1994.

Joutel, Henri. *Joutel's Journal of La Salle's Last Voyage*. Translated by Melville Best Anderson. Caxton Club, 1896.

Katzew, Ilona. *Casta Painting: Images of Race in Eighteenth-Century Mexico*. New Haven, CT: Yale University Press, 2005.

Kelley, Sean M. *Los Brazos de Dios: A Plantation Society in the Texas Borderlands, 1821–1865*. Baton Rouge: LSU Press, 2010.

―――. "'Mexico in His Head': Slavery and the Texas-Mexico Border, 1810–1860." *Journal of Social History* 37, no. 3 (2004): 709–23.

Kinnaird, Lawrence. *Spain in the Mississippi Valley, 1765–1794: Translations of materials from the Spanish archives in the Bancroft Library*. Vols. 1–3. Washington, DC: US Govt. Print. Off., 1949.

Klein, Herbert S. "The Colored Militia of Cuba: 1568–1868." *Caribbean Studies* 6, no. 2 (July 1966): 17–27.

Klooster, Wim. *Illicit Riches: The Dutch Trade in the Caribbean, 1648–1795.* Leiden: Brill, 1995.

Knaut, Andrew L. *The Pueblo Revolt of 1680: Conquest and Resistance in Seventeenth-Century New Mexico.* Norman: University of Oklahoma Press, 2015.

Knight, Frederick. *Working the Diaspora: The Impact of African Labor on the Anglo-American World, 1650–1850.* New York: New York University Press, 2010.

Kuethe, Allan J. "The Status of the Free Pardo in the Disciplined Militia of New Granada." *Journal of Negro History* 56, no. 2 (April 1971): 105–17.

Kuethe, Allan J., and Kenneth J. Andrien. *The Spanish Atlantic World in the Eighteenth Century: War and the Bourbon Reforms, 1713–1796.* New York: Cambridge University Press, 2014.

La Rosa Corzo, Gabino. *Runaway Slave Settlements in Cuba: Resistance and Repression.* Chapel Hill: University of North Carolina Press, [1988] 2003.

Landers, Jane G. *Black Society in Spanish Florida.* Urbana: University of Illinois Press, 1999.

———. "The Atlantic Transformations of Francisco Menéndez." In *Biography and the Black Atlantic,* edited by Lisa A. Lindsay and John Wood Sweet, 209–23. Philadelphia: University of Pennsylvania Press, 2013. https://doi.org/10.9783/9780812208702.209.

———. "*Cimarrón* and Citizen: African Ethnicity, Corporate Identity, and the Evolution of Free Black Towns in the Spanish Circum-Caribbean." In *Slaves, Subjects, and Subversives: Blacks in Colonial Latin America,* edited by Jane G. Landers and Barry Robinson, 111–45. Albuquerque: University of New Mexico Press, 2006.

———. "'Giving Liberty to All': Spanish Florida as a Black Sanctuary, 1673–1790." In *La Florida: Five Hundred Years of Hispanic Presence,* edited by Viviana Díaz Balsera and Rachel A. May, 117–41. Tallahassee: University Press of Florida, 2014.

———. "Gracia Real de Santa Teresa de Mose: A Free Black Town in Spanish Colonial Florida." *American Historical Review* 95, no. 1 (January 1990): 9–30.

———. "Spanish Sanctuary: Fugitives in Florida, 1687–1790." *Florida Historical Quarterly* 6, no. 3 (January 1984): 296–313.

Lane, Fernanda Bretones. "Spain, the Caribbean, and the Making of Religious Sanctuary." PhD diss., Vanderbilt University, 2019.

Lane, Kris E. "Buccaneers and Coastal Defense in Late-Seventeenth-Century Quito: The Case of Barbacoas." *Colonial Latin American Historical Review* 6, no. 2 (1997): 31.

———. *Colour of Paradise: The Emerald in the Age of Gunpowder Empires.* New Haven, CT: Yale University Press, 2010.

———. "In the Shadow of Silver: The Gold of New Granada under the Habsburgs." Invited lecture for Harvard symposium at I Tatti, Florence, 9 June 2016.

———. *Pillaging the Empire: Piracy in the Americas 1500–1750.* New York & London: Armonk, 1998.

———. *Quito 1599: City and Colony in Transition.* Albuquerque: University of New Mexico Press, 2002.

Lane, Kris E., and Mario Diego Romero. "Miners and Maroons: Freedom on the Pacific Coast of Colombia and Ecuador." *Cultural Survival Quarterly* 25, no. 4 (2001): 32–37.

Laprise, Raynald. "The Privateers of Saint-Domingue and Louis XVI's Designs on Spanish America, 1683–1685." *Terrae Incognitae* 39, no. 1 (2007): 68–82.

Larrea, Carlos Manuel. "Geographical Notes on Esmeraldas, Northwestern Ecuador." *Geographical Review* 14, no. 3 (1924): 373–87.

Leal, Claudia. *Landscapes of Freedom: Building a Postemancipation Society in the Rainforests of Western Colombia.* Tucson: University of Arizona Press, 2018.

Lentz, Mark W. "Black Belizeans and Fugitive Mayas: Interracial Encounters on the Edge of Empire, 1750–1803." *The Americas* 70, no. 4 (April 2014): 645–75.

Lewis, Laura A. "Negros, Negros-indios, Afromexicanos: Raza, Nación e identidad en una comunidad mexicana morena (Guerrero)." *Guaraguao* 9, no. 20 (2005): 49–73.

Lipsett-Rivera, Sonya. "*De Obra y Palabra*: Patterns of Insults in Mexico, 1750–1856." *The Americas* 54, no. 4 (1998): 511—39.

Lipsett-Rivera, Sonya, and Lyman L. Johnson, eds. *The Faces of Honor: Sex, Shame, and Violence in Colonial Latin America.* Albuquerque: University of New Mexico Press, 1998.

Lohse, Russel. "Slave-Trade Nomenclature and African Ethnicities in the Americas: Evidence from Early Eighteenth-Century Costa Rica." *Slavery and Abolition* 23, no. 3 (2002): 73–92.

Lokken, Paul. "A Maroon Moment: Rebel Slaves in Early Seventeenth-Century Guatemala." *Slavery & Abolition* 25, no. 3 (2004): 44–58.

López de Velasco, Juan. *Geografía y descripción universal de las Indias.* Madrid: Real Academia de la Historia, 1894.

Lovejoy, Paul. "The Impact of the Atlantic Slave Trade on Africa: A Review of the Literature." *Journal of African History* 30, no. 3 (1989): 365–94.

Macera, Pablo. *Los Jesuitas y la agricultura de la caña.* Lima: Tarea, 1988.

MacGaffey, Wyatt. *Religion and Society in Central Africa: The BaKongo of Lower Zaire.* Chicago: University of Chicago Press, 1986.

Mandrini, Raul. *Vivir entre dos mundos. Las fronteras del sur de la Argentina. Siglos XVIII y XIX.* Buenos Aires: Nueva Dimensión Argentina, 2006.

Mapp, Paul W. "Atlantic History from Imperial, Continental, and Pacific Perspectives." *William and Mary Quarterly* 63, no. 4 (2006): 713–24.

Markham, Clements R. *Reports on the Discovery of Peru.* London: Hakluyt Society, 1872.

Marquez, John C. "Freedom's Edge: Enslaved People, Manumission, and the Law in the Eighteenth-Century South Atlantic World." PhD. diss., University of Illinois at Urbana-Champaign, 2019.

———. "Witnesses to Freedom: Paula's Enslavement, Her Family's Freedom Suit, and the Making of a Counterarchive in the South Atlantic World." *Hispanic American Historical Review* 101, no. 2 (2021): 231–63.

Martínez, María Elena. *Genealogical Fictions: Limpieza de Sangre, Religion, and Gender in Colonial Mexico.* Stanford, CA: Stanford University Press, 2008.

Martínez Montiel, Luz María. "Our Third Root: On African Presence in American Populations." *Diogenes* 45, no. 179 (1997): 165–85.

Mason, William Marvin. *The Census of 1790: A Demographic History of Colonial California*. Menlo Park, CA: Ballena, 1998.

Matthew J. Clavin. *Aiming for Pensacola: Fugitive Slaves on the Atlantic and Southern Frontiers*. Cambridge, MA: Harvard University Press, 2015.

McCaa, Robert. "Calidad, Clase, and Marriage in Colonial Mexico: The Case of Parral, 1788–90." *Hispanic American Historical Review* 64, no. 3 (1984): 477–501.

McFarlane, Anthony. *Colombia Before Independence: Economy, Society, and Politics Under Bourbon Rule*. Cambridge: Cambridge University Press, 1993.

McKinley, Michelle. *Fractional Freedoms: Slavery, Intimacy, and Legal Mobilization in Colonial Lima, 1600–1700*. New York: Cambridge University Press, 2016.

McKittrick, Katherine. *Demonic Grounds: Black Women and the Cartographies of Struggle*. Minneapolis: University of Minnesota, 2006.

McKnight, Kathryn Joy. "Confronted Rituals: Spanish Colonial and Angolan 'Maroon' Executions in Cartagena de Indias (1634)." *Journal of Colonialism and Colonial History* 5, no. 3 (2004). doi:10.1353/cch.2004.0082.

Meacham, Tina L. "The Population of Spanish and Mexican Texas, 1716–1836." PhD diss., University of Texas at Austin, 2000.

Meiklejohn, Norman Arthur. "The Observance of Negro Slave Legislation in Colonial Nueva Granada." Ph.D. diss., Department of History, Columbia University, 1968.

Mena García, María del Carmen. *La sociedad de Panamá en el siglo XVI*. Sevilla: Excma. Diputación Provincial de Sevilla, 1984.

Merolla da Sorrento, Jerome. "A Voyage to Congo and several other Countries in the Southern Africk." In *A collection of voyages and travels, some now first printed from original manuscripts, others translated out of foreign languages, and now first published in English. To which are Added some Few that have formerly appear'd in English, but do now for their Excellency and Scarceness deserve to be Reprinted. In Four Volumes. With a General Preface, giving an Account of the Progress of Navigation, from its first Beginning to the Perfection it is now in, &c. The Whole Illustrated with a great Number of Useful Maps, and Cuts, all engraven on Copper*. 1704.

Metcalf, Alida. *Go-Betweens and the Colonization of Brazil: 1500–1600*. ProQuest Ebook Central, University of Texas Press, 2006. https://ebookcentral.proquest.com/lib/univtole-do-ebooks/detail.action?docID=3443173.

Miller, Joseph. *Kings and Kinsmen: Early Mbundu States in Angola*. Oxford: Clarendon, 1976.

———. *Way of Death: Merchant Capitalism and the Angolan Slave Trade, 1730–1830*. Madison: University of Wisconsin Press, 1988.

Millet, Nathaniel. "Borderlands in the Atlantic World." *Atlantic Studies* 10, no. 2 (2013): 268–95. https://doi.org/10.1080/14788810.2013.785197.

———. "Defining Freedom in the Atlantic Borderlands of the Revolutionary Southeast." *Early American Studies* 5, no. 2 (2007): 367–94.

Moreno, Juan Juárez. *Corsarios y piratas en Veracruz y Campeche*. Seville: EEHA, 1972.

Moten, Fred. *Black and Blur*. Durham, NC: Duke University Press, 2017.

Muñoz de Aronja, Pedro. "Descripción del gobierno del Chocó, sus pueblos de indios, el Número de estos, reales de minas, número de negros y esclavos para su laboreo." *Cespedesia* 45–46, suppl. 4 (1983): 461–72.

Murphy, Robert Cushman. "The Earliest Spanish Advances Southward from Panama Along the West Coast of South America." *Hispanic American Historical Review* 21, no. 1 (February 1941): 3–28.

———. "The Littoral of Pacific Colombia and Ecuador." *American Geographical Society* 29, no. 1 (February 1939): 1–33.

Navarrete, María Cristina. "Palenques: Maroons and Castas in Colombia's Caribbean Regions. Social Relations in the 17th Century." In *Orality, Identity, and Resistance in Palenque (Colombia): An Interdisciplinary Approach*, edited by Armin Schwegler, Bryan Kirschen, and Graciela Maglia, 269–96. Philadelphia: John Benjamins, 2017.

———. *San Basilio de Palenque. Memoria y tradición. Surgimiento y avatars de las gestas cimarronas en el Caribe Colombiano*. Cali: Universidad del Valle, 2011.

Naveda Chávez-Hita, Adriana. *Esclavos negros en las haciendas azucares de Córdoba*. Universidad Veracruzana, 1987.

Nichols, James David. *The Limits of Liberty: Mobility and the Making of the Eastern U.S.-Mexico Border*. Lincoln: University of Nebraska Press, 2018.

Nichols, Philip. "Sir Francis Drake Revived." In *Voyages and Travels: Ancient and Modern*, edited by Charles W. Eliot, 125–203. New York: P. F. Collier & Son, 1910.

O'Toole, Rachel Sarah. "'In a War Against the Spanish': Andean Protection and African Resistance on the Northern Peruvian Coast." *The Americas* 63, no. 1 (2006): 19–52.

Oropeza Keresey, Deborah. "La esclavitud asiática en el virreinato de la Nueva España, 1565–1673." *Historia mexicana* 61, no 1 (July 2011): 5–57.

Patiño Castaño, Diógenes, and Martha C. Hernández. "Arqueología e historia de africanos y afrodescendientes en el Cauca, Colombia." *Revista Colombiana de Antropología* 57, no. 1 (2021): 125–62.

Pearson, M. N. *The Indian Ocean. Seas in History*. New York: Routledge, 2003.

Pellicer de Touar, Joseph, *Mission evangelica al reyno de Congo por la serafica religion de los Capuchinos*. Madrid: Domingo Garcia i Morrás, 1649.

Peña Batlle, Manuel Arturo. *La rebelión del Bahoruco*. Santo Domingo: Liberia Hispaniola, 1970.

Pike, Ruth. "Black Rebels: The Cimarrons of Sixteenth-Century Panama." *The Americas* 64, no. 2 (2007): 243–66.

Ponce Leiva, Pilar, ed. *Relaciones Historico-Geographicas De La Audiencia De Quito: S. Xvi-Xix*. 2 vols., *V Centenario Del Descubrimiento De America*. Madrid: Consejo Superior de Investigaciones Cientificas, Centro de Estudios Historicos, Departamento de Historia de America, 1991–1992.

Ponce-Vázquez, Juan José. *Islanders and Empire: Smuggling and Political Defiance in Hispaniola, 1580–1690*. Cambridge: Cambridge University Press, 2020.

Porras Barrenechea, Raúl. *Los Cronistas Del Perú, 1528–1650*. 2 vols. Lima: Biblioteca Abraham Valdelomar, 2014.

Prado, Fabrício. *Edge of Empire: Atlantic Networks and Revolution in Bourbon Río de la Plata*. Oakland: University of California Press, 2015.

Premo, Bianca. *The Enlightenment on Trial: Ordinary Litigants and Colonialism in the Spanish Empire*. Oxford: Oxford University Press, 2017.

Price, Richard, ed. *Maroon Societies: Rebel Slave Communities in the Americas*. Garden City, NY: Anchor, 1973.

Proctor, Frank "Trey." *Damned Notions of Liberty: Slavery, Culture, and Power in Colonial Mexico, 1640–1769*. Albuquerque: University of New Mexico Press, 2010.

Rama, Angel. *Lettered City*. Durham, NC: Duke University Press, 1996.

Ramírez, Susan. *Provincial Patriarchs: Land Tenure and the Economics of Power in Colonial Peru*. Albuquerque: University of New Mexico Press, 1986.

Rappaport, Joanne, and Tom Cummins. *Beyond the Lettered City: Indigenous Literacies in the Andes*. Durham, NC: Duke University Press, 2012.

Rebagliati, Lucas. "Entre las aspiraciones de libertad y el derecho de propiedad: el patrocinio jurídico a los esclavos en tiempos de revolución, Buenos Aires, 1806–1821." In *El Asedio a la Libertad: Abolición y Posabolición de la Esclavitud en el Cono Sur*, edited by Florencia Guzman and Maria L. Ghidoli, 41–74. Buenos Aires: Biblos, 2020.

Recopilacion de Leyes de Los Reynos de las Indias. Madrid: Ivlian De Paredes, 1681.

Reid-Vazquez, Michele. *The Year of the Lash: Free People of Color in Cuba and the Nineteenth-Century Atlantic World*. Athens: University of Georgia Press, 2011.

"Report of Proceedings Relative to the Slave Trade in Guatimala." *African Observer: A Monthly Journal Containing Essays and Documents Illustrative of the General Character and Political Effects of Negro Slavery* (1828): 30.

Restall, Matthew. *The Black Middle: Africans, Mayans, and Spaniards in Colonial Yucatan*. Palo Alto, CA: Stanford University Press, 2009.

———. "Crossing to Safety? Frontier Flight in Eighteenth-Century Belize and Yucatan." *Hispanic American Historical Review* 94, no. 3 (July 2014): 381–419.

Richmond, Douglas W. "Africa's Initial Encounter with Texas: The Significance of Afro-Tejanos in Colonial Tejas, 1528–1821." *Bulletin of Latin American Research* 26, no. 2 (2007): 200–221.

Roberts, Neil. *Freedom as Marronage*. Chicago: University of Chicago Press, 2015.

Robles, Antonio de, and Antonio Castro Leal, eds. *Diario de sucesos notables (1665–1703)*. Mexico: Editorial Porrúa, 1946.

Rocha, Gabriel de Avilez. "Maroons in the Montes: Toward a Political Ecology of Marronage in the Sixteenth-Century Caribbean." In *Early Modern Black Diaspora Studies: A Critical Anthology*, edited by Cassander L. Smith, Nicholas R. Jones, and Miles P. Grier, 15–36. Cham, Switzerland: Palgrave Macmillan, 2018.

Rodrigues, Jaime. *De Costa a Costa. Escravos, marinheiros e intermediários do tráfico negreiro de Angola ao Rio de Janeiro (1780–1860)*. Rio de Janeiro: Companhia das Letras, 2005.

Rodríguez Demorizi, Emilio, ed. *Relaciones historicas de Santo Domingo*. 3 vols. Trujillo: Editora Montalvo, 1945.

Rodríguez, Frederick. "Cimarrón Revolts and Pacification in New Spain the Isthmus of Panama and Colonial Colombia, 1503–1800" (1979). *Dissertations*. 1804. https://ecommons.luc.edu/luc_diss/1804.

Rodríguez, Pablo. "La efímera utopía de los esclavos de Nueva Granada. El caso del palenque de Cartago." In *Tradiciones y conflictos: Historias de la vida cotidiana en México e Hispanoamérica*, edited by Pilar Gonzalbo Aizpuru and Mílada Bazant, 73–92. Mexico DF: Colegio de Mexico, 2007.

Rogers, Nicholas. "Caribbean Borderland: Empire, Ethnicity, and the Exotic on the Mosquito Coast." *Eighteenth-Century Life* 26, no. 3 (2002): 117–38.

Rogers, Woodes. *A Cruising Voyage Around the World*. London: Cassell, [1712], 1928. https://www.gutenberg.org/files/55538/55538-h/55538-h.htm#ill_007.

Romero, Mario Diego. "Sociedades negras: Esclavos y libres en la costa pacífica de Colombia." *América Negra* 2 (1991): 137–51.

Romoli, Kathleen. "Nomenclatura y población indígenas de la antigua jurisdicción de Cali a mediados del siglo XVI." *Revista Colombiana de Antropología* 16 (1974): 374–478.

Rumazo, José. *Documentos Para la Historia de la Audiencia de Quito*. 8 vols. Madrid: Afrodisio Aguado, S.A., 1948–1950.

Rupert, Linda M. "Contraband Trade and the Shaping of Colonial Societies in Curaçao and Tierra Firme." *Itinerario* 30, no. 3 (November 2006): 35–54.

———. "Marronage, Manumission and Maritime Trade in the Early Modern Caribbean." *Slavery and Abolition* 30, no. 3 (September 2009): 361–82.

———. "Seeking the Water of Baptism: Fugitive Slaves and Imperial Jurisdiction in the Early Modern Caribbean." In *Legal Pluralism and Empires, 1500–1850*, edited by Richard J. Ross, 199–231. New York: New York University Press, 2013.

Salomon, Carlos Manuel. *Pío Pico: The Last Governor of Mexican California*. Norman: University of Oklahoma Press, 2014.

Sánchez Mejía, Hugues R. "De arrochelados a vecinos: Reformismo Borbónico e integración política en las gobernaciones de Santa Marta y Cartagena, Nuevo Reino de Granada, 1740–1810." *Revista de Indias* 74, no. 264 (2015): 457–88.

———. "De esclavos a campesinos, de la 'roza' al mercado: Tierra y producción agropecuaria de los 'libres de todos los colores' en la gobernación de Santa Marta (1740–1810)." *Historia Crítica* 43 (2011): 130–55.

Sandos, James A. "Toypurina's Revolt Religious Conflict at Mission San Gabriel In 1785." *Boletín: Journal of the Mission Studies Association* 24, no. 2 (2007): 4–14.

Santos Gomes, Flávio dos. "Peasants, Maroons, and the Frontiers of Liberation in Maranhão." *Review (Fernand Braudel Center)* 31, no. 3 (2008): 379–99.

Sarmiento, Domingo Faustino. *Facundo: Civilization and Barbarism*. Berkeley: University of California Press, 2004.

Sartorius, David. "My Vassals: Free-Colored Militias in Cuba and the Ends of Spanish Empire." *Journal of Colonialism and Colonial History* 5, no. 2 (Fall 2004).

Schwaller, Robert C. *African Maroons in Sixteenth-Century Panama: A History in Documents*. Norman: University of Oklahoma Press, 2021.

———. "Contested Conquests: African Maroons and the Incomplete Conquest of Hispaniola, 1519–1620." *The Americas* 75, no. 4 (2018): 609–38.

———. "*Mulata, Hija de Negro y India*: Afro-Indigenous *Mulatos* in Early Colonial Mexico." *Journal of Social History* 44, no. 3 (Spring 2011): 889–914.

Schwartz, Stuart B. "Colonial Identities and the Sociedad de Castas." *Colonial Latin American Review* 4, no. 1 (1995): 185–201.

———. "Rethinking Palmares: Slave Resistance in Colonial Brazil." In *Slaves, Peasants, and Rebels: Reconsidering Brazilian Slavery, 103–36*. Urbana: University of Illinois Press, 1992.

Scott, Julius S. *The Common Wind: Afro-American Currents in the Age of the Haitian Revolution*. London: Verso, 2018.

Secreto, María Verónica. "Territorialidades fluidas: corsários franceses é tráfico negreiro no Rio da Prata (1796–1799). Tensões locais-tensões globais." *Topoi* 17, no. 33 (2016): 419–43.

Seed, Patricia. "The Social Dimensions of Race: Mexico City, 1753." *Hispanic American Historical Review* 62, no. 4 (1982): 569–606.

Sharman, J. C. *Empires of the Weak: The Real Story of European Expansion and the Creation of the New World Order*. Princeton, NJ: Princeton University Press, 2019.

Sharp, William Frederick. "El negro en Colombia: Manumisión y posición social." *Razón y fabula. Revista de la Universidad de los Andes* 8 (1968): 91–107.

———. "The Profitability of Slavery in the Colombian Chocó, 1680–1810." *Hispanic American Historical Review* 55 (1975): 468–95.

———. *Slavery on the Spanish Frontier: The Colombian Chocó, 1680–1810*. Norman: University of Oklahoma Press, 1976.

Sheridan, Richard B. "The Maroons of Jamaica, 1730–1830: Livelihood, Demography and Health." *Slavery & Abolition* 6, no. 3 (1985): 152–72.

Shumway, Jeffrey M. *The Case of the Ugly Suitor & Other Histories of Love, Gender, & Nation in Buenos Aires, 1776–1870*. Lincoln: University of Nebraska Press, 2005.

Sierra Silva, Pablo Miguel. "Afro-Mexican Women in Saint-Domingue: Piracy, Captivity, and Community in the 1680s and 1690s." *Hispanic American Historical Review* 11, no. 1 (2020): 3–34.

———. "The Pirate Link: Rethinking Early Charleston, Blackness and the 1683 Raid on Veracruz." Unpublished paper delivered at the Addlestone Library, College of Charleston, February 20, 2020.

———. *Urban Slavery in Colonial Mexico: Puebla de los Ángeles, 1531–1706*. Cambridge: Cambridge University Press, 2018.

Silverblatt, Irene. "Political Memories and Colonizing Symbols: Santiago and the Mountain Gods of Colonial Peru." In *Rethinking History and Myth: Indigenous South American Perspectives on the Past*, edited by Jonathan D. Hill, 174–94. Urbana: University of Illinois Press, 1988.

Sluiter, Engel. "Dutch-Spanish Rivalry in the Caribbean Area, 1594–1609." *HAHR* 28, no. 2 (May 1948): 165–96.

———. *The Gold and Silver of Spanish America, c. 1572–1648: Tables Showing Bullion Declared for Taxation in Colonial Royal Treasuries, Remittances to Spain, and Expenditures for Defense of Empire.* Berkeley: Bancroft Library, University of California, 1998.

Sluyter, Andrew. *Black Ranching Frontiers: African Cattle Herders of the Atlantic World, 1500–1900.* New Haven, CT: Yale University Press, 2012.

Socolow, Susan. "Spanish Captives in Indian Societies: Cultural Contact Along the Argentine Frontier, 1600–1835." *Hispanic American Historical Review* 72, 1 (1992): 73–99.

Sparks, Randy J. *The Two Princes of Calabar: An Eighteenth-Century Atlantic Odyssey.* Cambridge, MA: Harvard University Press, 2004.

Spear, Jennifer M. *Race, Sex and Social Order in Early New Orleans.* Baltimore: Johns Hopkins University Press, 2008.

Stark, David M. "Rescued from Their Invisibility: The Afro-Puerto Ricans of Seventeenth- and Eighteenth-Century San Mateo de Cangrejos, Puerto Rico." *The Americas* 63, no. 4 (April 2007): 551–86.

Steinberg, Philip E. *The Social Construction of the Ocean.* Cambridge, MA: Cambridge University Press, 2001.

Stern, Peter. "Gente de color quebrado: Africans and Afromestizos in Colonial Mexico." *Colonial Latin American Historical Review* 3, no. 2 (1994): 185–205.

Stevenson, William Bennet. *A Historical and Descriptive Narrative of Twenty Years' Residence in South America, Containing the Travels in Arauco, Chile, Peru, and Colombia; with an Account of the Revolution, Its Rise, Progress, and Results.* London: Hurst Robinson & Co.; [etc. etc.], 1825.

Stone, Erin Woodruff. "America's First Slave Revolt: Indians and African Slaves in Española, 1500–1534." *Ethnohistory* 60, no. 2 (2013): 195–217.

Sweeney, Shauna J. "Market Marronage: Fugitive Women and the Internal Marketing System in Jamaica, 1781–1834." *William and Mary Quarterly*, 3rd ser. 76, no. 2 (April 2019): 197–222.

Tardieu, Jean-Pierre. *Cimarrones de Panama. La forja de una identidad afroamericana en el siglo XVI.* Madrid: Iberoamericana, 2009.

Taylor, Joe Gray. *Negro Slavery in Louisiana.* Baton Rouge: Louisiana Historical Association, 1963.

TePaske, John J. "The Fugitive Slave: Intercolonial Rivalry and Spanish Slave Policy, 1687–1764." In *Eighteenth-century Florida and Its Borderlands*, edited by Samuel Proctor, 1–12. Gainesville: University Press of Florida, 1975.

Terrazas Williams, Danielle. *Capital of Free Women: Race, Status, and Economic Networks in Colonial Veracruz.* New Haven, CT: Yale University Press, 2022.

Texada, David K. *Alejandro O'Reilly and the New Orleans Rebels.* Lafayette: University of Southwestern Louisiana, 1970.

Thompson, Alvin O. *Flight to Freedom: African Runaways and Maroons in the Americas.* Kingston, Jamaica: University of the West Indies Press, 2006.

Thornton, John K. "African Dimensions of the Stono Rebellion." *American Historical Review* 96, no. 4 (1991): 1101–13.

———. "The Art of War in Angola, 1575–1680." *Comparative Studies in Society and History* 30 no. 2 (1988): 360–78.

———. *The Kingdom of Kongo: Civil War and Transition 1641–1718*. Madison: University of Wisconsin Press, 1983.

———. "Legitimacy and Political Power: Queen Njinga, 1624–1663." *Journal of African History* 32, no. 1 (1991): 25–40.

———. *Warfare in Atlantic Africa, 1500–1800*. London: UCL Press, 1999.

Tjarks, Alicia Vidaurreta. "Comparative Demographic Analysis of Texas, 1777–1793." In *New Spain's Far Northern Frontier*, edited by David J. Weber, 135–70. Albuquerque: University of New Mexico Press, 1979.

Tompson, Doug. "Between Slavery and Freedom on the Atlantic Coast of Honduras." *Slavery & Abolition* 33, no. 3 (September 2012): 403–16.

Torget, Andrew J. *Seeds of Empire: Cotton, Slavery, and the Transformation of the Texas Borderlands, 1800–1850*. Chapel Hill: University of North Carolina Press, 2015.

Torres Franco, Carmen Paulina. "De Abuelos Maternos, Nietos Indios: La 'desaparición' de las familias mulatas en la parroquia de Encarnación, Los Altos de Jalisco, Nueva España, 1778–1822." *Historia y Genealogía* 9 (2019): 93–103.

Tovar Pinzón, Hermés, Jorge Andrés Tovar Mora, and Camilo Ernesto Tovar Mora. *Convocatoria al poder del número: Censos y estadísticas de la Nueva Granada, 1750–1830*. Serie Historia, No. 1. Bogotá: Archivo General de la Nación, 1995.

Townsend, Camilla. *Tales of Two Cities: Race and Economic Culture in Early Republican North and South America: Guayaquil, Ecuador, and Baltimore, Maryland*. Austin: University of Texas Press, 2000.

Tratados De Tordesillas I–II. Transcribed and published online by the Universidad de Alicante. http://www.artic.ua.es/biblioteca/u85/documentos/1828.pdf.

Trouillot, Michel-Rolph. *Silencing the Past: Power and the Production of History*. Boston: Beacon, 2005.

Tubb, Daniel. *Shifting Livelihoods: Gold Mining and Subsistence in the Chocó, Colombia*. Seattle: University of Washington Press, 2020.

Twinam, Ann. *Miners, Merchants, and Farmers in Colonial Colombia*. Austin: University of Texas Press, 1982.

Usner, Daniel H. *Historia militar de Santo Domingo (documentos y noticias)*. 3 vols. Santo Domingo: Editora Búho, 2014.

———. *Indians, Settlers, & Slaves in a Frontier Exchange Economy: The Lower Mississippi Valley Before 1783*. Chapel Hill: University of North Carolina Press, 1992.

Utrera, Cipriano de. *Historia militar de Santo Domingo (documentos y noticias)*. 3 vols. Santo Domingo: Editora Búho, 2014.

Valdés, Dennis N. "The Decline of Slavery in Mexico." *The Americas* 44, no. 2 (1987): 167–94.

Vallet, Chantel Cramaussel. "La Evolución del Mestizaje en la Nueva España: Las

Aportaciones Recientes de la Historia Demográfica." *Habitus-Revista do Instituto Golano de Pré-Historia e Antropología* 14, no. 2 (2016): 157–74.

Van Young, Eric. *Hacienda and Market in Eighteenth-Century Mexico: The Rural Economy of the Guadalajara Region, 1675–1820.* 2nd ed. Lanham, MD: Rowman & Littlefield, 2006.

Vasconcelos, José. *La Raza Cósmica: Misión de la raza iberoamericana.* Notas de viajes a la América del Sur. Madrid: Agencia Mundial de Librería, 1925.

Vega, Garcilaso de la. *Historia General del Peru.* Cordoba: Viuda de Andres Barrera, 1617.

Vidal, Cécil. *Caribbean New Orleans: Empire, Race, and the Making of a Slave Society.* Chapel Hill: University of North Carolina Press, 2020.

———. "Private and State Violence Against African Slaves in Lower Louisiana During the French Period, 1699–1769." In *New World Orders: Violence, Sanction, and Authority in the Colonial Americas,* edited by John Smolenski and Thomas J. Humphrey, 92–110. Philadelphia: University of Pennsylvania Press, 2007.

Villar Ortiz, Covadonga. *La renta de la pólvora en Nueva España, 1569–1767.* Seville: Editorial CSISC, 1988.

Villarreal, Christina M. "Colonial Border Control: Reconsidering Migrants and the Making of New Spain's Northern Borderlands, 1714–1820." MA Thesis, University of Texas at Austin, 2015.

Vinson III, Ben. *Bearing Arms for His Majesty: The Free-Colored Militia in Colonial Mexico.* Stanford, CA: Stanford University Press, 2001.

———. *Before Mestizaje: The Frontiers of Caste in Colonial Mexico.* New York: Cambridge University Press, 2018.

———. "Fading from Memory: Historiographical Reflections on the Afro-Mexican Presence in Mexico." *Review of Black Political Economy* (2005): 59–72.

———. "Moriscos y lobos en la Nueva España." In *Debates históricos contemporáneos: africanos y afrodescendientes en México y Centroamérica,* edited by María Elisa Velásquez, 159–76. Mexico: Centro de estudios mexicanos y centroamericanos, 2013.

———. "Race and Badge: Free-Colored Soldiers in the Colonial Mexican Militia." *The Americas* 56, no. 4 (April 2000): 471–96.

Voisin, Erin E. "Saint Malo Remembered." MA thesis, Louisiana State University, 2008.

Wade, Peter. *Degrees of Mixture, Degrees of Freedom: Genomics, Multiculturalism, and Race in Latin America.* Durham, NC: Duke University Press, 2017.

Walker, Tamara J. *Exquisite Slaves: Race, Clothing, and Status in Colonial Lima.* New York: Cambridge University Press, 2017.

Weber, David J. *Bárbaros Spaniards and Their Savages in the Age of Enlightenment.* New Haven, CT: Yale University Press, 2005.

———. *The Spanish Frontier in North America.* New Haven, CT: Yale University Press, 1992.

Weddle, Robert S. *The Wreck of the Belle, the Ruin of La Salle.* College Station: Texas A&M University Press, 2001.

West, Robert C. *Atlantic Africa and the Spanish Caribbean, 1570–1640.* Chapel Hill: Omohundro Institute of Early American History and Culture and the University of North Carolina Press, 2016.

———. *Colonial Placer Mining in Colombia*. Baton Rouge: Louisiana State University Press, 1952.

———. "The First Great Waves: African Provenance Zones for the Transatlantic Slave Trade to Cartagena De Indias, 1570–1640." *Journal of African History* 52, no. 1 (2011): 1–22.

Wheat, David. *Atlantic Africa and the Spanish Caribbean, 1570–1640*. Chapel Hill: University of North Carolina Press, 2016.

Wheeler, B. Gordon. *Black California: The History of African-Americans in the Golden State*. New York: Hippocrene Books, 1993.

Wiersema, Juliet. "The Manuscript Map of the Dagua River: A Rare Look at a Remote Region in the Spanish Colonial Americas." *Artl@s Bulletin* 7, no. 2 (2018): 71–90.

———. "Importing Ethnicity, Creating Culture: Currents of Opportunity and Ethnogenesis Along the Río Dagua in Nueva Granada, c. 1764." In *The Global Spanish Empire: Five Hundred Years of Placemaking and Pluralism*, edited by John Douglass and Christine Beaule, 267–90. Tucson: Amerind Studies in Archaeology, University of Arizona Press, 2020.

———. "Map of the Course of the Atrato River and the Province of Zitará." Unpublished ms.

———. "Map of Curso del Río Atrato: A Case for Settlement in the Chocó." Unpublished ms.

———. "Map of the Río Atrato 1777." In *The History of a Periphery: Manuscript Maps of Colombia's Pacific Lowlands*. Austin: University of Texas Press, forthcoming.

Williams, Caroline A. *Between Resistance and Adaptation: Indigenous Peoples and the Colonisation of the Chocó, 1510–1753*. Liverpool: University of Liverpool Press, 2005.

Wilson, Kathleen. "The Performance of Freedom: Maroons and the Colonial Order in Eighteenth-Century Jamaica and the Atlantic Sound." *William and Mary Quarterly*, 3rd series, 66, no. 1 (2009): 45–86.

Worth, John E. "Forging a New Identity in Florida's Refugee Missions." Paper presented at the Missions and Frontiers in Spanish America symposium, 53rd International Conferences of Americanists, Mexico City, Mexico, July 19–24, 2009.

Wright, Irene A. "The Spanish Resistance to the English Occupation of Jamaica, 1655–1660." *Transactions of the Royal Historical Society*, 4th series, 13 (December 1930): 117–47.

Wright, Willie Jamaal. "The Morphology of Marronage." *Annals of the American Association of Geographers* 110, no. 4 (2019): 1134–49.

Zitomersky, Joseph. "The Form and Function of French-Native American Relations in Early Eighteenth-Century French Colonial Louisiana." *Proceedings of the Meeting of the French Colonial Historical Society* 15, (1992): 154–77.

CONTRIBUTORS

Cameron D. Jones is an award-winning author whose publications on the Spanish American borderlands include *In Service of Two Masters: The Missionaries of Ocopa, Indigenous Resistance, and Spanish Governance in Bourbon Peru* (Academy of American Franciscan History and Stanford University Press, 2018); and "The Evolution of Spanish Governance During the Early Bourbon Period in Peru: The Juan Santos Atahualpa Rebellion and the Missionaries of Ocopa," (*The Americas*, 2016), which received the 2017 Antonine Tibesar Award from the Conference on Latin American History. Jones was a doctoral fellow at the Academy of American Franciscan History in 2010. He teaches at California Polytechnic State University in San Luis Obispo, California.

Jay T. Harrison is an associate professor and chair of the Department of History at Hood College in Maryland where he also directs the college's program in public history. His research addresses the northern Spanish American borderlands of New Spain, indigenous history, and public history. He is the author of essays on missions and native peoples of northern New Spain and a coauthor of a public history monograph, *Almost Heaven: Fifty Years of Purgatory* (Durango, CO., 2015), which explores the history of one of Colorado's prominent western slope ski areas. A former doctoral fellow at the Academy of American Franciscan History (2008), Harrison served previously as director of the Center of Southwest Studies, a comprehensive museum, archive, and research library complex in Durango, Colorado.

Christina Marie Villarreal is an assistant professor of history at the University of Texas, El Paso. Her research focuses on the Texas-Louisiana borderlands, early America, fugitives from slavery, desertion, and sanctuary. Villarreal has received support for her research from the Ford Foundation, the Fulbright Program, The Institute for Citizens & Scholars, and the SSRC-Mellon Mays Program. In 2021–2022, Villarreal was a research fellow at the Clements Center for Southwest Studies at Southern Methodist University where she worked on her forthcoming manuscript, "Imperial Fugitives: Apostates, Deserters, and Runaways in Eighteenth-Century Texas and Louisiana Borderlands, 1714–1803."

Joseph M. H. Clark is an assistant professor of history at the University of Kentucky. His research examines the ways in which economic and political relationships that crossed colonial borders influenced the development of regionally specific

African diasporic identities, with a particular focus on Mexico and the Caribbean in the seventeenth century. His most recent book project, *Veracruz and the Caribbean in the Seventeenth Century*, studies African diaspora in the Mexican port city of Veracruz, with emphasis on the role of circum-Caribbean trade and migration in the construction of local concepts of race, ethnicity, religion, and status.

Anne M. Reid is an independent scholar whose research interests include eighteenth-century borderlands in colonial North America and Latin America. She served as the lead compiler of the Early California Population Project at the Huntington Library and has also been a visiting fellow at the Early Modern Studies Institute at the University of Southern California. She teaches at California State University.

Mark W. Lentz, associate professor of Latin American history and the History Program coordinator at Utah Valley University, is a historian of colonial Mexico, Central America, and the Atlantic World. His current interests include interpreters in the conquest and colonization of Yucatan and interethnic relations in colonial and early national Mexico and Guatemala. He recently published articles on indigenous-African relations in eighteenth-century Guatemala and Belize and the role of Jesuits in translation, conversion, and pedagogy in colonial Yucatan, and an article on creole and African-descent fluency and literacy in indigenous languages in the *Hispanic American Historical Review* that won the 2018 Best Article Prize at the Rocky Mountain Council for Latin American Studies. His first monograph, *Murder in Mérida, 1792: Violence, Factions, and the Law*, was published in June 2018 with the University of New Mexico Press's Diálogos Series. He was the 2015–2016 R. David Parsons Fellow at the John Carter Brown Library in Providence, Rhode Island.

Robert C. Schwaller is an associate professor of history at the University of Kansas. He received his PhD from Pennsylvania State University. His research focuses on the history of race and the experiences of African and Afro-descended individuals in early Spanish America. His book *Géneros de Gente in Early Colonial Mexico: Defining Racial Difference* (University of Oklahoma Press, 2016) examines the development of racial categories in early New Spain. His research has appeared in *The Americas, The Journal of Social History,* and *Rechtsgeschichte/Legal History,* among other journals. He currently serves as editor of *Ethnohistory*.

Juliet Wiersema is an associate professor of pre-Hispanic and Spanish colonial art history at the University of Texas, San Antonio. Her early research examined notions of constructed space in the art and archaeology of the Moche, a pre-Hispanic Andean culture without a written history. Her first monograph, *Architectural Vessels of the Moche. Ceramic Diagrams of Sacred Space in Ancient Peru* (University of Texas Press 2015), explores the relationship between portable architectural representations and monumental architectural remains. Her current work uses manuscript maps from eighteenth-century New Granada to unearth narratives about African autonomy, placemaking, indigenous resistance, and tenuous colonialisms in gold mining areas on the fringes of Spain's empire. Her current monograph, *Mapping the Periphery: Spanish Colonial Cartography from Colombia's Pacific Lowlands (1720–1820)*, will be published by University of Texas Press. Support for her research has come from the National Endowment of the Humanities, John Carter Brown Library, the Library of Congress, The Metropolitan Museum of Art, The Smithsonian Institution, and the Fulbright Program.

Charles Beatty-Medina is a professor of history at the University of Toledo, specializing in maroon societies in Colonial Latin America. He has published numerous articles and book chapters on the Esmeraldas maroons and marronage in colonial Latin America. These include "Caught Between Rivals: The Spanish-African Maroon Competition for Captive Indian Labor in the Region of Esmeraldas during the Late Sixteenth and Early Seventeenth Centuries" in *The Americas*; "Between the Cross and the Sword: Religious Conquest and Maroon Legitimacy in Colonial Esmeraldas" in *Africans to Colonial Spanish America*; and "Maroon Societies" (Oxford Online).

Rachel Sarah O'Toole is an associate professor of history at the University of California, Irvine, where she teaches classes on colonial Latin America, the African diaspora, and sex and gender. Her monograph, *Bound Lives: Africans, Indians, and the Making of Race in Colonial Peru* (Pittsburgh, 2012), received the 2013 Latin American Studies Association Peru Section Flora Tristán book prize. With Sherwin Bryant and Ben Vinson III, she coedited *Africans to Spanish America: Expanding the Diaspora* (2012), and with Ivonne del Valle and Anna More, she coedited *Iberian Empires and the Roots of Globalization* (2019). She has published articles on the construction of whiteness, masculinity within slavery, African diaspora identities, indigenous politics, and gender influences on racial constructions, and currently is completing her second monograph regarding the meanings of freedom in colonial Peru.

Alex Borucki is an associate professor of history at the University of California, Irvine. He is the author of *From Shipmates to Soldiers: Emerging Black Identities in the Río de la Plata* (University of New Mexico Press, 2015); and coeditor of *From the Galleon to the Highlands: Slave Trade Routes in the Spanish Americas* (University of New Mexico Press, 2020) and *The Rio de la Plata from Colony to Nations: Commerce, Society, and Politics* (Routledge, 2021). Apart from Spanish-language books and articles, he has published on the African Diaspora in the *American Historical Review*, *Hispanic American Historical Review*, *Colonial Latin American Review*, *The Americas*, *History in Africa*, *Itinerario*, *Atlantic Studies*, and *Slavery and Abolition*. He co-created the Intra-American Slave Trade Database, with Greg O'Malley (UC Santa Cruz), that adds nearly 30,000 slave voyages within the Americas to the Slave Voyages website at https://slavevoyages.org/american/about#methodology/0/en/.

INDEX

academic racism, ix

Africans/Afro-descendants: Afro-Belizeans, xv, 71, 72, 73, 74, 76, 79, 83nn24–25, 85n53; Afro-Brazilians, 173, 174, 176, 179, 181, 182–83, 186, 187, 189n26; Afro-Jamaicans, 51–52n24; Afro-Mexicans, 41, 45, 46, 49; Afro-Mexicans taken to Jamaica, 51–52n24; Afro-Mexicans taken to Saint-Domingue (Haiti), 41, 42; Afro-Mexicans sold as slaves in South Carolina, 41; anonymity, xiii; autonomy, 128n37; community formation, 128n37; defended and resisted empire, ix, 16; distinct cultural identities, xiv; free and enslaved African diasporas, xiv, 40, 46, 48, 49, 50, 105n11, 130n71, 171n87; free Blacks (*negros libres*), xi, xv, 4, 22, 24, 33n13, 33n19, 34n26, 44, 45, 46, 48, 49, 82n7, 100, 101, 104, 108–32, 174, 175, 176, 177, 179, 180, 182, 183, 184, 185, 186, 188n9; fugitive geographies, 27, 157, 161; hiding origins, xiii, 4, 7; holders of enslaved persons, xv, 120, 129n60, 130n66; indigenous enslavement of maroons, 24; knowledge and use of law, 122; liberation, xiii; linguistic diversity within, 131n91; male marriage to indigenous women, 14, 15–16; mine owners, xv, 108–32; resisting colonization, xi; retention of African languages, 124; self-emancipation/liberation, xiii, xiv, 20–37, 112; shaped Spanish hegemony, xi; social mobility, xi; suppression of indigenous rebellions, 16. *See also* racial-ethnic classification; racialized ethnonyms; racial (mis)identification; slavery/enslaved

Alabama, 22; Mobile, 20, 21, 49, 156. *See also* Spanish Gulf Coast Borderlands

Amazonia, 112

Argentina, x, 173, 175, 188n8, 188n13; Buenos Aires, xvi, 19n31, 51n23, 173–90; whitening of country (*blanquear el país*), x. *See also* Patagonia; Spain/Spaniards

Asians, x; Atlantic privateers' interest in Manila (Philippines), 150n6; chinos, 44; recruitment of labor, 56; South Asians enslaved in Nueva Galicia, 66n5

asylum/sanctuary, xiii, xiv, xv, 20, 21, 23–24, 25–26, 34n24, 34n26, 34n28, 70–86, 141; Fort Mose (Florida) as first free-Black settlement, 24; indigenous communities not reliable havens, 24; lack of uniform religious sanctuary, 24; Spain's granting of, 72; Spanish proposal to grant asylum to enslaved in Louisiana, 25. *See also* Africans/Afro-descendants; Belize; Guatemala

Bahía del Espíritu Santo, 43, 48, 52nn27–28, 53n37, 53n43. *See also* La Salle

Belize, xv, 24, 70, 71–72, 73, 74, 75, 76–77, 78–80, 81, 82, 82n6, 82–83n10, 83n14, 83n20, 85n46, 85n52, 85–86nn56–65, 86n67; Afro-Belizeans seeking conversion offered sanctuary, 76; Afro-Belizeans sold into slavery in Yucatán, 76; enslaved escaped to Guatemala, xv; formerly British Honduras, 73, 78, 82, 83n20, 86n65, 86n67; Spain concedes rights to British in, 73

Black Lives Matter, vii, ix

Brazil, xvi, 72, 137, 151n13, 173, 174, 175, 177, 179, 180, 181, 182, 185, 186, 187, 190; Rio de Janeiro, xvi, 177, 181, 182, 183–84, 185, 186, 189n31; Rio Grande do Sul, 177, 180, 181, 183, 185, 186. *See also* Africans/Afro-descendants

Britain/British, 8, 20, 21, 22, 24, 39, 40, 43, 44, 47, 48, 50, 51n14, 51n24, 70–71, 72, 73, 75, 76, 77, 78, 79, 80, 81, 82n1, 83n14, 83n19, 84n41, 85, 89, 96, 98, 99–100, 112, 136, 137, 146, 147, 148, 152n21, 153n40, 188n3; acquired *La Florida* (Saint Augustine, 1763), 21; alliance of convenience with Spain, 77; Belize (British Honduras), 71, 73, 80, 82; competition with Spain, 135; corsairs, 96; created Georgia colony to reduce marronage, 24, 48; defeated Spain as part of the Seven Years' War, 6; Drake, Francis, 92, 96, 99–100, 102, 106n26, 145–46, 147, 153n39; enslaved escape to Spanish territory, xv;

217

Velasco, Gerónima de, 118–20, 129n60; holder of enslaved workers, 116; *negra libre*, 125; owner of Real de Santa Rita gold mine, 116, 119; sister of Velasco, Miguel de, 116. *See also* Colombia; Velasco y Solimán, Miguel de

Velasco y Solimán, Miguel de, 116, 118–20, 124, 129n53, 129n56; brother of Velasco, Gerónima de, 116; descendants owned houses, mines, and *cuadrillas* of enslaved workers, 116; holder of enslaved workers, 116, 118; mine owner, 116; *negro libre*, 116; owned the San Antonio and other gold mines, 116, 118, 119; paid the crown mining tax, 118; *vecino*, 124. *See also* Colombia; Velasco, Gerónima de

Venezuela, 72, 105n1, 105n16, 106n44, 172n101; Nueva Granada viceroyalty, 109. *See also* Nueva Granada

Yucatán (Mexico), xv, 38, 71, 72, 75, 76, 77, 78, 80, 81–82, 82–83n10, 84n35, 84n38, 84n43, 85n53, 133, 151n8; African males married Mayan women, 14; attacks on Belize, 77; Belizean enslaved denied asylum, xv; Belizean enslaved escape to, 75. *See also* Belize; marronage; Mexico